Soviet Strategy Toward
Western Europe

Soviet Strategy Toward Western Europe

Edited by

EDWINA MORETON
GERALD SEGAL

London
GEORGE ALLEN & UNWIN
Boston   Sydney

George Allen & Unwin (Publishers) Ltd,
40 Museum Street, London WC1A 1LU, UK

George Allen & Unwin (Publishers) Ltd,
Park Lane, Hemel Hempstead, Herts HP2 4TE, UK

Allen & Unwin Inc.,
9 Winchester Terrace, Winchester, Mass 01890, USA

George Allen & Unwin Australia Pty Ltd,
8 Napier Street, North Sydney, NSW 2060, Australia

First published in 1984

British Library Cataloguing in Publication Data

Soviet strategy toward Western Europe.
1. Soviet Union – Foreign relations – Western
Europe   2. Europe, Western – Foreign
relations – Soviet Union
I. Moreton, Edwina   II. Segal, Gerald
327.47'04   DK67 .5.W/
ISBN 0–04–330337–4

Library of Congress Cataloging in Publication Data

Main entry under title:
Soviet strategy toward Western Europe.
1. Europe – Foreign relations – Soviet Union –
Addresses, essays, lectures.   2. Soviet Union – Foreign
relations – Europe – Addresses, essays, lectures.
3. Europe – Foreign relations – 1945–   – Addresses,
essays, lectures.   I. Moreton, Edwina.   II. Segal,
Gerald, 1953–
D1065.S65S694   1984   327.4704   83–15895
ISBN 0–04–330337–4

Set in 11 on 13 point Garamond by Nene Phototypesetters, Northampton
and printed in Great Britain by Billing and Sons Ltd, London and Worcester

Contributors

Hannes Adomeit is a senior staff member of the Stiftung Wissenschaft und Politik in Munich, Federal Republic of Germany. He has also held teaching and/or research posts at the IISS (London), Institute of Soviet and East European Studies (Glasgow), Queens University (Kingston, Ontario). He is the author of *Soviet Risk Taking and Crisis Behaviour* (Allen & Unwin, 1982) and co-editor of *Foreign Policy Making in Communist Countries* (Saxon House, 1979).

Karen Dawisha is a lecturer in the Department of Politics, University of Southampton, and a Rockefeller Foundation International Affairs Fellow at the London School of Economics. She is the author of *Soviet Foreign Policy Toward Egypt* (Macmillan, 1979), and co-editor of *Soviet–East European Dilemmas* (Heinemann, 1981) and *The Soviet Union in the Middle East* (Heinemann, 1982).

Lawrence Freedman is Professor of War Studies, King's College London. He was previously head of policy studies at the Royal Institute of International Affairs, London. He is the author of *U.S. Intelligence and the Soviet Strategic Threat* (Macmillan, 1977), *Britain and Nuclear Weapons* (Macmillan, 1980), *The Evolution of Nuclear Strategy* (Macmillan, 1981), and co-author of *Nuclear War and Nuclear Peace* (Macmillan, 1983).

R. A. Mason is an Air Commodore, Director of Personnel Ground (RAF). He is a specialist on the role of air power in strategic studies and international relations and with special reference to the Soviet Union. He has edited *Air Power in the Nuclear Age* (Macmillan, 1978), *Readings in Air Power* (Royal Air Force, 1979), *The Royal Air Force Today and Tomorrow* (Ian Held, 1982), and co-edited *Air Power in the Nuclear Age* (Macmillan, 1983).

Edwina Moreton is a member of the editorial staff of the *Economist* specializing in Soviet and East European Affairs. She was previously a lecturer in Politics at the University College of Wales, Aberystwyth. She is the author of *East Germany and the Warsaw Alliance* (Westview,

1978), and co-author of *Nuclear War and Nuclear Peace* (Macmillan, 1983).

Gerald Segal is a lecturer in the Department of Politics, University of Leicester. He was previously a lecturer in International Politics at the University College of Wales, Aberystwyth. He is the author of *The Great Power Triangle* (Macmillan, 1982), co-author of *Nuclear War and Nuclear Peace* (Macmillan, 1983), editor of *The China Factor* (Croom Helm, 1982), *The Soviet Union and East Asia* (Heinemann, 1983), and co-editor of *Soviet Strategy* (Croom Helm, 1981).

Jane Sharp is a Visiting Scholar at the Peace Studies Program, Cornell University. She was previously a research fellow at the Center for Science and International Affairs, Harvard University. She has written widely on arms control issues in such journals as *Arms Control*, *The Bulletin of the Atomic Scientists*, *International Security* and *Survival*. She is a member of the Board of Directors of the Council for a Livable World, Washington, DC.

Angela Stent is an assistant professor in the Department of Government, Georgetown University (Washington). She is the author of *From Embargo to Ostpolitik* (Cambridge University Press, 1982) and 'Soviet energy and Western Europe', *The Washington Papers*, No. 19.

Contents

Introduction

Gerald Segal and Edwina Moreton

Europe is not at peace. Neither deterrence nor détente constitute real peace, although Europe has had no war since 1945.
This uncertain state of affairs, which some have called a 'cold
war', has existed largely unchanged since 1945. As the primary
focus of East–West tension, Europe is where cold war lines were
first drawn, and where the stakes remain highest. But cold war is
by definition an ambiguous state of affairs, and thus Europe's
most powerful cold war actor, the Soviet Union faces dilemmas
and predicaments in its strategy towards Western Europe rather
than clear-cut policies and goals.

Our central theme is therefore the predicaments of Soviet
power.[1] But at no stage should one forget the centrality of
Europe for Soviet foreign policy, even though crises over Berlin
no longer dominate the headlines. Because of more obvious
tensions in other regions of the world Soviet foreign policy in
the Middle East, towards China, or in START may at times appear
more crucial. But these issues can only be dealt with by the
Soviet Union, because the most crucial balance of forces in
Europe appears relatively stable. However, Moscow is under no
illusion that stability means peace, or that its relations with
Western Europe are any less fundamental to its strategic outlook.

If Europe is so stable, then why produce a book on Soviet
policy in the area? The answer is in three parts. First, the
question of Soviet policy towards Western Europe is rarely
analysed in anything longer than an article. To be sure there
have been numerous excellent article-length studies of various
dimensions of Soviet policy, but few books that attempt a more
comprehensive analysis. The occasional volume that does

1

appear often seems to suffer from two weaknesses. First, the difficult grey areas of Soviet foreign policy dilemmas are often forced into unsuitable black and white categories of assertions of straightforward Soviet objectives. The very term 'cold war' points to one of the greyest of areas. Secondly, previous analyses have rarely drawn so heavily on the work of European scholars. This is not to suggest that Europeans have a monopoly on truth about Soviet policy in the area, but it is true that Europeans tend to have a distinctive view. Living on the same continent as the Soviet Union, and not entirely trusting the United States to defend them, the West Europeans have learned to appreciate to a greater extent the grey areas of East–West conflict. At a time of renewed concern over the policies being pursued by the United States, it is now more crucial than ever that the Europeans be better understood.

Understanding European concerns has become more urgent with the growth of the anti-nuclear movement in Western Europe. Today's 'peace movements' are not necessarily correct in their grasp of the issues at stake, but they should not be dismissed as being mere 'tools of the Communists'. The peace movements express real and important disquiet about the potential for future conflict in Europe. They remind us that Europe is not at peace. The peace movements also force us to reassess our view of Soviet strategy towards Western Europe. These protesters rightly argue that at the core of their government's policy is an assessment of a 'Soviet threat'. They challenge us to substantiate that assessment and justify our willingness to live with the second best option of deterrence rather than peace.

The third reason for taking another look at Soviet strategy is the increased sense of political uncertainty in Western Europe. This is not to suggest that Europe is any less stable than before, or that Soviet strategy has become any more hostile. The notion that we might prefer the instability of a Berlin crisis to present wrangles over pipelines and sanctions, is to fail to appreciate that some distance has been travelled towards peace on the war–peace continuum. The real roots of recent uncertainty about Soviet policy are to be found both in Western perceptions and in Soviet realities. The West in general, but the Europeans in particular, seem now to question their policy priorities in a way that was not done when prosperity and peace seemed more easily attainable. In the recent recessionary atmosphere, with the election of a right-wing American President, and above all the demise of détente, West Europeans seem less confident about their future and about the choices before them.

What is more, the Soviet Union seems to face difficult choices of its own. The deterioration in détente is as much a cause of concern in Moscow as it is in London or Bonn. The Soviet economy is also anything but robust and priorities are questioned. But above all, this is a period of succession in the Soviet leadership. The long anticipated end of the Brezhnev era has now come, and some have suggested that the Andropov era and beyond could be very different. Certainly if there were to be changes, then the European theatre, as Moscow's most important priority, would be likely to be affected.

Issues in Soviet Policy

The contributors to this volume do not suggest that Soviet objectives can be readily listed. While other analysts might suggest with great confidence that Soviet policy is clear cut and unchanging, we have found no such certainty. What emerges from our analyses is several themes of Soviet policy, many of which are characterised by dilemmas, while others have been seen to change over time. To suggest that there is a Soviet code of behaviour, let alone that Moscow can be drawn into agreeing to a code of conduct, is to simplify a far more complex reality. In place of such simplicity, we offer an analysis of seven of the central elements of Soviet strategy in Europe.

(A)   LIMITED POWER

It might seem strange to argue that the massive Soviet military power arrayed against Western Europe along the eastern side of the iron curtain has serious limitations. The argument is based on two premises. First, military power is largely matched by countervailing NATO military power. It is not necessary to get involved in arcane disputes about the balance of tanks in a given area or the relative advantage of airforces to suggest that the West is far from defenceless. Only the most radical maintain that the Soviet Union already has sufficient military advantage to risk launching an attack on NATO and expect to get away with it. This is not to say that Soviet military power does not pose a threat, but it is to stress that so long as the relative military balance remains as it is, Soviet strength is severely limited.

Secondly, military power rarely translates simply into political power. When advantages are in the realm of $2\frac{1}{2}$ to 1 in tanks or 25 per cent in medium-range bombers, how is it possible to suggest that the Soviet Union has specific political leverage. Obviously no such direct linkage can be made. Nevertheless, there are those in the West who point to such Soviet advantage, when even hawkish Kremlin generals might be more cautious. This self-inflicted wound on the part of some analysts of assuming Western weakness has the danger of becoming a self-fulfilling prophecy. If we believe ourselves to be vulnerable when we are not, then the enemy obtains an advantage – whether political or military – that he does not deserve. The 'window of vulnerability' on the strategic level is a case in point.[2] Scare-mongering is seen by some as a necessary tactic to obtain defence spending in a democracy, but in the long run it is counter-productive. To 'cry wolf' when the wolf is off licking other wounds, will undermine democratic consensus in the justifiable need to retain sufficient countervailing power. The scare-mongers in the end serve Soviet interests, and undermine the very Western security they seek to protect.

(B)   DILEMMAS OF POWER

Some might suggest that Soviet objectives are fairly obvious – to safeguard its own national security and improve its position at the expense of its adversaries. This attitude of 'what's mine is mine, and what's yours is negotiable' is hardly an unusual objective for any power, and tells us little about the operational objectives of Soviet strategy.

In fact, the more closely specific objectives are analysed, the more apparent it is that the Soviet Union faces conflicting priorities in Europe rather than neatly defined goals. Contributors to this volume have made clear that the most difficult dilemmas involve the United States and Germany. Does the Soviet Union want United States power removed from Europe, or does the United States presence help sustain the rationale for Soviet control of its part of Europe? Does the Soviet Union want a united Germany, thereby splitting West Germany from NATO, or does it fear the growth of German power in Europe? Does the Soviet Union want détente with Western Europe for the trade and security gains it brings, or does it fear the spread of noxious ideas that seem to accompany liberalisation across cold war lines?

Certainly in the last twenty years it is hard to claim that the Soviet Union has been successful in achieving any clear-cut objective in Europe. Instead Moscow seems to have settled for the management of the dilemmas of power.

(C)   GENUINE DIVIDE BETWEEN EAST AND WEST

The current belief on one wing of the European peace movement that there are no real divisions between East and West is one that is rejected as clearly in Moscow as in Washington. It should also continue to be rejected in West European capitals. In the mass of statements deploring the dangers of the arms race and the sterility of East–West conflict, the core values of Western society are often lost. There is no such illusion in the Soviet Union: real differences of system and ideology divide East and

West. Of course ideology is neither a rigid doctrine nor is it necessarily a practical guide for action in the Kremlin, but ideology still exists as a prescription for a different social order in Europe's Eastern half than exists in the Western half.

There may be legitimate doubts as to just how much risk the Soviet Union is willing to take in pursuit of its ideological objectives, but the calculation of risk is affected by the presence of countervailing power. Without this balance, the risks to the Soviet Union are lowered. Both sides of the East–West divide appreciate that while military power is not always a useful instrument to attain ideological objectives, they need sufficient power to deter the opponent. Hence the extraordinary development of permanent military alliances whose purpose is not to fight. NATO and the Warsaw Pact are at one and the same time symbols of the real divide in Europe, and evidence of why those divisions cannot be allowed to grow wider.

(D)   NEUTRALISM OR FINLANDISATION?

If there were no countervailing NATO threat, might the Soviet Union lower its guard as well? This argument appeals to those who urge West European neutrality along the model of Sweden, Switzerland or Austria. The Soviet Union would no doubt be pleased to see such a trend, but the Soviet reaction is by no means so predictable. Soviet ideology certainly does not accept the possibility of neutrality for anything but a transition to socialism. Soviet practice has only accepted the neutrals that now exist because there was countervailing Western power behind them. The Soviet withdrawal from Austria after the Second World War was hardly done out of the goodness of its heart, nor is Sweden's independence tolerated simply out of fear of Swedish national self-defence plans.

Similarly, the notion that there could exist nuclear-free zones in Europe, even on the scale of specific towns or counties in Western Europe, must be a source of much hilarity in Moscow.

Certainly in times of war, Soviet doctrine makes no provision for limited tactics to avoid such free zones, and even in 'peace', nuclear armed submarines have a disturbing habit of appearing in neutral waters. Neutralism, where it exists in Europe, is a luxury at present supported by Western power, and in war likely to be ignored by both sides.

(E) THE SUPERPOWERS AS EQUAL IMPERIALISTS

The Soviet Union is involved in Western Europe by geography, while the United States is present by invitation. Moscow is inevitably deeply concerned about politics in Western Europe. The United States has been invited by NATO allies to help balance Soviet power. Furthermore, the United States is seen as broadly sharing the values and interests of Western Europe. While it may be true that some Americans might hope to fight a limited war in Europe, should nuclear weapons ever be used, rather than involve their own territory, a far larger number of Americans wonder why they have to put up with noisy and ungrateful European allies and would favour withdrawing behind the walls of fortress America. The choice is largely up to the West Europeans.

If West Europeans are so concerned that United States policy is harming their interests and the Soviet Union can be better dealt with without Washington's shrill anti-Soviet rhetoric, then the invitation to Washington in support of European defence can be withdrawn. The step has not been taken, largely because United States interests are not seen as so divergent from those of the West Europeans and because the Europeans have been reluctant to put their money where their mouth is, and pay the extra required to defend themselves.

There is a good case to be made for a middle ground among Europeans between subservience to or rejection of United States power. But that too would require greater West European co-operation and defence spending. Europeans could benefit from formulating their more moderate views on the Soviet military threat and trade with Moscow, and then negotiating from strength with their American allies. It is debatable however whether the Soviet Union would really be pleased to see a resurgent Western Europe, even if it were in the cause of greater moderation in policy towards Moscow. For example, European wild cards, such as De Gaulle's France, make it more difficult for the Soviet Union to have confidence in the outcome of nuclear weapons negotiations with the United States.

(F)   THE CASE FOR DIALOGUE

Having discussed themes reflected by the 'hard-line' spectrum of opinion – real divisions between East and West and the need for preparedness in Europe – one complementary theme should be noted. 'Détente' is in the interests of both the Soviet Union and the West. There are real dangers of war that must be controlled, real benefits from mutual trade, and real rewards in greater social contact, especially for the German nation. Détente helps contribute to stability in all these spheres, and it is this very stability, so the argument runs, that is the single most important post-war gain for both East and West in Europe. Neither war nor even tension can be in the interest of either side.

Détente in itself, it should be noted, is little more than atmosphere, but it does reflect genuine acceptance of stability in certain areas. Both those on the extreme 'right' and the extreme 'left' who dismiss détente either as failing to go to the heart of the disputes, or as failing to stop the onward march of Soviet power, expect too much from the process. Europe is more stable than it was during the crises of the 1950s, but it is not at peace. Those who attack détente and claim the 1980s to be a dangerous decade, all too easily forget the major reductions of tensions that have been achieved since the superpowers stared each other down in Berlin. Nor has détente given the Soviet Union anything it did not already have. The Helsinki accords in

1975 accepted the Soviet dominated post-war borders, but that was a formal recognition of a long established fact; it was not a Western concession.

(G) COMPETITIVE CO-EXISTENCE

Our single, uniting theme is therefore 'competitive co-existence'. Competitive, because the Soviet Union and the West Europeans are divided by fundamental differences of ideology and interests. But 'co-existence' is also vital, because of the awesome conventional and nuclear threat hanging over Europe. Unbridled competition brings the risk of war closer and hence limits are enforced. It is in the self-interest of East and West that the competition be resolved by non-military means.

Competitive co-existence is a term better understood by Soviet policy makers – who have based much of their post-war policies on it – than hitherto by those in the West. A shot of such realism would do the Western debate no harm at all. Competition will continue, whether it be Western anxiety over Polish instability or Soviet economic failures, or Soviet interest in Western recession and Europe's anti-nuclear movements. Recognition of competing and opposing interests forms the natural foundation of East–West dialogue.

Perspectives on Soviet Strategy

The choice of how to analyse Soviet strategy towards Western Europe offers almost as many options as the Kremlin has strategies. This book selects four dimensions of Soviet policy. Not only is it important to assess both the internal and external dimensions of Soviet policy, but the main powers and the main issues confronting Moscow deserve a mention. No analysis should make immodest claims about its scope, but it is hoped that this more varied approach will better illuminate the different aspects of Soviet policy. The price paid is invariably some degree of overlap between chapters, especially in the final two sections.

The first section assesses the importance of the domestic dimension to Soviet policy-making. There is a tendency among students of Soviet foreign policy to overestimate the centrality of Soviet domestic policy by suggesting that Soviet strategy is primarily a result of internal pressures. The opposite tendency is to focus entirely on external policy pressures and see the domestic politics of an authoritarian state as little more than a 'black box'. The two chapters in this volume stake out the middle ground, arguing that domestic politics in part contribute to defining Soviet policy, but in other ways the domestic dimension is a filter or a prism, sifting and refracting external pressures. Domestic pressures can rarely be neatly isolated so as to provide simple explanations on their own for Soviet foreign policy.

Karen Dawisha takes up this problem of Soviet images as filters for policy when tackling the question of the role of Soviet ideology. She suggests there should be little doubt that ideology remains important, despite fashionable tendencies to dismiss its relevance. Where the critics do have a point is that the ideology is primarily relevant for discussions of 'first principles', but does not serve as a guide for Soviet action. Dawisha makes it plain that the ideological principles retain an enormous degree of flexibility, in part as a result of their eclectic origins. Ideology can in no way serve as a guide, for example, on the question of whether and how to trade with Western Europe, or how to deal with policy dilemmas with the United States and Germany. This does not, however, invalidate the role of ideology, but merely limits it. To prove the lack of validity of ideology requires evidence of contravention of sacred principles. Such cases are not evident, even though there are many where ideology offers no clear code of conduct. Where ideology does remain central is on the question of the inevitable conflict between East and West. While not prescribing how such conflict should be conducted, there should be few illusions that in the final Soviet analysis, capitalist and communist systems are irreconcilable.

Hannes Adomeit reinforces this complex view of Soviet strategy by suggesting that Soviet decision-making follows no pre-arranged pattern. Simplistic Western models would have us believe that relatively independent institutions vie with each other for power in the Kremlin in accordance with the hallowed rules of bureaucratic politics. While this view may be an improvement on simple totalitarian explanations, it fails to do justice to the more sophisticated decision-making process. Adomeit suggests that, to be sure, there are important institutions involved in Soviet foreign policy-making, but on particular issues their participation is expected and relied upon rather than won as a result of bureaucratic in-fighting. This participatory explanation is made even more complex by the existence of divisions within institutions, thereby creating cross-cutting cleavages in policy-making. However, Adomeit's non-bureaucratic approach does not imply the absence of domestic debates on Soviet policy. Such disagreements certainly do take place, but they are often between participants sitting on a delicately balanced see-saw. Sudden shifts of weight are difficult to achieve as consensus politics tends to ensure that movements in one direction tend to be counterbalanced by shifts in the opposite direction. Thus external pressures also affect the see-saw and help encourage some movement along its length, but it is enormously difficult to calculate with any certainty how the crowd on the see-saw will shift. Adomeit urges the importance of studying these movements and alignments, but cautions about drawing over-arching lessons from the study.

The buffeting winds of external pressure on Soviet policy of course come from many different directions. To pretend to cover all of them would require far more space than publishers are inclined to allow. This study has concentrated on the Soviet Union's two main great power rivals, the United States and

China, along with Germany, at the expense of other important dimensions, such as Soviet–East European relations.[3]

Lawrence Freedman plainly points out that no single aspect of Soviet policy is as crucial as superpower relations. Thus Soviet strategy towards Western Europe has been directly linked with Western Europe's main external ally, the United States. This linkage, essentially embodied in NATO, has continued to pose dilemmas for Soviet policy. From the early post-war period when Europe was the Soviet Union's hostage for good American behaviour, to the present when American power in Europe helps legitimise Soviet control over Eastern Europe, Moscow has never clearly opposed the United States's presence in Europe. When push comes to shove the Soviet Union seemed satisfied to settle for a calm, if antagonistic Western Europe, if that meant a more managed superpower relationship. In some respects it is Soviet policy that helps keep United States power in Western Europe, even if the West Europeans sometimes seem less than welcoming. Certainly Moscow's declarations that it would not allow the United States to fight a limited nuclear war in Europe suggests that the linkage of Western Europe and the United States that so worries NATO strategists, is in important ways dependent on Soviet policy. Freedman makes it clear that these apparent ambiguities and dilemmas in Soviet strategy towards United States policy in Western Europe are unlikely to be easily resolved.

Edwina Moreton's discussion of the problems of divided Germany reinforces the line taken in several other chapters – namely that Soviet policy is characterised more by dilemmas than simple strategies. Nowhere is this more evident than in Soviet policy towards Germany, where the fundamental question of whether to seek a united or divided Germany remains unresolved. Moreton does not, however, argue that these grey-area choices lead to an abandonment of an active Soviet German policy. Bonn is still seen as the linchpin to Soviet strategy in Western Europe, and in recent years as some sort of communication channel to the West as a whole. Moreton does not argue that West Germany can serve as an interpreter in East–West relations, for it is firmly wedded in the Western alliance. But Soviet policy will continue to focus on the possibilities of prising Bonn away from NATO policy where leverage can be gained and benefit can be accrued. Recent Soviet overtures to the West Germans, especially in a time of otherwise fairly frigid East–West relations, point both to the importance of the German problem for Soviet strategy, as well as to the enduring difficulties for Moscow in achieving any success.

Gerald Segal's analysis of the potential China factor in Soviet strategy reveals an almost minimal role for Peking. In keeping with the Chinese saying, 'distant water cannot quench fires', it is plain that China's role in Soviet strategy towards Western Europe is almost entirely secondary. West Europe is an area of primary military, political and economic concern for Moscow, such that whatever mischief the Chinese may get up to elsewhere in the world, its effect on Europe is marginal. Segal does however point to some areas where the China factor deserves greater attention. The difficulties of Soviet placement of SS-20s with 'swing' capability against China or Western Europe poses important complications for arms control talks. What is more, if there is a China factor in Soviet strategy, it originates in Soviet fears of a two-front war. Thus in times of serious Sino–Soviet tension, as in the fifteen years from 1963 until the late 1970s, détente with Western Europe takes on added importance. Similarly, given the icy blasts of a somewhat colder war in Europe, the significance of the recent limited Sino–Soviet détente should not be underestimated for Soviet strategy towards Europe.

While one might debate the nature of Soviet strategy towards individual states, certain themes have wider relevance. There are those who argue that such an issue-centred approach alone can reveal the outlines of a Soviet strategy. The contributors to this volume have found no such coherence, and indeed have noted just as many dilemmas of policy whether applied to one country or to Western Europe as a whole.

Tony Mason braved the thicket of Soviet military policy and emerged with no clear picture of an over-arching Soviet strategy towards Western Europe. Mason argues that the starting point of Soviet strategy is of course to maintain sufficient military power to guarantee Soviet security. But as in the case of ideology, the utility of the security principle becomes harder to ascertain when applied to more specific policy problems. Mason suggests that Soviet military power is extremely difficult to translate into usable political influence, despite Soviet superiority in certain sectors. The bluntness of the military instrument is not un-recognised in the Kremlin. But this is not to say that there is no 'Soviet threat'. Mason makes clear that the failure to offer countervailing military power to Soviet forces in Europe would abdicate the responsibility of defence. This is not to suggest the necessity for precise matching of Soviet power in every category, but sufficient overall opposing power dare not be abandoned. Thus while Mason may note sympathetically the Soviet motives for SS-20 deployment, he also makes clear that it would be folly for the West to abandon attempts to offer credible countervailing power. Like the other contributors, Mason urges vigilance, albeit not hysteria, in the face of Soviet military power in Europe.

Soviet economic policy, as with military policy, can hardly be fitted into neat categories of objectives. Angela Stent makes plain that two fundamental Soviet goals – economic benefits and economic instruments of leverage – are often in conflict. Not surprisingly then Soviet policy makers have debated the way in which economic tools might be used. Similarly, it is not surprising that Moscow finds it impossible to manipulate its economic ties to pressure the West Europeans. The Soviet need to import Western goods, its limited foreign currency and con-flicting domestic priorities, all mean that while Moscow will continue to see an adversary relationship with the West Euro-peans, it will be unable and unwilling to effectively wield the economic weapon.

In the final chapter, Jane Sharp identifies several broad Soviet objectives in arms control negotiations and suggests, like the authors of many of the previous chapters, that the practice of Soviet policy is far from consistent and coherent. Pragmatism is not surprising in the complex field of defence strategy where weapons development is rapid and military doctrine is regularly adjusted. In the Soviet case, the fluctuating negotiating process is made even more uncertain by such problems as the need to garrison extra troops to control as well as to defend Eastern Europe. Jane Sharp also reinforces the conclusions of previous chapters that Soviet policy, even regarding the United States' presence in Europe, is characterised by dilemmas. The Soviet policy of threatening to respond to a United States nuclear threat in Europe as if it were a threat from the United States itself, coincides with the West European desire to link United States and West European security. Such paradoxes in Soviet policy are more the rule than the exception.

Is There a Soviet Strategy?

In a sense the title of this book is a misnomer. The contributors to this volume might be more satisfied with 'Soviet Strategies Towards Western Europe', but even in this plural case, they would all argue that Soviet policy is too complex to be encompassed neatly in this way. That, however, is no reason for shrugging our shoulders in despair. Much like the complexity of the nuclear weapons debate in Europe, the intricacies of arguments about grey areas of Soviet policy makes it all the more urgent to spend time in their assessment.

As this book goes to press these twin issues of Soviet strategy towards Western Europe and the nuclear danger have tended to blend into each other. The year of the Euro-missiles – 1983 – will be one of intense debate over at times bewilderingly complex issues. The contributors to this volume have tried to help that debate forward by asking the right kinds of questions about the issues at stake, even if they do not pretend to offer all the answers. Europe is neither at peace nor at war. Soviet strategy is neither uncontrollably aggressive nor meekly defensive. In the end we are condemned to compete and co-exist with Soviet power in Western Europe.

Notes to Introduction

1 For four recent books on other aspects of Soviet strategy taking a similar balanced view, see Karen Dawisha and Philip Hanson (eds), *Soviet–East European Dilemmas* (London: Heinemann, 1981); Adeed Dawisha and Karen Dawisha (eds), *The Soviet Union in the Middle East* (London: Heinemann, 1982); Gerald Segal (ed.), *The Soviet Union in East Asia* (London: Heinemann, 1983); John Baylis and Gerald Segal (eds), *Soviet Strategy* (London: Croom Helm, 1981).
2 For a full analysis of the centre ground in the nuclear weapons debate see Gerald Segal, Edwina Moreton, Lawrence Freedman, and John Baylis, *Nuclear War and Nuclear Peace* (London: Macmillan, 1983).
3 On Soviet–East European relations see Dawisha and Hanson (eds), *Soviet Dilemmas*.

Part I

The Domestic Dimension

1

Soviet Ideology and Western Europe

Karen Dawisha

The late 1960s and the early 1970s was a period of détente not only in politics but also in political science, a period in which much was written suggesting that the USSR was a 'system' like any other, that ideology was 'dead' and that increased international interdependence plus the effects of the scientific–technological revolution inevitably would transform socialist society into a more Western-style liberal and democratic system. This has not happened; and now in the long shadow still cast not only by the invasion of Czechoslovakia in 1968, but also by the excommunication of the Eurocommunists throughout the 1970s and the crushing of Solidarity in Poland in 1981, more than ever before, any analyst of Soviet policy towards Western Europe must address these questions: What *is* the role of ideology in Soviet politics? What are the component parts of that ideology and how does it affect the making of policy towards Western Europe? And, finally, how does practice differ from precept, and what difficulties and strains have arisen as a result of contrasts between ideology and its application?

Soviet Ideology

Before discussing the role of ideology in the formulation of Soviet policy, it is necessary first to define it both as a general

19

concept and as a specific input into decision-making in the USSR. As is true with most theoretical concepts, there exists a wide range of opinion on the definition of ideology. C. Wright Mills conceptualises ideology merely as a vague 'social reality'.[1] Richard Lowenthal expands on this theme by citing Marx's definition of ideology as 'a distorted reflection of social reality in the consciousness of men, used as an instrument of struggle'.[2] Marx, in the *German Ideology*, extends this quasi-personal and private notion of ideology when he states that 'we set out from real, active men, and on the basis of their real life process, we demonstrate the development of the ideological reflexes and echoes of this life process. The phantoms formed in the human brain are also, necessarily, sublimates of their material life process.[3] How different is the definition provided by the official Soviet *Filosoficheskii Slovar* almost a century later: ideology is 'a system of definite views, ideas, conceptions and notions adhered to by some class or political party . . . and is a reflection of the economic system predominant at any given time'.

Many of these definitions contain references to values, beliefs and norms, others emphasise ideology as a system of guidance for behaviour, whether it be struggle against a state or actions supportive of a state. Because ideology does fulfil, to borrow the phrase coined by Talcott Parsons, a functional requisite by serving as a system of guidance in which societal values are transmitted into action, it can be seen that this link is a *constant* factor in the process which occurs in any society when norms are transformed into policies. This view implies that a society's ideology need not be a tightly-woven, interdependent or logical system of beliefs, relevant at all times and in all situations. Like a many-sided prism, a particular aspect of the ideology in a given situation may reflect the image given by a value through a series of vectors which direct possible action. In a changed situation, a different facet of the ideology might receive the values and transform them into another set of policy alternatives. With the link between values and actions in mind, one can go on to discuss the specific elements of Soviet ideology which over time have contributed to the formulation of its policy toward Europe.

The Soviet Conception of Europe

The Soviet conception of Europe is contradictory. The source of that contradiction is deeply embedded both in Soviet history and Soviet ideology. Dating from 1836 with the publication by Peter Chaadeyev of the 'First Letter', Russian political life was divided into the two schools of 'Slavophils' and 'Westernisers'. Although the split between these two groups is not as clear-cut as is sometimes presented, nevertheless, the Westernisers did seek to introduce 'enlightened' Western ideas and political institutions into Russia against the objections of most Slavophils, who in their determination to defend Russian traditions and in their conviction of the moral superiority of the Russians over European peoples, turned their backs on the 'contagion' of Western civilization.

Eurocentric by nature, Marxism once it took root on Russian soil should have resolved this argument decisively in favour of the Westernisers. For Marx and Engels both believed Europe to be the natural home of the eventual socialist revolution, not only because they saw in it an economic system close to collapse but also because they believed that culturally and educationally the European proletariat was most equipped to build a new social order on the ruins of the old. Admittedly, they conceded, for example, in the introduction to the first Russian edition of the *Communist Manifesto*, the possibility of the small peasant communes in rural Russia making a direct transition to socialism, but nowhere did they conceive it to be possible that this sleepy feudal giant of Russia would ever, or could ever, be the standard-bearer for socialism in Europe.

It took first Lenin and then Stalin to change the centre of gravity toward Muscovy. Lenin's major theoretical contribution on the subject came in his work on *Imperialism, the Highest Stage of Capitalism*. Here, while maintaining that true socialism could only be established in Europe, where capitalism was most developed, he recognised that capitalism there had been able to postpone its demise by expanding into underdeveloped countries in search of cheap labour and materials and additional markets. Only by depriving Europe of its new lifeline to the colonies could capitalism be sufficiently weakened so as to allow the proletariat and its vanguard to rise up and over-throw the bourgeois state. The revolution in Russia helped in this effort in several ways: it was a blow to European capitalists who had significant investments in Russian banking and industry; it was a beacon of hope, a symbol of socialism to the working classes and left-wing intelligentsia of Europe, and it was also seen by Lenin as an important home-base, safe-haven, hide-out, and arms cache all rolled into one for European revolution. Thus to the extent that the European communists were asked to subordinate their own struggle to the defence of the Russian Revolution, it was primarily because they conceived of it as both the ideological avant-garde and the material rear-guard of their own revolution. Although by the time of Lenin's death in 1923 much had been done to establish Russian hegemony over the international communist movement, nevertheless the object of this exercise, in Lenin's eyes, was to better co-ordinate all revolutionary forces in order to achieve the more speedy collapse of capitalism *in Europe*. Lenin was by inclination, therefore, if one may draw an over-simple com-parison, a Westerniser, someone who on the one hand saw his major role as 'keeping the revolution warm' for Europe while on the other hand working feverishly to raise the cultural and political consciousness of the Russian people in order that the revolution would not be distorted out of all proportion while 'in a holding pattern' over Moscow. However, even Lenin had occasion to doubt whether this would be possible and whether even the Bolsheviks themselves were not gradually falling under the influence of those autocratic reflexes of centuries of tsarist rule. Thus, shortly before his death, in his report to the Eleventh Party Congress in 1922, Lenin despaired:

> The economic power in the hands of the proletarian state of Russia is quite adequate to ensure the transition to communism. What then is lacking? Obviously what is lacking is culture among the . . . communists. If we take Moscow with its 4700 communists in responsible positions, and if we take that huge bureaucratic machine, that gigantic heap, we must ask: who is directing whom? . . . [The Communists] are not directing, they are being directed.[4]

Stalin did not suffer from any similar self-doubts about where the capital of the international communist movement should be. Faced with the failure of the European revolution and the rise of fascism and militant ultra-nationalism in Germany and other European states, Stalin came to power in conditions which allowed, and some would say necessitated, a totally different conception of Europe.

Stalin never conceived of Russia as having a place *in* Europe or even of being an extension of European culture and civilization. He did not adhere to the Leninist view that the revolution stood the chance of being weighed down by Russian culture. On the contrary he extolled 'Russian' values and constantly denigrated the corruption and consumerism which were rife amongst the European bourgeoisie and proletariat alike, and saw little of value which the Russians could extract with benefit from Europe. (He thought more highly of the United States, exhorting Party members in Moscow, for example, to combine 'Russian revolutionary sweep' with 'American efficiency' in order to achieve the proper Leninist style of work.[5]) Equally, he eschewed the notion that the USSR was merely a staging post for the emplantation of socialism in its natural home – Germany. On the contrary, although he conceded that Germany may have been the heartland of socialism in the 1840s when Marx and Engels wrote the *Communist*

23

Manifesto, Stalin felt that by the beginning of the twentieth century, 'because Russia was the only country in which there existed a real force capable of resolving the contradiction of imperialism in a revolutionary way . . . the centre of the revolutionary movement was bound to shift to Russia'.[6]

Out of this rejection of Europe as the natural centre of proletarian revolution came the development of 'Socialism in One Country', which marked the final ascendancy of Slavophil reflexes *vis-à-vis* Europe. No longer was Europe seen as verging on the brink of collapse: it was militarily strong and Stalin, upon hearing Hitler's classification of Slavs as one of the races destined for extinction, became convinced that Germany was preparing to renew the war against Russia left unfinished by Napoleon. Stalin stalled for time with the Nazi–Soviet Pact of 1939 while he sought to rally the rest of Europe, but the immobility of other European leaders in the face of fascism convinced him that while publicly they may not have employed the same racist rhetoric as Hitler, nevertheless they too, in Stalin's estimation, shared the Fuhrer's basic hostility towards Russia. The call went out, increasingly therefore, from the late 1930s onward not only to defend socialism but also, and more importantly, to defend a great civilisation, a great culture, a great people. The strength of ultra-patriotism and ultra-nationalism was such during this period that in the words of the Soviet historian Konstantin F. Shteppa, 'a new Slavophilism negating Western influence extolled Chernyshevsky, Lenin, and Stalin at the expense of Marx himself'.[7]

If Socialism in One Country evolved before the outbreak of the Second World War, and to some extent as a defensive reaction to German preparations for it, nevertheless the experience of the war, when Russia saw itself to be standing alone against fascism, even further lowered the esteem in which Europe was held by Stalin and all those Soviet leaders who rose up through the ranks during that period. It was Europe that had given birth to fascism, it was Russia that had killed it.

Thus the Party line drew the consistent distinction between

'the decisive role of the USSR . . . its consistent, honest policy in *international* relations with the members of the anti-Hitler coalition, and, on the other hand, the perfidious, mercenary and treacherous policy of the Anglo–American imperialists in this war'.[8]

This perceived failure of Russia's allies to come to its aid when under attack sowed the seeds for the continued chauvinistic elevation of Russia as the natural and permanent centre of the post-war international communist system, and the simultaneous denigration of all things European, including certain aspects of Marxism. Thus, such was Stalin's power that by 1949 in his 'On the Article of Engels "The External Policy of Russian Czarism"', he was able to condemn Marx and Engels openly for their negative appraisal of Russian foreign policy *under the Czar*![9] Having opened the floodgates for 'creative Marxism', Stalin and his influential minister of culture, A. A. Zhdanov, enunciated the famous 'Two-Camp Theory' which both reflected and strengthened the post-war division of the world into two great power blocs. In ideology this also led to the rigorous fight against 'cosmopolitanism', in which Party officials were warned against 'blackening the past of the Great Russian people and understating its role in world history'. The exhortation continued:

Experience proves that any undervaluation of the role and significance of the Russian people in world history is directly tied in with admiration for foreign lands. Nihilism in the evaluation of the great achievements of Russian culture and the culture of the other peoples of the USSR is the reverse side of fawning before the bourgeois culture of the West.[10]

It goes without saying that much of the more chauvinistic excesses inherent in the post-war conception of Europe died with Stalin. It was no longer so permissible to exhort the virtues of the Russians as a people, particularly now that socialism had at last spread to parts of Europe and in particular to the eastern sector of divided Germany. Nevertheless, the experience of the war and the view of Europe which dominated Soviet ideology during the war moulded a whole generation of Soviet people and their leaders, and thus even though the Party line under both Khrushchev and Brezhnev enunciated the principles of peaceful co-existence and détente in Europe, nevertheless the experiences and ideological reflexes of that period have left their firm imprint upon the current Soviet conception of Europe, and in particular upon the way they assess the correlation of forces in the European theatre.

Correlation of Forces

In the USSR today, as in the past, the application of ideology to current operative policy issues is determined by calculating what the Soviets call the correlation of forces (*sootnoshenie sil*). In the West, while the systematic comparison of one's own capabilities relative to the adversary's is usual in military science, it is only the socialist countries which carry this over into the making of foreign policy. It was Lenin who once imbued the assessment of the correlation of forces with an aura of scientific near-infallibility by stating that 'we, Marxists, have always been proud of the fact that by a strict calculation of the mass forces and mutual class relations we have determined the expediency of this or that form of struggle'.[11] Thus current Soviet assessments echo Lenin when they boldly assert: 'This knowledge of the laws of social development allows Soviet foreign policy to look confidently to the future and gives it the strength of scientific prevision'.[12] In fact, however, the Soviets themselves recognise that there is incredible flexibility of interpretation in divining actual and potential shifts in the alignment of forces. Indeed, with the continued emphasis on 'creative Marxism' it is claimed that it is not only the application of Marxist principle but also 'flexibility, realism and willingness to accept reasonable compromises [which] make Soviet foreign policy highly effective . . .'.[13]

Keeping these general caveats in mind, it is possible to analyse some of the key principles inherent in the correlation of forces, and to examine the extent to which that calculus is shaped both by ideology and by the various and often conflicting conceptions of Europe discussed in the previous section. Within this context, three elements of the correlation of forces deserve further discussion:

1 Soviet policy must take into account, and seek to manipulate, the total correlation between class forces, and not just the balance of power between states.
2 Short-term policy must serve long-term goals.
3 Regional policy should be determined with reference to global strategy.

The first aspect in the 'classical' Soviet conception of the correlation of forces then is that international relations is concerned with the interaction not primarily between states and governments, as in the Western conception, but between the two main class forces – socialism and capitalism. Thus, because the focus of the Soviet vision is on the dialectical relationship between these class forces, the USSR has absolutely no qualms about openly supporting any communist party or separatist group which helps to 'tilt the balance in favour of socialism'. Thus seen from this 'pure' or overly-stark perspective, one is able to draw a black and white distinction between on the one hand the Western powers in Europe interested in the stability of the state and the status quo of the system, and the Soviet Union and its allies, on the other hand, committed to a continual reassessment of that status quo utilising non-state actors and undermining the very structure of the state system.

In reality, however, the Soviet view of the interaction of class forces in Europe turns out to be not so different from the state-

27

centric approach of the West Europeans. This is primarily due to two factors: the Soviet leadership has lost faith in Euro-communism, of which more below, and also, and more importantly, socialism now has boundaries in Europe. That is to say, the distinction between the promotion of socialism as a class force on the one hand and the protection of the interests of the community of socialist states on the other is blurred because socialism is no longer seen by the Soviet leaders in an abstract or dynamic way but rather in more geographic and static terms. Socialism now has capitals, rivers, plains and populations which have to be protected; and as a result, the security of the socialist system and the interests of the state *qua* state have been elevated to primary importance when analysing the correlation of forces in Moscow.

What are the implications for Soviet policy in Europe of this redefinition of socialism to mean above all the system of socialist states headed by the Soviet Union? Its primary impact is that Soviet policy becomes bloc policy, in the sense that Soviet policy toward Western Europe is formulated in such a way as to maintain its position in Eastern Europe. Whatever interests the Soviet Union may have in pursuing any policy toward Western Europe, therefore, those interests and that policy will be secondary to the greater interest of maintaining Soviet control over Eastern Europe. This axiom is relevant equally in times of cold war and détente, with the major difference between the two phases being the degree of co-operation and, crucially in Soviet terminology, 'peaceful co-existence' between the two different social systems, *not* the lessening of Soviet control over the bloc. This was precisely the lesson that the Czechs were forced to learn in 1968 – e.g. that détente did not mean the loosening of the ties binding Prague and Moscow. 'The borders of socialism are immutable', as the Soviets continually re-minded the Czechs in 1968, and if any political or economic bridges were going to be built between East Europe and West Europe, they would have to be built with Russian plans and by Russian engineers. Only after Soviet troops had driven this point home directly to the people of Czechoslovakia, and indirectly to other East European and West European leaders, was the way clear for the process of *Ostpolitik* which culminated in the signing of the Helsinki Final Act – praised in the West as signifying the Soviet commitment to lower the barriers between East and West, but hailed in Moscow as the final recognition by the West that those barriers do in fact legitimately exist and that Europe is forever divided into two sectors. Thus the USSR, by signing the Final Act, further indicated the extent to which Soviet leaders, in calculating the correlation of forces in Europe, increasingly view 'class forces' as being a term practically synonymous with 'the balance of power between the socialist and capitalist state systems'.

The fact that Moscow adheres to a more state-centric definition of the balance in power leaves open the issue of its attitude toward and support for the communist parties of Europe. When Lenin was surveying the chances of a revolution in Europe, he obviously looked to the communist parties there to provide the avant-garde of that movement. But when it came to protecting the nascent Soviet republic, Lenin, in a series of trade agreements and treaties, from Brest-Litovsk to Rapallo, did not hesitate to deal with and even implicitly to strengthen the very governments his Eurocommunist allies were seeking to destroy. This policy was strengthened under Stalin when European communists in the Comintern were forced to support policies which fluctuated wildly between the ultra-leftism of the late 1920s to the popular front period of the 1930s and then even accommodation with fascism for the brief period after the 1939 Nazi–Soviet Pact. These shifting policies mirrored Moscow's state interests but were formulated with total disregard for the local conditions under which the European communists were operating. And in the ultimate show of 'realpolitik', once the alliance between the USSR and the Western powers was forged, Stalin abandoned the European communists altogether and abolished the Comintern.

These trends continue in the Soviet attitude toward Eurocommunism, with the difference that the protection of Soviet and bloc security has become an even greater determinant of Soviet policy and the prospect of a communist party coming to power (by whatever means) anywhere in Europe has further receded in Soviet calculations. The result has been an inevitable rift between the two groups as Moscow continually reasserts its view that unswerving loyalty to the notion of Soviet infallibility is an inalienable part of being a good socialist. The Prague Spring expressed and reinforced many of the aspirations of Eurocommunists for a more 'intellectual' and reform-minded communism. But the Soviet reaction to it left Eurocommunists in no doubt on three scores: one, that the maintenance of Soviet control over Eastern Europe was the corner-stone of Moscow's strategy toward Europe as a whole; two, that Moscow would never yield its position as the *fons et origo* of communist doctrine to any other communist party; and three, that the Kremlin willingly accepted that its invasion of Czechoslovakia would damage beyond repair the popularity of the communist movement in Europe for decades.

This view of the Prague Spring and the ultimate Soviet invasion of Czechoslovakia despite Eurocommunist objections illustrated more clearly than any other action since the 1956 Hungarian uprising the absolute priority Moscow attached to long-term strategy – the second aspect of the correlation of forces. This assessment of Soviet priorities was stunningly displayed by Brezhnev himself during the negotiations with the Dubček leadership following the invasion. An account of Brezhnev's remarks was subsequently published by Zdenek Mlynar, a secretary of the Czechoslovak Communist Party, who was present at the time. Mlynar states:

> Brezhnev spoke at length about the sacrifices of the Soviet Union in the Second World War: the soldiers fallen in battle, the civilians slaughtered, the enormous material costs. At such a cost, the Soviet Union had gained security, and the guarantee of that security was the postwar division of Europe

and, specifically, the fact that Czechoslovakia was linked with the Soviet Union 'forever' . . . 'For us', Brezhnev went on, 'the results of the Second World War are inviolable, and we will defend them even at the cost of risking a new war . . . So what (he asked Dubček) do you think will be done on your behalf? Nothing. There will be no war. Comrade Tito and Comrade Ceausescu will say their piece, and so will Comrade Berlinguer. Well, and what of it? You are counting on the Communist movement in Western Europe, but that won't amount to anything for fifty years.'[14]

This passage aptly displays both the Soviet assessment of Eurocommunism and the extent to which the dominant Soviet image of Europe has been shaped by the Soviet experience during the Second World War, as discussed in the previous section. And even more than a decade after the Prague Spring, despite the improved relations with Europe which were a feature of the 1970s, the events in Poland in 1980 and 1981 illustrated that this basic assessment of Europe and Euro-communism was still very operative. The growth of Solidarity, talk about reform communism, and openly anti-Soviet be-haviour evoked fears in Moscow that Poland might become a less reliable member of the Warsaw Pact, thus upsetting the balance of power in Europe. The Polish events also reminded the Soviets that thirty-five years of alliance between Warsaw and Moscow had done little if anything to bury the anti-Russian biases of the Polish people or to convince them that by nature and by culture they belonged on the eastern divide of Europe. Thus the Soviet leadership, in its exchange of polemics with the Poles, continually equated anti-socialism and anti-Sovietism, and repeatedly reminded the Poles of how many Russian lives had been sacrificed to achieve peace in Europe. The following quote, from the Politburo letter to the Polish leadership, illustrates these points. Its subject is the existence of an 'unchecked campaign' against the USSR:

31

Its main objective is to vilify and cast aspersions on the world's first socialist state and on the very idea of socialism, to enkindle among Poles hostility and hatred of the Soviet Union and the Soviet people, to break the bonds of the brotherly friendship linking our nations and as a result to wrest Poland out of the socialist commonwealth, and to liquidate socialism in Poland herself . . .

The Soviet people, which has made vast sacrifices to liberate Poland from fascist bondage, which has selflessly helped and continues to help your country today, has the full moral right to demand that an end be put to the anti-Soviet impudence in Poland.[15]

The Soviet Union rejected as unjustified interference any Eurocommunist comment on the Polish situation, in much the same way as they had scorned it in 1968. The events in Poland, and Soviet reaction to them, thus underlined the continuing validity into the 1980s of the second of the three aspects of the correlation of forces, namely that long-term strategy takes precedence over short-term policy – defined in this context to mean the Soviet Union's immutable adherence to the post-war division of Europe.

But what of the third principle inherent in the correlation of forces – that regional policy should be determined with reference to global strategy? This postulate is particularly applicable to Europe due to the centrality of Europe in Soviet global calculations. It is less so in other areas contiguous to the Soviet border where the interests of maintaining the security of the Soviet border can come into conflict with global strategy. It was arguably the case, for example, that the Soviet invasion of Afghanistan was designed to prevent an unpopular and increasingly anti-Soviet regime from destabilising the situation on the Soviet Union's southern perimeter (regional policy) but that at the same time it reflected negatively upon the Soviet Union's relationship with the United States and its general standing internationally (global strategy). Indeed President Brezhnev's subsequent admission that the USSR had been 'surprised' by the international reaction to the invasion suggests that while they may have attempted to make a correct assessment of the impact of invasion upon this aspect of the correlation of forces, they had miscalculated.

Of course, the relationship between regional and global strategy is much more intimately connected in Europe. The current bipolar world rose up out of, and then came back to haunt, a bifurcated Europe. For the Soviet Union, détente both globally and in Europe was never about redrawing the map of that continent. Rather, détente was about the final and universal acceptance precisely of a divided Europe. Admittedly, it allowed for greater co-operation, more exchanges, and higher trade levels, but only within the context of acceptance of the status quo in Europe. Thus, for example, Moscow hailed the Soviet–West German Treaty signed in August 1970 not so much because of the tangible benefit détente might bring for the peoples of both countries but because, in the words of *Pravda*, it 'marked the acknowledgement by realistic forces in the West of post-war realities'.[16] It can be said, therefore, that although in all other regions of the world, including even the Far East, the Soviet Union attempts to formulate a regional policy which will serve its global strategy, Europe is the one region where the Soviet Union would sacrifice its own position globally in order to maintain its position regionally.

There was a time, in the early and mid-1960s, when some West European leaders felt that Moscow might be changing its policy, that the Soviet Union's interest in a stable East–West relationship in Europe was such that it would accept greater East European autonomy. Thus this Soviet interest in détente, skilfully exploited by de Gaulle and characterised by Brandt, in defining the objectives of *Ostpolitik*, as 'transformation through rapprochement', seemed likely to lead to a greater independence both of East Europe from Moscow and West Europe from the United States. The Soviet Union, of course, had then, and still has, a great interest in encouraging the Europeans to pursue a policy more independent of Washington, since to do so would in the first instance weaken the NATO alliance and possibly also ultimately reduce the chances of Europe being used as the launching pad for any American-inspired offensive against the Soviet bloc. The Soviet Union, therefore, had every interest in decoupling Europe from the United States, but not if the price was to be a simultaneous decoupling of Eastern Europe from Moscow. This was, of course, the quintessential feature of the Brezhnev Doctrine, namely that the states of the socialist commonwealth were more than a mere alliance of sovereign states – they formed a single organic unity, which as a whole represented a major force in international politics. The unity of those states was imperative for the defence of socialism, and therefore for one state to pursue an alien and individual policy was anti-socialist, short-sighted and serving of narrow sectional and national interests as opposed to global strategy. These charges, levelled against the Czechs, the Romanians and then the Poles whenever they have attempted to move closer to Europe, have at their roots the Soviet interest in maintaining the security of the Soviet bloc both from direct military threat and from the subversive effects of European culture.

Europe will always be a central focus of Soviet policy-makers. This is not only because of the psychological attractions of Europe for the Russian and East European peoples but also because of the repeated European invasions of Russia which tend to be at the forefront of all Russian considerations and which seem at times to obliterate any other view of Europe which the Kremlin could have drawn out of its long Russian and Marxist past. The exclusiveness of Marxist ideology in the formulation of Soviet policy toward Europe is therefore open to doubt, but what seems more certain is that adherence to Marxism exhorts Soviet leaders to develop a more clearly defined strategy which integrates Moscow's short-term goals with her long-term plans and at the same time places Europe within the context of Soviet global strategy. Having said that ideology sets the parameters for policy formulation, yet the ideas, the content of that policy are heavily affected by security considerations. Europe remains in the Soviet *Weltanschauung* essentially a region which both militarily and culturally the Soviet Union seeks security from. There is the occasional Westernising echo to be heard in the walls of the Kremlin, but the basic reflex remains firmly Slavophil.

Possibilities for Change

And what of the future? Is Moscow likely to remain welded to this essentially cocoon-like response toward and conception of Europe? Will its hostile attitude toward Eurocommunism be forever unyielding and is there no hope of reform-minded communism being allowed to develop anywhere within the Soviet sphere? The answer to any of these questions necessarily remains in the realm of conjecture, but certain developments might lead to the revision of Soviet doctrine. The first possibility for change lies in the inevitable transition to the next generation of Soviet leaders – men not conditioned by the reflexes of the Second World War, and with no direct experience of the need to protect their Western borders. These men, schooled during the Sino–Soviet dispute, the Vietnam War, and the decades of troubles in the Middle East and South Asia might tend to regard the threat from Europe as secondary to the threat from other areas on the Soviet periphery. The normalisation of relations with China in particular has come to have great priority in recent years, as witnessed for example by President Brezhnev's Baku speech of 25 September 1982[17], and therefore a new generation of Soviet leaders who diversified Soviet concerns away from obsession with the 'threat from Europe' would really only be reinforcing a trend which has been growing for some time.

This trend would be strengthened if Moscow could be further convinced that co-operation with Europe would serve its own interests. In particular if such co-operation weakened American hegemony over the Atlantic Alliance, this would most certainly be in Moscow's interests. At the same time, the Soviet Union's failure to close the technology gap has strengthened the nascent symbiosis between East and West Europe whereby Soviet raw materials are exchanged for West European technology. Not only do economic advantages in such agreements accrue to both sides, but politically, as the fierce debates over the West European defiance of American efforts to boycott the delivery of gas pipeline equipment to the USSR testify, Moscow reaps enormous political advantages by splitting the Alliance. In the realm of disarmament, too, the Soviet Union has much to gain in fostering ties with those West European countries most cautious about the deployment of American nuclear missiles on their territory.

It is precisely on these issues that Moscow stands the most chance of finding new common ground with those elements of the European left ostracised by Moscow since the late 1960s. It is remarkable and ironic, but true none the less, that Euro-communism, born as it was largely out of disgust with Soviet actions in Czechoslovakia in 1968, should, fifteen years later, be directing much of its energies toward the reduction of American influence in Western Europe rather than Soviet influence in Eastern Europe. To the extent, therefore, that Eurocommunism is supportive of the broader trend in Europe undermining the American position there, it certainly will be supported by Moscow. But as long as the ruling governments themselves in countries such as West Germany, France and even Britain on certain trade issues defy American pressures, then the Soviet leadership is hardly likely to encourage any com-munist party activity in Western Europe which might upset this trend.

In planning for the years to come, the current generation of Soviet leaders have focused more and more on solving the urgent problems of their economy. The need for a shift from extensive to intensive development, the demands of consumers for more food, better housing and services and more luxury items, the growing demographic imbalance in the location and composition of the work force, the massive investments that will be required to exploit Siberian-based natural resources and the related awareness of the need for energy conservation to prevent possible future shortfalls – all of these problems can be expected to loom ever larger in the preoccupation of the next generation of Soviet leaders. Such an introversion of the Soviet system need not, and probably would not, bring about any radical transformation or liberalisation of domestic processes, nor would it necessarily result in any substantial alteration in the basic Soviet conception of Europe or the assessment of the correlation of forces there. But it could have a discernible effect on Soviet behaviour by making Soviet leaders more prone to crisis management rather than crisis exploitation, to co-operation rather than conflict, and to the political and economic advantages of reducing arms rather than stockpiling them. This is the logical outcome of the pressures which have built up in the Soviet system. However, analysts have in the past frequently been amazed at the ability of the Soviet leadership and bureaucracy to withstand, ignore, suppress or just misconstrue such pressures, muddling through, simultaneously absorbing and smothering any far-reaching demands for innovation.

In such a climate, the Soviet military machine has for over a decade been able to claim the lion's share of resources by virtue simply of its greater efficiency, power and purposiveness compared with other sectors of the economy. The introversion of the Soviet economy would therefore depend on the ability of those atrophied sections of the bureaucracy to regain their strength and weaken the influence of the military. Such an outcome would demand both the strong support of the new First Secretary and the willingness of the West not to challenge the Soviet Union in a way which would strengthen the military card. This argument may be appreciated in many European capitals, but in Washington the very fact of Alliance differences over the handling of the Soviet Union is taken as proof of the extent to which Europe has fallen under Soviet influence. It is indeed possible, therefore, that the outcome of the crucial debate over resource allocation which will inevitably accompany the succession to the post-Brezhnev era and which will decide whether there will be any substantial changes in Soviet policy towards Europe will be shaped, if not determined, by the European conception of the Soviet Union and how Washington reacts to it.

Notes to Chapter 1

1   C. Wright Mills, *The Marxists* (London: Pelican, 1962), p. 14.
2   Richard Lowenthal, 'The Logic of One-Party Rule', in *Russia under Khruschev*, ed. A. Brumberg (London: Methuen, 1962), p. 29.
3   Karl Marx, *German Ideology* (London: Lawrence & Wishart, 1965), p. 14.
4   V. I. Lenin, *Selected Works in Three Volumes*, Vol. 3 (Moscow: Progress Publishers, 1971), p. 695.
5   J. V. Stalin, 'The Foundations of Leninism', in *The Essential Stalin* (London: Croom Helm, 1973), p. 184.
6   Stalin, 'Foundations of Leninism', pp. 95–7.
7   Konstantin F. Shteppa, *Russian Historians and the Soviet State* (New Brunswick, NJ: Rutgers University Press, 1962), p. 147.
8   'Zadachi sovetskikh istorikov v oblasti novoi i noveishei istorii', *Voprosy istorii*, no. 3 (1949), p. 7.
9   'Zadachi sovetskikh', pp. 3–4, in referring to the article states: 'In this article of genius, J. V. Stalin with complete persuasiveness, showed the mistaken views of Engels in the 1840s with regard to the external policy of Russia . . . [Stalin] showed that the role of the last stronghold of reaction . . . more and more was transferred from Russia to the imperialistic bourgeois states of Western Europe . . .'
10 'Protiv obyektivizma v istoricheskoi nauke', *Voprosy istorii*, no. 12 (1948), p. 11.
11 V. I. Lenin, *Sochineniya*, Vol. 22 (2nd edn, Moscow: Gostpolitizdat, 1929), p. 265.
12 I. D. Ovsyany *et al.*, *A Study of Soviet Foreign Policy* (Moscow: Progress Publishers, 1975), p. 12
13 Ovsyany *et al.*, *A Study*, pp. 16–17.
14 Zdenek Mlyner, *Night Frost in Prague* (London: C. Hurst & Co., 1980), pp. 239–41.
15 Polish News Agency text as reprinted in *The Times*, 19 September 1981.
16 *Pravda*, 13 August 1970.
17 Reported in *The Times*, 27 September 1982.

2

Soviet Decision-Making and Western Europe

Hannes Adomeit

Some of the most striking features of developments in the Soviet Union during the Brezhnev era were the internationally unparalleled stability of the Soviet leadership, the almost complete absence of institutional change (and in some instances the undoing of institutional changes made by Khrushchev), the constant reiteration of standard ideological formulas, declining economic growth rates, and falling productivity.[1] Yet at first sight, paradoxically, the USSR in the same period embarked on a vigorous armament programme, rising to parity with the USA in the strategic sphere, improving its traditional superiority over NATO in the conventional weapons in Central Europe, and acquiring naval and airlift capabilities to intervene, or support intervention, in close proximity to the Soviet homeland (e.g. in Afghanistan) or in distant regions (e.g. Angola or Ethiopia). At the same time it has, since 1969, conducted policy toward the West under the traditional slogan of 'peaceful co-existence' and the more modern one of détente (*razryadka*), first applying it to both the United States and Western Europe and then, after the outbreak of the 'new cold war' in Soviet–American relations at the end of 1979, more selectively to Western Europe. In each and every phase, however, Soviet policy was remarkably flexible, combining the approach of 'speaking softly' – and

39

sometimes not so softly – with that of carrying a 'big stick', utilising both 'inter-imperialist contradictions' (e.g. differences of interest and policy between the United States and Western Europe) and 'intra-imperialist' conflicts (e.g. the opposition of Western European 'peace' movements to government plans of deploying new medium-range nuclear systems).

According to Lenin (and essentially he was right on that point), 'There is no more erroneous or harmful idea than the separation of foreign from internal policy'.[2] But, as follows from the above enumeration of contradictory elements, the *character* of Soviet foreign policy is different from that of Soviet domestic politics. The provincialism and narrow-minded vindictiveness against dissent and reformism at home stands in stark contrast to the Soviet Union's profile as a global power with commitments ranging from Cuba to Vietnam, world-wide diplomatic representation and Party contacts, scientific activities from pole to pole and in space, far-flung fishing operations (including fishing for intelligence), and considerable and expanding commercial operations. This curious contradiction needs explanation. More specifically, it is appropriate to ask what sort of mechanism of policy-making it is that is transforming domestic retrenchment into external activity.

There are a number of broad possibilities which could serve as guidelines to answer that question. First, it could be argued that the apparent difference in the character of Soviet domestic and foreign policy reflects loss of ideological momentum domestically but continuation of such momentum internationally. Secondly, as a stronger variation of this theme, it is conceivable – contrary to the point made above by reference to Lenin – that there *is* a strict separation of the domestic and foreign policy spheres, each one following its own logic and dynamics. (To make the point clear here and now, there is not much evidence for this.)

Thirdly, external dynamism could be interpreted as a compensation of sorts for internal weakness, a process whereby international glory serves to divert attention from domestic drabness and latent discontent. If so, there would be parallels to nineteenth-century European imperialism which, too, showed a marked tendency to neglect social, economic and political reform but emphasised the glory of empire-building abroad. To that extent the dichotomy is perhaps more apparent than real: in both spheres of activity, domestic politics and foreign policy, it would be the primary rationale of policy to maintain and expand power. Seen from these perspectives Soviet foreign policy appears as the logical extension of, rather than a puzzling contradiction to, domestic politics.

Fourthly, it could be argued that the contradiction between domestic stagnation and foreign policy expansionism was characteristic merely of the second half of the 1970s but that it began to lessen in the last two years of the Brezhnev era. The economic shortcomings at home and the 'burden of empire' in Eastern Europe (notably Poland) began to place significant constraints on Soviet foreign policy ambitions. These limits, to conclude the argument, can be expected even more thoroughly to affect Andropov's policies – in Europe and elsewhere.

Endorsement or rejection of any of these arguments crucially depends on an accurate diagnosis of the forces at work in the Soviet system. It hinges on whether there exist pressures – by individuals, groups or institutions – which may be at odds with the present conduct of domestic or foreign policy. It is also tied to answering the question of whether those individuals, groups or institutions adopt congruent attitudes on issues of domestic (including economic) politics and foreign policy (including intra-bloc policies and relations between the CPSU and the international communist movement).

To put analysis of these problems in some kind of order it is appropriate to begin by looking at some of the broad, long-term factors of Soviet policy-making, above all ideology, power and the bureaucracy. Based on the discussion of bureaucracy an attempt will be made to illuminate in some detail the interests and probable influence of some of the bureaucracies. Considering that the rise of the Soviet Union to military–strategic parity with the USA was achieved by relying on an economic base that is only little more than half as big as that of the United States; taking into account Western estimates of Soviet defence expenditures as being between 11 and 13 per cent of GNP, growth rates in defence spending as having been at a constant 4 per cent throughout the Brezhnev era, and the share of machinery allocated to meet military 'needs' as being one third of the total output; bearing in mind also that Soviet military aid to developing countries considerably exceeds economic aid and that a significant and rising portion of Soviet foreign exchange earnings derives from the export of weapons, it is appropriate to focus in some detail on the role of the military in foreign policy-making. Not least because of Andropov's career background, it is then necessary to focus upon the power and possible role of the political police (KGB) and military intelligence (GRU). Next, as economic and military problems are closely linked, and as it is possible to see the Soviet emphasis on heavy industry and military power as the result of a series of defeats for such interest groups or bureaucracies promoting economic reform, it is necessary to look also at the likely foreign policy interests and attitudes of economic administrators, 'technocrats', managers and the 'agricultural lobby'. This leads to an examination of the question of whether it is possible to tie military, political, economic and ideological factors into one single framework of analysis. The final section deals with the possible scope and likely direction of political, ideological and economic change under Andropov and asks how the West could influence such changes as are advantageous to its own interests.

The 'End of Ideology'

Western specialists on Soviet affairs are likely to react to any discussion of the role of ideology in Soviet foreign policy with expressions of *déjà vu* and boredom, and the comment that there is nothing more to say on a problem that has been discussed *ad infinitum* and for all practical purposes 'solved'.[3] The alleged solution presents itself in the form of wide agreement with the view that ideology may have explained something of Soviet foreign policy in the early period (i.e. before Stalin came to power) but that there had been a long evolutionary process, as a result of which national or state interests of the USSR had superseded the ideological dimension of Soviet politics.[4] Brest-Litovsk, the proclamation of the New Economic Plan (NEP), entry in the League of Nations, the Hitler–Stalin pact, the XX Party Congress and the Sino–Soviet split are taken as landmarks supposedly demonstrating the increasingly deep contradiction between national and state interests and ideology.

This perceived contradiction is seen as being reinforced by another. 'Ideological' is usually associated with 'irrational', 'reckless' and 'adventurist' but put in sharp contrast to 'pragmatic', 'opportunist' and 'realistic'. As a consequence, ideology as a factor influencing Soviet policy-making is being eroded in the mind of the Western analyst when he or she is faced with instances where Soviet representatives display diplomatic skill, act as shrewd and calculating businessmen or pay much attention to military power as an instrument of furthering state interests.

A sub-theme of this perceived contradiction between ideology and pragmatism is the view that the ideological content of foreign policy is equivalent to the degree of Soviet support to world revolution, more specifically, the extent to which the Soviet Union is willing to employ military force on behalf of local communists in various areas of the world. As a result, ideology in Soviet foreign policy-making is being eroded in the perception of the Western analyst when the Soviet leaders apparently close their eyes to the oppression of local communists while engaging in co-operation with the oppressors at the state level (as in many countries of the Arab world), stand by with folded arms as Marxist regimes are being crushed (as in Chile) or fail to exploit alleged or real advantages for deepening the 'crisis of capitalism' (as in the wake of the oil crisis after 1973).

These two contradictions as seen by Western analysts add up to a third one, namely that between *ex post facto* rationalisation (*Rechtfertigung*) and *ex ante* motivation (*Antrieb*), the argument being that the Soviet state is indeed an ideology in power but is merely providing legitimacy to action, i.e. can no longer be regarded as a guide to action. Proof of this thesis is derived from the undoubtedly valid observation that Marxist–Leninist doctrine has served to justify all sorts of policies. At the inter-Party level it has been used to justify projected governments of national union (Italy), adventurous disregard of mathematical majorities (the Portuguese CP in 1975) and hesitation with regard to popular-front tactics (France). It has been used to justify *massive* military aid to fraternal countries (Hungary, Czechoslovakia), progressive regimes (Ethiopia, Afghanistan) and national liberation movements (MPLA in Angola), or *none* at all (as recently in Lebanon).

Several reservations with regard to these contradictions are well in place. First of all, if it is true that the Soviet state is an ideology in power it follows that the contradiction between ideological and state, or national, interests is more apparent than real. What is at issue is not a matter of nationalism supplanting ideology but supplementing it.[5] The reconciliation of apparent contradictions was provided long ago by Stalin in his dictum that 'An internationalist is ready to defend the USSR without reservation, without wavering, unconditionally'.[6] The essence of this doctrinal assertion, of course, is the idea that what serves to enhance Soviet power internationally, simultaneously increases the prospects of world revolution.

From a practical political point of view it would be very comforting if one could accept the idea that such an assertion was nothing but cynicism and pretension out of touch with the reality of world politics. It is not wise to adopt such a view. Dynamic interrelationships between Soviet support for revolutionary transformations abroad, the occasional success of such transformations, and benefits for Soviet power and foreign policy do remain. Cuba is perhaps the best example of such

44

interrelationships. Castro's turn from a brand of liberalism to Marxism-Leninism almost provided the USSR with an extensive strategic-nuclear benefit in 1962 (if Khrushchev's idea of a *fait accompli* had worked out as he had anticipated it would); in the latter half of the 1970s it was Cuban troops who put the Marxist-Leninist MPLA into power in Angola and pulled the chestnuts out of the fire for Mengistu's regime in Ethiopia; and in the same period – rivalries between Hanoi and Moscow notwithstanding – the Vietnamese communists helped spread Soviet influence to Vietnamese-controlled Laos and Cambodia, and provided the USSR with strategic advantages in South-east Asia. The Soviet leadership, one suspects, is still deeply affected by the idea that revolutionary transformations are first and foremost a blow to imperialist influence and control: in Cuba, Nicaragua and perhaps elsewhere in Latin America; in Vietnam, Laos, Cambodia and potentially elsewhere in Asia; in Angola, Mozambique and in other African countries; and – if possible – also in Europe. Certainly, not every revolutionary or pseudo-revolutionary transformation *per se* can be regarded as strengthening the power of the Soviet state, and not in all cases is it possible to say that a Western loss is automatically a Soviet gain. This is the 'objective' state of affairs. Yet it appears that the Soviet leadership is untiring in its optimism that if the correlation is not direct and immediate it will ultimately turn out to be so.

As for the contradiction between ideology and pragmatism, careful distinctions need to be made. To speak of Soviet ideology is to speak of Leninism which is largely an adaptation of Marxism to the Russian social, economic and political setting, providing a set of policy prescriptions and advice on tactics. Such advice can be summed up in the firm belief that the ends justify the means and that manoeuvering, flexibility, pragmatism and opportunism are necessary attributes of policies at home and abroad. To that extent, opportunism or pragmatism can be a reflection of ideologically conscious policy rather than a con-tradiction to it. As the editor of *Izvestiia* put it seventy years ago at a time of undoubted relevance of ideology for policy-making, 'We are convinced that the most consistent socialist policy can be reconciled with the sternest realism and most level-headed practicality'.[7]

To turn to the argument that ideology is merely *ex post facto* justification rather than motivation of policy, on this point too it is useful to express reservations because the distinction looks neat in theory but is not very persuasive in practice. This is perhaps best shown by an analogy. For a tribal medicine man the sacred myths and rituals involving the healing power of snake skins, goat blood and monkey tails are undoubtedly a source of legitimacy for the power he exerts. This is so irrespective of whether he is a complete cynic. Nevertheless, the myths, rituals and taboos can assume important motivating functions under two conditions. The first one is a belief on the part of the medicine man that his power will be improved if he can spread the myths to other tribes. The second is the appearance of internal or external critics who dare call the assumed healing powers of myths and medicine men a deplorable hoax and/or deliberate deception; this is likely to call forth vigorous counteraction.

Both of these conditions exist in Soviet foreign policy. Concerning the first condition there are the hopes connected with spreading Marxism-Leninism to the national liberation movements of the Third World. Concerning the second condition, the widespread cynicism about ideology among the Soviet population and the (at present almost crushed) activity of dissidents in the USSR; the mass support for industrial and rural *Solidarność* and, as a result, the almost complete collapse of the authority of the Communist Party in Poland; the challenge of the 'new communist internationalism' presented by the non-ruling Italian, Spanish and other West European parties but supported also by the ruling party of Yugoslavia; and the new theme in the West about 'managing the decline of the Soviet empire' with the taking of sanctions to maintain or induce change in Eastern Europe (Poland), all point in the same direction, namely, that the Soviet leadership *nolens volens* cannot relegate ideology to a place of secondary importance. It is possible to summarise, therefore, that an evolutionary process has taken place. The original ideological fervour (the utopian, revolutionary or missionary aspects of ideology) and the humanistic, emancipatory content of Marxism have given way in the Soviet Union to a greater emphasis on legitimacy. To that extent, there has been a transformation in the functions of ideology. What it does not mean, however, is that ideology no longer matters in Soviet foreign policy.

The Ends of Power

As with the standard dichotomies between ideology and national interest, and ideology and pragmatism, it is unwise to make a rigid distinction between ideology and power. An effective, persuasive ideology can be an important means of exerting influence, and to that extent constitutes a form of power; conversely, power in its traditional dimension (i.e. military and economic power) can be an effective instrument to spread ideology. This is the general frame of reference.[8] Looking specifically at Soviet foreign policy it is obvious that a shift of emphasis has taken place.

In the pre-Second World War era the Soviet political leaders often had to make a virtue of necessity, namely to attempt to expand influence with the help of local Communist Parties without being able to come to their aid. In fact, due to the vulnerability of the Soviet state precisely the opposite was the rule: the local Parties had to come to the aid of the Soviet Union, the most noteworthy examples being the popular front tactics of the 1930s and the support required of the various Communist Parties for the Hitler–Stalin pact. The Second World War dramatically altered this state of affairs. Military power, either in the form of direct involvement, deterrence or threat, or in the form of weapons deliveries, could be and was used to further

47

Soviet state interests, as well as in attempts to achieve and safeguard 'revolutionary transformations' abroad, first in Eastern
Europe, later in the Middle East, South-east Asia and Africa and,
finally, in Afghanistan.

Although the use of military power in direct or indirect form
is not an unambiguous success story, and although there is no
direct correlation between growth in Soviet military power and
growth in political influence, it is fair to say that the Soviet
leaders believe that, roughly, there *is* such a correlation. So far,
they have had no negative experience with military strength,
only with military weakness; and so far they have had no
traumatic lesson of defeat taught to them as it was to the
Germans and the Japanese in the Second World War, and the
Americans in Vietnam. (The failure thus far to stifle the
resistance of the *mujaheddin* in Afghanistan is a serious international embarrassment but not a 'Soviet Vietnam': Soviet
casualties are in the hundreds, not thousands, economic costs in
millions of rubles, not billions, and these costs have to be set
against the benefits from the extraction of gas and raw materials
from the country, military-strategic advantages in South-west
Asia, and the Soviet conviction that – as in Poland in 1980–1 –
superior military strength will ultimately lead to the demoral-
isation and defeat of the opponent.)

The Soviet leaders are probably quite aware of the fact that
due to the failure of Marxist-Leninist ideology and the Soviet
system to inspire the *intelligentsia* of the West and Japan, the
lack of cultural penetration outside the Soviet bloc and the
decline of the Soviet Union as a model of development for the
Third World, it is the status of the USSR as a *military power* equal
to that of the USA which ensures that Moscow's point of view is
taken into account. It is this status which, in Soviet perceptions,
time and again forces the United States to the negotiating table
on arms control. It is, finally, this very status which, as seen
from Moscow, plays a crucially important role in Soviet–West
European relations in as much as Western Europe is largely
instrumental in frustrating US attempts at isolating the USSR,

conducting a coherent policy of sanctions against the Soviet Union or embarking on a large-scale joint effort to restore the East–West military balance. To this has to be added the important function which the armed forces have in building 'socialist man', namely in instilling discipline and patriotism, and in helping to break down nationality barriers.[9]

All these factors reinforce each other. They warrant the conclusion that for the Soviet leadership military power is just as important for safeguarding Soviet security as for extending political influence abroad. It remains, therefore, high on the list of priorities in domestic resource allocation – an observation that will be of relevance later in the discussion of the role of the military in Soviet policy-making.

Endless Bureaucracy

In addition to ideology and power, Soviet policy-making proceeds in the context of a third factor of major importance: the bureaucracy. Despite, as Soviet political leaders and commentators repeatedly put it, the on-going 'scientific-technological revolution' (NTR: *nauchno-tekhnicheskaya revo-lyutsiya*) and the complex demands it creates, Soviet politics, society and economics remain overshadowed by the Tsarist past, not only as regards the tradition of absolutism and autocracy but also the bureaucratic tradition, including rigid adherence to administrative routine, red tape, procrastination, intriguing, scheming and infighting, and a general indifference to the plight of the individual. The Stalinist period did much to resurrect the all-pervasive power of the bureaucracy. Socialism in the Soviet Union, as Trotsky was to note, suffered a profound bureaucratic degeneration.

Many Western analysts, drawing on Max Weber's theory of bureaucracy, look at the USSR as one 'large complex bureaucracy' and at Soviet society as having one 'bureaucratic command structure'.[10] They note the 'far wider scope of government' in the Soviet Union as compared to Western political systems, 'the limited character of the public political process'[11] and the system of *nomenklatura* (central allocation of important posts in the hierarchies of Party and state). They also point out that

> in the USSR, despite distinctions between Party, government, social organisations, etc., there is an important sense in which all are part of one great single hierarchy . . . It is as if the Establishment division of the British Treasury guided or approved all appointments, from the editorship of a provincial newspaper or a trade union secretaryship in Scotland up to a ministerial appointment and down to a managerial post in the Midlands.[12]

As argued by Astrid von Borcke, the Soviet political system still aims at asserting the primacy of politics over society, and it attempts to treat the whole social life as one unified organisation.[13] Any diminution of the leading role of the Party is held by the top leaders to 'jeopardise the achievements of socialism' (read: their own power position).[14] Although the Party's claim that it is expressing a 'scientifically founded common interest excludes public policy in the sense of competition of ideas, leaders and interests, the exclusion of social, economic and political groups, except for those sanctioned and controlled by the Party, has the result of allocating to the bureaucracy an important integrative function in the body politic. (This, too, was noticed by Trotsky. He argued that the means of production belonged to the state. 'However, the state belongs to the bureaucracy.') Hence, if the Soviet system is one of the most bureaucratised in the modern world, this is so not only because bureaucracy is implementing policy but also and mainly because it is exclusively the various bureaucracies which are authorised to participate in the decision-making process.

This type of bureaucratisation shows features *sui generis* which so far have not sufficiently been recognised conceptually. It is a politicised bureaucracy. Its main loyalty does not belong to any particular office or concrete purpose, in accordance with the Weberian concept of 'rational rule', but to the Party – a phenomenon expressed in the term *partiinost'*. Hence, the authority of an official depends less on the office itself than on the degree of political protection he receives; the main criterion for his appointment or advancement is political reliability; and 'the advancement and protection of sectional interests and commitments depends mainly on the behind-the-scenes efforts of sympathetic officials'.[15] The essence of politics in the Soviet Union, therefore, can be regarded as lying in the interaction between powerful leaders, their adherents and the organisations over which they preside.[16]

Many of the basic problems, goals and interests of the regime find their expression in the positions and the interaction of the big bureaucracies. While it is true that the regime has been able to counteract the tendencies towards autonomy inherent in all bureaucracies – because of the role of the Party, the system of *nomenklatura* and a number of specific features, such as informal relations as in cliques and family circles – it is also valid to assume that each big organisation is in partial conflict with every other; and although all the bureaucracies do have basic goals in common, foremost among which the safeguarding of the regime, they do form nevertheless only a 'coalition' of sorts. Of course, political struggle in the Soviet system does not proceed in the form of electoral contests. But politics cannot be abolished. This is the reason why administrative processes are affected by it, and the result produced is that of a form of 'crypto-politics'.[17]

But just as with ideology and power, there have been important changes that have affected Soviet bureaucracy. In the early stages of industrialisation it was possible to concentrate efforts on a few tasks of major importance. Coercion and genuine pioneering spirit combined to produce impressive rates of growth in industry. Indeed, in the initial stages of development, centralisation and the command economy made good sense – despite the absence of computer technology.

However, as most Western and some East European economists argue, modern industrial society requires a higher degree of specialisation and diversification of functions than in the past; it creates dynamics of its own that can neither be anticipated in detail nor entirely be regulated from above. In such a state of affairs terror becomes counterproductive. A premium is put on voluntary co-operation and initiative at lower levels of decision-making.

The result of this development for the purpose of the present inquiry is to say that tendentially modern industrial society increases autonomy of the individual bureaucracies and potentially enhances their role in foreign policy-making. More detailed consideration of this problem will show whether these tendencies and potentialities have found their reflection in the actual state of affairs in the Soviet Union.

There are some affinities in conceptual approach between the consideration of bureaucracy and bureaucracies, and the focus on interest groups in the study of policy-making in the USSR. According to Gordon Skilling's introduction to the anthology *Interest Groups in Soviet Politics*:

> There can be no doubt that communist society, in spite of its monolithic appearance and the claims of homogeneity made by its supporters, is in fact as complex and stratified as any other, and is divided into social classes . . . Each group has its own values and interests, and each its sharp internal differences, and all are inescapably involved in conflict with other groups.[18]

Skilling's central assumption, that the Soviet political system passed through a period of transition and had arrived at a stage characterised by an increased activity of political interest groups, is shared by many other Western analysts, by Jerry Hough, for instance, who expressed these images in the term 'institutional pluralism' of Soviet society and politics,[19] and by Milton Lodge who traced élite-group attitudes in a content analysis of Soviet periodicals.[20] What, then, are those 'interest groups' in the Soviet setting?

Judging from the table of contents of the anthology by Skilling and Griffiths, Soviet interest groups include the Party *apparatchiki*, the security police, the military, the industrial managers, the economists, the writers, and the jurists. In this list one might also want to include the specialists of international affairs at the various institutes of the USSR Academy of Sciences, and the Foreign Ministry's Institute of International Relations (IMO), a category which can be called the *institutchiki*. As this enumeration shows, there is a great deal of overlap between the two approaches because all of the important interest groups are at the same time officially sanctioned bureaucracies. On this basis the following argument has been developed by Western observers: the interests represented by the leaders of the various groups are primarily functional interests; attitudes and the direction of influence exerted can be inferred, or predicted, from the axiom of 'Where you stand depends on where you sit'.[21]

But this is precisely where major problems arise. Is it really safe to assume that the leaders on top of the various bureaucracies are primarily functional representatives of the various bureaucracies, or are they representatives of the Politburo in the bureaucracies? Assuming that the former is largely true, what exactly are the interests of the various bureaucracies in foreign policy? (So far, most of the Western discussion has been limited to examining the role of the various bureaucracies and interest groups in domestic politics.) Assuming that one can arrive at a reasonably accurate reconstruction of interests, the problem that arises next is to see whether attempts are being made by the interest groups/bureaucracies to exert influence on foreign policy in a direction corresponding with their interests and attitudes. Finally, if such attempts are made, it would be interesting to see whether they are effective for all types of decision, e.g. decisions concerning day-to-day business, decisions of principle and far-reaching consequence, and decisions in international crises. These are complex questions which cannot be answered within the limited scope of this article (if at all). But it is useful at this stage to abandon the broad framework of ideology, power and bureaucracy and probe more deeply into the roles played by specific bureaucracies, organisations and institutions.

The Role of the Military

Analysis of interests and attitudes of the Soviet military and Party military relations has been shaped significantly by the writings of Roman Kolkowicz, by his view that there existed some kind of adversary relationship between the Soviet military and the Party, the military stressing professional autonomy, nationalism, detachment from society, heroic symbolism and élitist organisational goals, the Party emphasising ideological orthodoxy, proletarian internationalism, social involvement, anonymity and egalitarian ideals.[22] This theme is taken up by Kolkowicz in his contribution to Skilling and Griffiths's anthology where he argues that the military's relations with the Party are characterised by instability, but that there had been 'noticeable success in the efforts of the military to obtain institutional autonomy'.[23] As an extension of this argument, it seemed to many observers at the time that the appointment of Marshal Grechko to full membership in the Politburo in April 1973 was a manifestation of this very trend of allegedly greater institutional autonomy and increased influence of the military in policy-making.

However, this line of reasoning, stressing the conflicting nature of Party military relations and the growing influence of the Soviet military is too simplistic, and perhaps even misleading. Military-patriotic education, discipline, devotion to duty, conservatism, and ideological orthodoxy are preferences which are shared by the military as well as by the Party *apparatchiki*. To assume a discrepancy between the current interpretations of proletarian internationalism and nationalism is problematic in itself, but to divide these principles in terms of Party/military conflict is even more problematic. Assumptions that the military is always the advocate of a high degree of professionalism, innovation and technical expertise evade the question of whether it is not precisely the Party that utilises the central *apparat* to give new ideas and military science a push and introduce them into the armed forces, often against conservative and traditional elements in the military. This would be true in particular for the foundation of the Strategic Rocket Forces under Khrushchev. But it would be even more correct with regard to the Soviet Navy, traditionally a weak branch of the armed forces at a disadvantage *vis-à-vis* the other branches: it is hardly conceivable that the expansion of its role could have been achieved without the active support of the political leadership (and, most likely, against resistance by other branches).[24]

In the light of these arguments, it would appear that the consistent practice of appointing military professionals to the post of Defence Minister and Grechko's inclusion in the Politburo were not the harbingers of 'Bonapartism' or a rise to power of the military at the expense of the Party, nor indications of greater institutional autonomy of the military, but manifestations of a deliberate policy by the Party to ensure effectiveness of control and speedy implementation of politico-military decisions taken at the level of the Politburo or the Defence Council.[25] Similarly, Ustinov's appointment to the post of Defence Minister in April 1976 should not be taken as a reversal of the respective fortunes of the Party and the military (i.e. as a victory of the Party over the military) and the ascendancy of civilian over military priorities; it is more likely the result of a number of things, partly a reward for long services rendered, partly a response to the necessity of co-ordinating increasingly complex decisions in defence economics, and hence partly an indication of the Soviet leadership's awareness of interrelationships between an efficient economic and scientific-technological base and effective military power.[26]

But what about those instances where the Soviet military

played a role in domestic power struggles? It is fair to argue that where it did play a role it did so not in the form of pushing itself into the political limelight to further its own power ambitions as a politicised institution and at the expense of the Party, but because it was invited in, for a limited time span, by the political leadership or a major faction of it. This applies to all the three major instances that are relevant in this context: the arrest and execution of Beria and the curtailment of the power of the secret police in 1953–4; the help the military gave Khrushchev in 'reversing a mathematical majority' in the Presidium in June 1957; and the support it extended to the Presidium in removing Khrushchev from office in October 1964.

A fourth example often cited to underline the conflicting nature of the relationship between the military and the Party is the dramatic ouster of Marshal Zhukov from his posts of Defence Minister and full membership of the Presidium in October 1957 by a plenum of the Central Committee, and the nature of the charges subsequently levelled against him.[27] However, a convincing reconsideration of the Zhukov affair shows that it was primarily an episode 'occasioned by the actions of one man under particular circumstances'; it was undoubtedly a conflict between Zhukov and Khrushchev; and this conflict was inflated by the 'atmosphere of Soviet élite politics'. But it is

> hazardous indeed to assume that the clash between the two was a manifestation of some more profound conflict between the institutions of which they were formal heads. Conflicts do perhaps 'rage in the Kremlin', but the combatants are not necessarily surrogates for larger social structures.[28]

There is another conclusion that emerges from the analysis of the Zhukov affair:

> A revised understanding should spur reconsideration of the dichotomous way in which Soviet military politics has been

interpreted in the West, in terms of an image of army and Party locked in implacable conflict and able to agree only on temporary truces. On the contrary, elements of consensus are often as important in this relationship as elements of conflict.[29]

This is not to say that there is a complete absence of conflict over politico-military affairs in the USSR. Yet the nature of conflict is less likely to be dominated by such esoteric concepts as 'professionalism', 'élitism', or 'social involvement' than by highly practical questions, such as budgetary allocations for the various branches of the armed forces, the size of the ground forces, the role and functions of the Soviet Navy, the technical and political implications of armed forces reductions in Central Europe, and the limitation of strategic arms. Also, when conflict does occur it is unlikely to divide the major protagonists into two well-defined camps (i.e. the military versus the Party) but it will produce opinions and attitudes cutting across institutional lines.

A framework of analysis constructed along these lines will provide a useful safeguard against the idea that 'the Polish model' will ultimately come to be adopted in the Soviet Union; that the Party's waning legitimacy, its withering resilience and its inability to reverse economic decline will ultimately lead to non-ideological, military-technocratic rule by the military.[30] The problem with this argument is that it is inaccurate – even for Poland. Far from representing a Latin-America-style putsch by the military against authority, the head of the military *and* the Party (and the government as well) felt obliged to restore communist control through emergency measures. He, Jaruzelski, did so by using the military as a shield and a screen but relying heavily on internal security forces.[31] Behind the shield and screen, the Party – however much eroded its legitimacy may have been – continued to assert its leading role. In the USSR, use of security forces and the military to deal with any serious challenge to the authority of Party and state is highly probable (although it is difficult to see how such challenge could come about); the transformation of government to some sort of non-ideological, military-technocratic rule, however, is not.

It is on the basis of these considerations that the question of the role and influence of the Soviet military in *foreign policy* could most appropriately be analysed. Kolkowicz writes that in what 'may be described as generic to all military establishments', one of the 'functional interests' of the Soviet military is the 'maintenance of a certain level of international political tension in order to provide the rationale for large military budgets and allocations'.[32] While this may be correct, it tells us nothing about attempts by the military to exert influence on Soviet foreign policy, about effectiveness of these attempts when they are made, or about the problem of whether hard-line attitudes imply support of the military for ventures which require the acceptance of military risks, as in Berlin in 1961 or in Cuba in 1962, or whether they work for or against military commitments as, let us say, in the Middle East, Angola, Ethiopia or Afghanistan.

This last point is of particular importance. Surely, no elaborate quantitative content analysis is needed to prove the obvious, namely that military newspapers and journals, almost everywhere, will have a tendency to stress military aspects of international relations and exaggerate threats to security, real or imagined. As for the Soviet Union, the columns of *Krasnaya zvezda* (Red Star) and *Kommunist vooruzhennykh sil* (Communist of the Armed Forces) will obviously tend to emphasise themes such as the incurable aggressiveness of imperialism. For reasons of intimidation of addressees abroad, notably in Europe, and morale-building at home, they will tend to stress the ability to wage and win war – even, until quite recently, *nuclear* war. But to conclude from this that the Soviet military is prone to adventurism and exerts a role to that effect in foreign policy would be hazardous.

First, it is necessary to question the way in which the attitudes of the military are usually established. The procedure adopted is typically to compare the content of military newspapers and journals, e.g. *Krasnaya zvezda* and *Kommunist vooruzhennykh sil*, with non-military journals, say, *Pravda*, which leads to the (foregone) conclusion that the military has different attitudes and hence advocates different policies from those of the Party. The problem with this procedure lies in the fact that, although the masthead of *Krasnaya zvezda* – the main newspaper of the Soviet armed forces – tells the reader that it is an 'organ of the Ministry of Defence', the newspaper is actually edited under the auspices of the Main Political Administration (MPA) of the Army and Navy, i.e. by an organ of the Party! The bi-weekly journal *Kommunist vooruzhennykh sil* is also edited by the MPA. It follows from this that if military attitudes are, in fact, established in the way as outlined one would most likely be retracing the political line handed down from the Party to the armed forces rather than establishing genuine military opinion. Seen from these perspectives, it is not at all surprising to read, in a study of the Soviet military and Soviet policy in the Middle East in 1970–3 as reflected in various Soviet military periodicals, that 'Each of the organs under investigation presented a uniform and consistent line' and that '*Kommunist vooruzhennykh sil* aligns itself consistently and unequivocally with the forward line of *Krasnaya zvezda*'.[33]

A related pitfall is the selection of views expressed by particular officers without regard to their career background and institutional attachment. This is true in particular for inferences frequently drawn in the West from statements of such notorious hardliners as Colonels Rybkin and Bondarenko. Both of them are not professional officers but political officers attached to the MPA. For opinion of the military, or sections or branches thereof, it is necessary to turn to the writings of professional officers. But some caution is advised even then because such writings may be commissioned or even provided by Party organs. Such practice is not uncommon in the Warsaw Pact countries.

A final pitfall rests in the tendency of Western analysts to establish a direct causal relationship between the hard-line, forward-oriented 'attitudes' of the military, as expressed in military periodicals, and a successful role of the military in foreign policy-making. The above quoted analyst of Soviet policies in the Middle East, 1970–3, consequently summarises that one could infer from the evidence the 'evolving importance of the military as a political pressure group' because of the fact 'that in all the cases [of changes in Soviet policy in the Middle East] referred to in the foregoing analysis the military's "advice" was . . . heeded and followed'.[34]

It is at this point that one comes up against the same analytical problem in foreign policy as in Soviet domestic politics, that is, to distinguish between preferences of the military and the political leadership. Soviet military and political leaders alike have stressed, even during the height of détente, that there remains not only a certain level of international tension, but a 'fundamental contradiction between imperialism and socialism in the world arena' and hence the necessity for vigilance, military preparedness and the strengthening of combat readiness. Up to 1973/4 (i.e. until it became politically in-expedient to continue doing so), the higher sense of 'realism' attributed to Western statesmen was explained by the *institut-chiki*, the political leadership and, of course, the military as the direct result of significant changes in the correlation of forces in favour of socialism, that is, primarily by the growth of Soviet military power. Although such confident assertions are no longer publicly made, the Soviet leadership in all likelihood remains convinced that political accommodation can be brought about in Europe (and elsewhere) by maintaining superior military forces at all levels of the East–West arms competition.

What this means for the analysis of foreign policy-making in the Soviet Union is pointed out clearly by Malcolm Mackintosh who concludes on the basis of three case studies (the Middle East crisis of 1967, the invasion of Czechoslovakia in 1968, and

SALT) that 'when a foreign policy adopted by the leadership coincides with military views, it is difficult to distinguish whether the policy was initiated by the Party or by the military'; that in cases where the views of the armed forces might differ from those of the Party leaders, 'there is nothing to suggest any diminution of the Party's ultimate primacy in foreign policy decision-making'.[35]

Also, Mackintosh's case studies, this author's own case studies (Berlin 1948, the Middle East 1956 and Berlin 1961), as well as impressions gained from looking at other cases (e.g. Cuba 1962), only serve to underline the point that far from advocating risky and adventurous schemes abroad, the Soviet military is tendentially an advocate of caution, taking a conservative approach to the commitment of Soviet military forces outside the immediate Soviet-bloc area.[36] If this is correct, the hard-line, forward-oriented themes struck in the military periodicals, and as expressed in the speeches of the Soviet military leaders, appear to have a variety of purposes. They can be devices, as mentioned above by reference to Kolkowicz, to secure and legitimise large allocations for the defence sector. They can serve to support the general ideological theme of the ultimate victory of socialism over capitalism. And they can be a boost to morale in the armed forces because too differentiated or too peaceful a picture of international politics would erode the effectiveness of the leadership's call for vigilance. But taken by themselves they are not necessarily indications of a hard line on the substantive issues of East–West conflict.

It is on the basis of this discussion that preference should be given to the third of the four broad categories suggested at the beginning of this chapter for explaining the (on the surface) puzzling contradiction between domestic retrenchment and external commitment. The display, maintenance and expansion of power, both at home and abroad, find two strong advocates in the Soviet political system: the Party *apparatchiki* and the military. A large majority of these two powerful bureaucracies evidently believes that the social and economic costs of expansion will appear less painful against the background of enhanced superpower status and increasing global influence. Where on these issues must the security apparatus be expected to stand?

The Security Apparatus

Contrary to confident predictions made at the beginning of the 1970s that 'the power and influence of the police and security agencies in the USSR will diminish',[37] there has been a quite remarkable rise in political influence of these agencies – even prior to Andropov's appointment as Party leader. In the course of the 1970s the KGB continued to maintain the world's largest secret network of troops, guards, informers and analysts, totaling about 400,000 to 500,000 men and women, and internally and externally it succeeded in upgrading its power, profile and representation. This was manifest not only in the representation of the KGB in the Politburo (in 1973) but also in the increased number of candidate members of the Central Committee (since 1976) and the promotion of former KGB or internal security chiefs to leading posts in the Union republics, including the post of First Secretary (Geydar Aliyev in Azerbaidzhan and Eduard Shevardnadze in Georgia).[38] This was followed by the ascendancy of Andropov, which began in earnest with his appointment to the Politburo in 1973 (see above), continued with his assumption of major portions of Suslov's responsibilities in the Central Committee in May 1982 and culminated in his election as Party chief in November of the same year. Along with him rose Aliyev, his former subordinate and protégé, to full member of the Politburo and later to First Deputy Chairman of the Council of Ministers where he is apparently waiting in the wings to replace the current chairman, Tikhonov. (Aliyev is 59 years old, Tikhonov 77.) His own and Aliyev's transfer notwithstanding, Andropov clearly does not want to weaken his hold over the security apparatus: Vitaly

Fedorchuk, another one of his former subordinates in the KGB (First Deputy), was first made chief of that organisation, and later transferred to the Ministry of Internal Affairs (MVD) to become its head. Viktor Chebrikov, yet another subordinate (KGB chief in the Ukraine), in turn, was made chairman of the KGB.

In sum, the succession at the top proceeded much more quickly and smoothly than many Western analysts of the USSR had expected; Andropov – at least to the outside observer – seems firmly implanted; and the role of the KGB in the Soviet political system has been further strengthened. This process, moreover, is bound to continue as 'corruption' has been identified by the new Party leader as one of the major evils afflicting Soviet society and the economy. The problem is only that the Soviet system is built on privilege which, looked at from the point of view of the non-privileged, is but a form of corruption. The official sector of the economic system, furthermore, greatly relies on *tolkachi* (people with some power and good connections to speed up important deliveries, provide access to additional finance, secure trained manpower where needed etc.) who operate in a grey area between legality and illegality. Finally, there is the quite large unofficial economy, which makes life more bearable for many people by providing essential services, better agricultural products and even some consumer goods, but which definitely is illegal and often involves corruption. Anti-corruption campaigns, thus, are faced with the daunting task of deciding upon what is functional and what dysfunctional to the system. Generally, however, they do not have much to do with any higher moral conviction of those who launch them. As almost everyone up to the very top is vulnerable to corruption charges, they are primarily to be regarded as a useful means for building up and consolidating power.

By virtue of his experience in and personal connections with the KGB, as well as by authority of his new office, Andropov can effectively utilise the security services in *foreign policy*. This is of some significance as the KGB is just as or perhaps even more important for information gathering, processing and analysis, and the implementation of foreign policy, than the Ministry of Foreign Affairs. Officers of the KGB and the GRU, its military subsidiary, ordinarily occupy a majority of embassy posts, composing as much as 80 per cent of the staff in some Third World countries. Many *bona fide* diplomats who leave Moscow for assignment abroad are forced in their new posting to work almost exclusively for the KGB. While taking up a large share of diplomatic posts at embassies and in the United Nations, the KGB also stations its men abroad in other guises, e.g. as staff members of Tass, Aeroflot, Novosti and commercial delegations.[39] KGB resources abroad are significantly augmented by the intelligence services of the Warsaw Pact countries and Cuba. The Soviet Union dominates these services so completely that they can for all practical purposes be considered mere extensions of the KGB.[40] The East Europeans and Cubans are, on the other hand, valuable auxiliaries precisely for the reason that they are often not perceived in the West as acting for the Soviet Union. From the Soviet point of view, this is particularly advantageous in certain high-risk operations for which the USSR wishes to avoid blame in case of failure.

It is important to bear in mind, however, that the KGB may provide information and help in the implementation of policy but *does not itself make policy*. Policy is made in the Politburo, and in that body even Andropov may find it difficult to set aside the principle of 'collective leadership'.[41] Secondly, despite Andropov's long tenure of office in the KGB, from 1967 until 1982, one should not forget that his career is not that of an ordinary *Chekist* who rose up through the ranks. His is a typical *Party* career, which started in the Komsomol in Jaroslavl' (1937–40), continued with various Party offices in Petrozavodsk (1940–51) and ambassadorial postings in Budapest (1951–7), and finally took a steep rise upward with the job of head of the Central Committee department for relations with the ruling communist parties in Moscow (1957–67).

Thirdly, the sordid involvement of the secret police in the mass murders under Lenin and Stalin, the continued, though now more subtle, suppression of dissidents, and the suspected role of the KGB in training guerrillas and terrorists for use abroad should not cloud one's view about possibilities for change in Soviet domestic and foreign policy. Precisely because the KGB is the best informed of all Soviet institutions and has been less constrained than any other organ by formalities and 'socialist legality', it may come to be regarded by the political leadership both as a vehicle of change and as the main guarantee against change getting out of control.

Increased reliance on the KGB, however, may also mean that foreign policy will become more effective. This applies in particular to Soviet policy towards Western Europe. Ever since the – from the Soviet point of view – eminently successful campaign in 1977–8 against the deployment of enhanced radiation weapons (the 'neutron bomb') in Europe,[42] the Soviet leadership has placed high hopes on invalidating NATO's dual-track decision by a dual-track approach: negotiating from positions of strength in Geneva while attempting to undercut the Western negotiating position with the help of Western 'progressive' and 'peaceloving' forces, including environmentalists, 'freeze' and 'unilateralist' movements. The KGB quite obviously did not invent these movements. Yet along with the Central Committee's international department (head: Boris Ponomarev, deputy: Vadim Zagladin) and the international information department (head: Leonid Zamyatin), it has used these movements to further Soviet foreign policy objectives.[43] If, then, Andropov – using the services of the security apparatus – were to adopt more flexible policies in the USSR and abroad, would he be aided by the economic bureaucracy?

The Role of Economics and Economic Interest Groups

To turn to economic interest groups as the assumed proponents of a policy that seeks to create feedbacks between East–West economic exchanges and domestic economic reform, and between external détente and internal liberalisation, one must first try to identify with some precision the dramatis personae. Six broad categories are relevant in the present considerations: (1) the Politburo and the central Party bureaucracy; (2) the central planning and administrative organs, including Gosplan and the economic ministries; (3) the First Secretaries of the provincial Party committees (*obkoms*); (4) the managers; (5) economists, sociologists and other experts; and (6) 'all the rest': collective farmers, workers, and consumers.

Clearly, not much political power and influence rests in the last two categories of the enumeration: the collective farmers, workers and consumers (category 6) do not appear in an autonomous organised fashion on the Soviet national political scene. Their interests are assumed, deduced and – perhaps surprisingly – met, although at a painfully slow pace. Economists, sociologists and other experts (category 5) generate ideas, some of them progressive and reformist, but their power base is non-existent, their access to central decision-making limited and their role in implementation of decisions marginal. Also, it would appear that the overwhelming majority of them is quite satisfied with the professional, material and status rewards that the regime seems quite willing to offer and is therefore not prepared to risk privileges by engaging in dissident activities.

There is broad agreement among Western analysts that there is little enthusiasm for reform among the central planning and administrative organs (the second category) and stiff opposition by the First Secretaries of the *obkoms*, the provincial Party committees (third category) and that it is these two groups which are in a powerful position to delay, distort or misdirect almost any sort of reformist venture. This is so despite the fact that they are often in conflict with each other. The reasons for their lack of reformist enthusiasm are not difficult to reconstruct. The *obkom* First Secretaries – Soviet prefects – play an important 'horizontal' co-ordinating role in the economy intersecting and often improving the 'vertical' flow of instructions from the ministerial bureaucracies.[44] Because of the cumbersome planning mechanism the *obkom* First Secretaries act as intermediaries and arbiters among the managers. This role, at the local level, as well as the role of the central planning and administrative organs, would be much eroded if the basic features of the reforms of 1965 were to be introduced on a large scale in the 1980s. Some of these features include expansion of direct contacts between enterprises, expansion of production associations (*firmy* or *ob"edineniya*), aggregate orders to form the basis of the production plan, reduction of central indicators, establishment of incentive funds for financing capital investments by enterprises, and introduction of new success indicators (sales, profit and profitability). Reform attempts of this kind tend to accentuate what many observers see as a basic conflict between power and efficiency.[45] And, in fact, whenever in the past such conflict became acute, efficiency had to yield.

The only category that is assumed to benefit from economic reforms, and for this reason to support them, is that of the managers (category 4). Alexander Yanov, a former Soviet journalist, is a strong advocate of this point of view. Summing up his own experiences he paraphrases a Soviet enterprise director to the effect that the Soviet managers have been accustomed to thinking independently. They want to throw off the shackles of Party control and interference. They would be willing to introduce innovative, fundamentally new modes of work organisation and be 'ready to experiment day and night'. And they believe that given a free reign they could not only reach but even surpass, by a wide margin, world standards of labour productivity.[46]

This may be painting a much too favourable picture of the Soviet manager. Obviously, innovation can only mean uncertainty and disruption, at least initially. Decentralisation of economic decision-making can only mean that the enterprise director has to take responsibility for his decisions – something he can often avoid now. It is not surprising, therefore, to read that a limited sample of factory directors interviewed by Yanov thought that the proportion of their colleagues who would actively want to participate in a major reconstruction of the Soviet economy was only between 25 and 30 per cent![47] This picture is rounded off by taking into account that many of the politically important managers work in the ministries, which – as Yanov argues – are opposed to experimentation.

The views of the Politburo (the first category) are difficult to ascertain. However, given the complexity and depth of the economic problems in the USSR (e.g. falling factor productivity, declining rates of investment in industry, a growing energy shortage, severe setbacks in agricultural production, a hopelessly outdated machinery pool, a completely inadequate transport system, and rates of growth of defence expenditures which surpass those of the economy as a whole) it would be surprising, indeed, if there weren't significant differences of approach. Attempts have been made by Western analysts, with the aid of Kremlinological research techniques, to reconstruct some of these differences for the 1960s and 1970s. In their view, the respective positions which leaders in the Politburo adopt flow from the functions they fulfil: Kosygin, then chief of the state apparatus, in favour of the 1965 reform and its variants; Brezhnev, as chief of the Party, by and large opposed.[48]

Whereas it is quite possible that this reconstruction of the respective positions taken by these two leaders is correct, there is a problem with juxtaposing the differences of approach according to functional criteria. Offices of the state (including those in the economic hierarchy) and the Party are often interchangeable, and officials at the top often hold jobs in both hierarchies.[49] Examination of the educational and occupational composition of the CPSU membership and of its leading bodies suggests that no sharp distinction can be made between the two groups; and that the relation between economic managers and *apparatchiki*, particularly at the higher levels, may more accurately be seen as one of interpenetration and mutual absorption than conflict.[50]

The conclusion which one has to draw from this is that none of the six groups examined (with the possible exception of the politically least powerful) can be regarded as a thoroughly convinced advocate of reform. If, despite that, economic reform in the Soviet Union is not inconceivable, it is because of the clearly expressed worry by the top leadership about a weakening power base. In one of his last speeches before his death, for example, Brezhnev stated that in foreign policy 'more than words are necessary. Policy can only be effective if it is based on real economic and military power.'[51]

Domestic economic reform, however, would have to be forced upon reluctant and recalcitrant bureaucracies, managers and workers. Only a determined leadership at the top (such as Andropov's?) would be able to achieve some success. These considerations provide the necessary background for discussion of possible linkages between domestic economic reform and political change in the USSR, and between changes in domestic and foreign policy.

Policy Linkages

One widely accepted framework of analysis for the examination of policy linkages is that of an inner logic that links a revisionist attitude in foreign affairs to revisionism at home and in doctrine, and similarly translates sectarianism, or Stalinism, or conservatism into a totality of interlocking views on both internal and external affairs.[52] In the view of Alexander Dallin, who developed this framework of analysis, there is congruence of elements either of the left (ideology, orthodoxy, internationalism, mobilisation, adventurism, priority of heavy industry and emphasis on vigilance and arms efforts) or the right (pragmatism, reformism, nationalism, gradualism, relaxation of tensions, priority of light industry and emphasis on agriculture and consumer goods production), such congruence simultaneously affecting doctrine and behaviour, domestic, intra-bloc and foreign policy, and policy in the international communist movement.[53]

As for the bureaucracies, institutions or interest groups advocating this or that particular line of policy, there are correspondingly assumed to exist two major benches, on one sitting the exponents of the military-industrial complex (including the military, the supervisors of defence industry and those engaged in heavy industrial production, ideologues and orthodox Party *apparatchiki*), and on the other the members of the agricultural and consumer goods lobby, the economic reformers, the pragmatists and experts. Vernon Aspaturian speaks of two similarly broad groupings, a 'security–productionist–ideological' coalition and a 'consumptionist–agricultural–public sector' coalition.[54]

This framework of analysis was applied to the interpretation of Soviet policy in the era of détente. 'Soviet pronouncements in 1970–72', one author wrote, 'suggest a new preponderance of the moderates and their continued alliance with the consumer goods and agricultural lobbies'; speculation is warranted to the effect 'that the advocates of gross strategic parity with the United States have carried the day over those pushing for a serious try to achieve strategic superiority . . .'[55]

It would, of course, be foolish to dismiss the idea that policy linkages exist in the Soviet context. However, with the benefit of hindsight it is painfully evident that the suggested framework of analysis yielded inaccurate or inadequate explanations and predictions of Soviet policy. Coherence, i.e. a unified approach, may very well exist but so far its main direction and purpose has not been to create feedbacks between influx of Western technology and domestic reform but precisely the opposite: to delay, circumvent or make unnecessary basic reforms in the command economy, to strengthen the performance of the Soviet economy, to broaden the scientific-technological base of the USSR and to make a determined effort at achieving military superiority at all levels of the East–West arms competition.

There are, however, more general problems with the framework of analysis. First, it lends itself to the fostering of simplistic ideas, in particular the notion that Soviet domestic politics and foreign policy inevitably and incurably call forth a fundamental split in the leadership between 'hawks and doves', which, as one Kremlinologist characteristically wrote, manifested itself 'on every major issue' of politics.[56]

Secondly, the dichotomy into left and right may be a useful framework for analysing certain periods in the history of Soviet foreign policy, but it is doubtful whether it is of help in the analysis of the present era. Current Soviet domestic, intra-bloc and, more generally, foreign policy, as well as policy of the CPSU within the international communist movement, is characterised by increasing complexity. Simple solutions, if they ever existed, are no longer available. Confrontation with one major power (say China) may require compromise with another (e.g. the United States). This applied to the late 1960s and early 1970s; today the position of the two powers has almost been reversed. Similarly, in Europe, a hard line towards one country (say, West Germany in 1966–8) may be accompanied by a soft line toward another (e.g. France, precisely for the reason of bringing pressure to bear on West Germany by virtue of a Franco–Soviet rapprochement). Isolation of one Eurocommunist Party leader (Carrillo) may go hand-in-hand with attempts at maintaining friendly relations with another (Berlinguer).

Thirdly, the framework is incapable of solving contradictions not only when it comes to specific issues of policy but also when one looks at individual Soviet leaders in their assumed role as representatives of functional interests and bureaucracies. For instance, Molotov has correctly been regarded as one of the foremost examples of a 'leftist' in the Soviet context, due to his orthodox Stalinist outlook, his emphasis on priority production of heavy industry, etc., yet at the same time there is convincing evidence that he warned against any leftist adventurism in the Middle East.[57] Khrushchev is being regarded as the prototype of all the elements of the right, yet at the same time his was a most serious and most direct approach to the diplomacy of threat and superpower confrontation.[58]

To Suslov has been attributed a consistently left outlook and a hard line on ideological and foreign political matters, ranging from China to the 1961 Berlin crisis, from vigorous encouragement of the national liberation struggles to support for the Portuguese CP's attempt in 1975 to win power through revolutionary means, but at the same time he is being credited with having been strongly opposed to Soviet intervention in Czechoslovakia.[59] For the first years of office as Party leader, Brezhnev was regarded as the prototype of the unimaginative, orthodox *apparatchik*, as an advocate of close co-operation with the military and the military–industrial complex (due to his association of long standing with both) but soon came to be seen as the chief architect of détente, as the flag-bearer of the moderates and the agro-consumer complex. Andropov, finally, in his capacity as ambassador to Budapest in 1956 and as head of the KGB in 1968 is said to have played a major role in the Soviet decision to intervene in both Hungary and Czechoslovakia, yet at the same time he is reported as having protected the Hungarian economic reforms[60] and as being a liberal in the Soviet context.[61] Clearly, something is amiss.

Fourthly, the framework has a tendency to overlook or belittle one of the most typical and basic features of Soviet policy, namely the deliberate balancing of policies of the left by elements of the right so as to maintain overall coherence of policy. This basic feature can be traced all the way back to Lenin. When in 1921 the New Economic Policy was being promulgated, with all the – from the Bolshevik point of view – possible negative consequences, such as erosion of ideological fervour and the danger of slipping back to capitalism, this was attempted to be held in check by the imposition of increased discipline in the Party by the outlawing of 'factionalism'. Similarly, the Soviet verbal emphasis on détente, arms control agreements, the authorisation of contacts with the West on selected levels, increase in East–West economic exchanges, and some gestures to assuage Western opinion aroused by harsh treatment of dissidents, all these elements are often accompanied by extensive efforts to impose ideological orthodoxy and discipline in the Soviet bloc. To take one major example, Brezhnev's peace offensive, which began in the spring of 1969, coincided with a much more severe turning of the screw in Czechoslovakia: only when 'normalisation' had been achieved to relative Soviet satisfaction, and the seeds of reformism seemingly been contained, did the USSR embark upon détente policies abroad. Finally, the unprecedentedly large arms build-up of the 1960s and 1970s was accompanied by more arms control initiatives than ever before. All this points to basic coherence of policy but not to left–right congruence. Still, an 'inner logic' linking issues of the left and of the right may exist. So far, however, i.e. ever since NEP, the Soviet leadership has not taken the risk of giving this logic full scope to develop. This, too, could change.

The Foreign Policy Elite: Change of Generation

The argument as it has been developed thus far emphasises coherence of policy and consensus about basic principles of foreign policy rather than internal conflict, and suggests that distinctions between 'hawks' and 'doves' in the Soviet leadership are blurred. Such differences as may exist are most likely not clear-cut or permanent, following primarily functional lines, but variable, the variation depending on particular foreign policy issues as well as the relative political influence and individual preferences of the decision-makers. Soviet policy, therefore, typically consists of differing dosages of 'hard' *and* 'soft' lines, repression *and* reform, expansionism *and* détente. The relatively high degree of political continuity, policy coherence and leadership consensus rests on a number of factors. One of them is the similarity of background, age, experience, career pattern and outlook of the top foreign policy-makers.

However much the current leaders may regret it, neither have the achievements of Soviet gerontology progressed far enough to make them (the Soviet leaders) immortal, nor is it true, as Kirilenko once asserted, that seventy years of life in the Soviet Union is 'considered only middle age'.[62] A change of generation is inevitable. It will take place soon. And it will go far beyond the rise of Andropov and the new appointments he has made so far. The question is only, what will the next generation be like, and what policies are they likely to adopt?

Undoubtedly, one of the starting points for well-founded conjectures about future trends in foreign policy-making is to emphasise the high degree of professionalisation and specialisation that has taken place in the middle echelons of the foreign policy establishment, both in the Central Committee apparatus responsible for international problems and in the Ministry of Foreign Affairs. Middle-level officials in these two organs, who are now in their late 40s and 50s, are often graduates from MGIMO (Moscow State Institute for International Relations, which is under the auspices of the Ministry of Foreign Affairs), and they have broad experience within their respective institutions and/or in journalism dealing with international problems. A virtual explosion of international relations institutes under the auspices of the Academy of Sciences of the USSR has taken place in the post-Stalin era, and in several instances it is a well established fact that the more important heads of these institutes have some role in foreign policy-making *vis-à-vis* non-communist countries. This is true, for example, for G. A. Arbatov (Director of the Institute of the USA and Canada and a member of the CC) who is said to have had access to Brezhnev and to have advised him, as well as the CC apparatus, on US–Soviet relations; significantly, Arbatov owes his rise to influence largely to Andropov who made him head of a consultative group in 1964 and who will probably now draw on his services again.[63]

The conclusions often drawn from all this are (1) that the coming generation of the Soviet foreign policy elite will not only be better trained and better informed but will also contribute to making Soviet foreign policy more 'rational', more amenable to compromise and accommodation, and hence will make the USSR easier to deal with, and (2) that the processes of professionalisation and specialisation in the sphere of foreign policy are merely part of an overall increase in the role of experts as opposed to that of Party officials.

Some caution is well advised as regards both propositions, but particularly the latter. Previous patterns of promotion clearly establish the fact that specialists may find their way to the corridors and ante-rooms of power but not to the seat of power itself. As for the top echelons of rule, Party officials are more than twice as likely to become members of the Politburo as state officials.[64] Similarly, patterns of political succession in the Soviet Union show that those leaders in control of the *Party* (i.e. Stalin, Khrushchev and Brezhnev) were in the best position to win supreme power. This pattern cannot be regarded as having substantially been modified in 1982 since Andropov's career, as noted, is mainly that of a Party official put in charge of the KGB, not that of a 'security specialist' who rose up through the ranks. Finally, those leaders who appealed to 'hard'-line, dogmatic, fundamentalist or uncompromising sections of the Soviet power elite, who had good contacts with and promised support for the military (Khrushchev in 1953–4 and Brezhnev in 1964–5) succeeded in outmanoeuvering rivals who (like Malenkov in 1953–5) were pursuing 'soft' options and appealing to some real or imaginary 'agricultural and consumer-goods lobby'.

As for the middle and lower echelons of power, too, there is no evidence to suggest that the Party apparatus is losing its role as the main channel of promotion and the prime instrument of rule. The provincial (*oblast'*) Party secretaries, in particular, continue very much in their role of Soviet 'prefects' essentially holding together the Soviet political, ideological and economic system.[65] They are at the same time an important force of retardation to be reckoned with at the top. There is, for example, much reason to believe that some of Khrushchev's more far-reaching reformist schemes were brought to a halt not least because of the *oblast'* Party secretaries' obstructionism and opposition. Last but not least, the process which can be seen at work today in the Soviet system is not one of *replacement* of the Party officials by non-Party specialists but an *increase in the educational and technical skills* of the officials.

Applied to the realm of foreign policy this means, among other things, that the type of leaders to emerge at the top in domestic power struggles will most likely originate in the – comparatively narrow, parochial and conservative – Party ranks; these leaders will acquire expertise in their new area of responsibility while at the same time drawing on the advice of foreign policy specialists. However, when it comes to entrusting power, authority and influence to foreign policy professionals the leaders will most likely continue to be reluctant to do so.[66]

Prospects of Change and its Policy Implications

Soviet domestic politics, economics and foreign policy, to sum up, will continue to be shaped by the Party. Trends of professionalisation and the brief period of détente in East–West relations have not led to a 'de-ideologisation' of the Soviet system, a relegation of Marxism-Leninism to the rubbish heap of Soviet history or an increase in autonomy for various social and political groups. The Party continues to cling to its 'leading role' in politics and society and is unlikely to step aside now and voluntarily accept a lesser role.

This, however, is not to say that the dichotomy between domestic rigidity and foreign policy expansionism must continue indefinitely. Precisely because of the fact that in the more than sixty years of its rule the Party has shown itself remarkably resilient and adaptable (one need only think of the civil war and the Second World War), it may respond to the current erosion of its legitimacy and lagging economic performance in ways which break the established patterns. In particular, the relationship between Soviet domestic politics and foreign policy may change.

This relationship in the 1970s, to revert to the questions posed in the introduction, *was* most likely one of external assertiveness to divert attention from internal drabness, repression and corruption. It *was* to a considerable extent characterised by the intent to prove – if need be with the help of the Cubans and Vietnamese – that the 'correlation of forces' was inexorably and irreversibly continuing to shift in favour of socialism. And it was probably conditioned by three major factors: (1) the attempt at utilising large-scale Western technology imports in order to modernise the Soviet economy; (2) the temptation of 'cashing in' on newly developed power projection capabilities – indirectly in Europe and directly in the Third World; and (3) the (correct) calculation that US determination to recommit military power to oppose Soviet, Cuban or Vietnamese intervention would decisively be weakened by the post-Vietnam and post-Watergate syndrome.

These conditions for the previous patterns of interplay between domestic and foreign policy, however, may no longer apply in the years to come. The Soviet stress on the military aspects of the East–West relationship in the second half of the 1970s has already led to large increases in US military expenditures, a stridently anti-Soviet mood and hence made Soviet intervention a much more risky affair. This very fact tends to force the USSR inward, to concentrate the collective mind of the Soviet leadership on the solution of internal problems. Western attempts at redressing the tilted military balance at the conventional and nuclear level in Central Europe, restoring deterrence, providing NATO's doctrine of 'flexible response' with greater credibility and denying to the Soviet leadership military options which it may think it has in Europe, therefore, are useful measures as they tend to reinforce this tendency.

Less useful, however, are policies which emphasise deterrence and, beyond that, provide for maximum exploitation of Soviet weaknesses, curtailment of East–West economic exchanges and across-the-board sanctions to *compel* the Soviet Union to embark on domestic change.

Although it is quite true that Soviet foreign policy will not change in any fundamental way unless the Soviet domestic system changes (i.e. unless a much lesser role is allocated to one of the primary determinants of East–West antagonism: Soviet ideology), such change cannot, should not and need not be forced upon the Soviet leadership from the outside, for several reasons. First, the channels in the Soviet system through which external pressure can move upward so as to change the policies of the leadership are weak or non-existent. Secondly, the leadership in turn, conscious of prestige and the Soviet Union's status as a military superpower, will do its utmost to avoid giving the impression that it can be 'pushed around', particularly when it comes to questions pertaining to Soviet domestic politics and to the USSR's pre-eminent position in Eastern Europe (e.g. Poland). Thirdly, conflicts and contradictions are inherent in Soviet society and politics. The pressures for change are already there, and they are increasing. Any major effort to disrupt or 'destabilise' the Soviet system or that of any other Eastern European country from the outside is bound to strengthen the hand of the hard-line, orthodox Party *apparatchiki* and thus retard autonomous processes of adaptation. Such efforts, in short, are generally counterproductive.

Fourthly, the political support needed for an unbalanced strategy based exclusively on military strength to work is either lacking altogether (e.g. in Western Europe) or cannot be sustained for long (in the United States). Conversely, a balanced Western approach which mixes confrontational, competitive and co-operative elements; which, in particular, is determined and strong enough to frustrate Soviet military moves outside Europe and deny success to Soviet interference in Western security policy in Europe but at the same time confident enough to trade according to mutual – Soviet and Western – advantage (e.g. gas for pipes financed by credit on commercial terms; grain for hard currency), such a strategy would command much broader support in the West. It is also an approach that could more easily be sustained in the long run. It is, finally, a policy that would make experimentation and reform appear less risky to any Soviet leadership intent on trying this tack.

Soviet–West European relations could improve, i.e. become more relaxed and 'normal', if such a policy were to be adopted by the West. Put differently, these relations would change for the better if each of the major protagonists in the failed détente experiment of the late 1960s and early 1970s were to learn the right kind of lesson from it. For the Soviet Union the lesson to learn (and it probably has already done so) is that co-operation with the West can at best alleviate some of the pressing economic problems but not solve them without major domestic reform. For the United States it is that a modest level of trade and economic co-operation, as well as scientific exchanges, will neither 'Finlandise' Western Europe nor 'bail out' the Soviet Union. For Western Europe it is that without effective deterrence and determination to redress the military balance in Central Europe, détente policies will be interpreted by the Soviet leadership as weakness, tempt it to play off Western Europe against the United States and delay necessary processes of internal reform in the Soviet Union.

Notes to Chapter 2

1   This chapter is a revised and updated version of the author's 'Soviet Foreign Policy Making: The Internal Mechanism of Global Commitment', in Hannes Adomeit and Robert Boardman (eds), *Foreign Policy Making in Communist Countries: A Comparative Approach* (Farnborough: Teakfield, 1979), pp. 15–48.

2   V. I. Lenin, *Sochineniya*, vol. 15 (4th edn, Moscow: Gostpolitizdat, 1935), p. 67.

3   The best examples of such discussion were in the 1950s and 1960s, in particular chapter 17, 'The Relations of Ideology and Foreign Policy', of Barrington Moore's *Soviet Politics: The Dilemma of Power* (Boston, Mass.: Harvard University Press, 1950); the debate between Richard Lowenthal, Samuel Sharp and R. N. Carew Hunt in *Problems of Communism*, vol. VII, no. 2 (March–April 1958), pp. 10–30, and ibid., vol. VII, no. 3 (May–June 1958) pp. 50–2; Zbigniew Brzezinski, *Ideology and Power in Soviet Politics* (New York: Praeger, 1962); and Alfred G. Meyer, 'The functions of ideology in the Soviet political system', *Soviet Studies*, vol. XVII, no. 3 (January 1966), pp. 273–85.

4   As part of this thesis of the 'erosion of ideology', William Zimmerman has advocated the view that Soviet and Western perspectives on the international system are essentially similar; see his *Soviet Perspectives on International Relations, 1956–1967* (Princeton, NJ: Princeton University Press, 1969): 'Soviet policy in the 1970's', *Survey*, vol. XIX, no. 2 (Spring 1973), esp. pp. 193–4; and 'Elite perspectives and the explanation of Soviet foreign policy', *Journal of International Affairs*, vol. XV, no. 1 (1970), pp. 84–98.

5   This is a point made by Alexander Yanov, *Détente after Brezhnev: The Domestic Roots of Soviet Foreign Policy*, Policy Papers in International Affairs (Berkeley, Calif.: Institute of International Studies, 1977).

6   J. Stalin, *Sochineniya*, X, p. 45.

7   Steklov in *Izvestiya*, 15 March 1918, as quoted by E. H. Carr, *The Bolshevik Revolution*, vol. III, Pt 5 (Harmondsworth: Penguin, 1971), p. 79.

8   Vernon Aspaturian has expressed this as follows: 'Soviet ideology itself defines 'national interest', 'power', and 'world revolution' in such a way as to make them virtually as indistinguishable and inseparable as the three sides of an equilateral triangle'; see his 'Ideology and National Interest in Soviet Foreign Policy', in Aspaturian, *Process and Power in Soviet Foreign Policy* (Boston: Little, Brown and Co., 1971), p. 331.

9   The importance of compulsory military service in ethnically mixed units as an integrative tool is analysed by Ellen Jones, 'Minorities in the Soviet armed forces', *Comparative Strategy*, vol. III, no. 4 (1982), pp. 285–318.

10 Alfred G. Meyer, 'USSR Incorporated', *Slavic Review*, vol. XX (October 1961) pp. 369–76, esp. p. 370; similar views are expressed in his *The Soviet Political System* (New York: Random House, 1965). This reference as quoted by Jerry F. Hough, 'The bureaucratic model and the nature of the Soviet system', *Journal of Comparative Administration* vol. V, no. 2 (August 1973), pp. 13–67, esp. p. 135. An analysis of Western views on Soviet bureaucracy can be found in Hough's article.

11 T. H. Rigby, 'Hough on political participation in the Soviet Union', *Soviet Studies*, vol. XXVIII, no. 2 (April 1976), pp. 257–61, esp. p. 258.

12 Alex Nove, 'History, hierarchy and nationalities: some observations on the Soviet social structure', *Soviet Studies*, vol. XXI, no. 1 (July 1969), pp. 71–92, esp. p. 76.

13 In her contribution to *Sowjetunion 1976–77: Analyse und Bilanz*, the Yearbook on Soviet affairs edited under the auspices of the Bundesinstitut für ostwissenschaftliche und internationale Studien, Cologne. The following summary is essentially a condensed version of A. von Borcke's article.

14 'Every diminution of the leading role of the Party jeopardises the achievements of socialism', Brezhnev wrote in *Voprosy istorii KPSS*, no. 12 1970, p. 107.

15 Rigby, 'Hough on political participation', p. 258.

16 Joel C. Moses, 'Regional cohorts and political mobility in the USSR: the case of Dnepropetrovsk', *Soviet Union* (Philadelphia), no. 3, Pt 1 (1976), pp. 63–89.

17 The term is T. H. Rigby's. This ends the summary based on Astrid von Borcke's article.

18 H. Gordon Skilling, 'Interest Groups and Communist Politics: An Introduction', in H. Gordon Skilling and Franklyn Griffiths (eds), *Interest Groups in Soviet Politics* (Princeton, NJ: Princeton University Press, 1971), p. 13.

19 Jerry F. Hough, 'The Soviet system: petrification or pluralism?', *Problems of Communism*, vol. XXI, no. 3 (March–April 1972), pp. 25–45.

20 Milton C. Lodge, 'Soviet elite participatory attitudes in the post-Stalin period', *American Political Science Review*, vol. LXII, no. 3 (September 1968), pp. 827–39; Lodge, *Soviet Elite Attitudes Since Stalin* (Columbus, Ohio: Bell & Howell, 1969).

21 This is the aphorism that looms large in Graham T. Allison's bureaucratic politics model, e.g. in his *Essence of Decision: Explaining the Cuban Missile Crisis* (Boston: Little, Brown & Co., 1971), p. 176.

22 Roman Kolkowicz, *The Soviet Military and the Communist Party* (Princeton, NJ: Princeton University Press, 1967), p. 21.

23 Roman Kolkowicz, 'The Military', in Skilling and Griffiths (eds), *Interest Groups in Soviet Politics*, pp. 135–6. This writer agrees very much with the opposite line of reasoning adopted by William E. Odom, 'The Party connection', *Problems of Communism*, vol. XXII (September–October 1973), pp. 12–26, and by Matthew P. Gallagher and Karl F. Spielmann, Jr, *Soviet Decision-Making for Defense* (New York: Praeger, 1972), pp. 40–3.

24 It is of considerable significance that the political leadership did go along with the ambitious and far-reaching plans for naval expansion and the allocation of an important peacetime role to the Soviet Navy as advocated in the series of articles by Gorshkov in *Morskoi sbornik* in 1970 and in the expanded, book version of these articles, *Morskaya moshch gosudarstva*, published in 1976. The naval expansion does not mean that the Soviet Navy is now superior to its American counterpart. What it does mean, however, is that the USSR has built up power projection capabilities which have to be taken into account by local actors as well as the United States. Concerning these problems see Michael McGwire, 'The rationale for the development of Soviet seapower', *US Naval Institute Proceedings*, vol. CVI, no. 5 (May 1980), pp. 155–83 and Jürgen Rohwer, 'Admiral Gorshkov and the influence of history upon sea power', ibid., vol. CVII, no. 5 (May 1981), pp. 150–75.

25 Prior to Ustinov's appointment there were only two exceptions to the general practice of appointing military officers to the post of Defence Minister: Trotsky and Bulganin.

26 This problem is explored further by Hannes Adomeit and Mikhail Agursky, 'The Soviet military-industrial complex', *Survey*, vol. XXIV, no. 2 (Spring 1979), pp. 106–24. See also Karl F. Spielmann, 'Defense industrialists in the USSR', *Problems of Communism*, vol. XXV, no. 5 (September–October 1976), pp. 52–69.

27 Zhukov was said to have: (1) plotted the overthrow of the regime; (2) disagreed on policy matters with civilian leaders; (3) sponsored a 'cult of his own personality'; (4) administered the military establishment in an 'incorrect and non-Party manner'; and (5) attacked the military Party organs; see Timothy J. Coulton, 'The Zhukov affair reconsidered', *Soviet Studies*, vol. XXIX, no. 2 (April 1977), pp. 158–213, esp. p. 190.

28 Ibid., pp. 212–13.

29 Ibid., p. 212.

30 This is a point made – surprisingly – by such an astute analyst of the Soviet Union as Michel Tatu. He argues that the Soviet armed forces as an institution are strong. They are an 'adult', modern and well-educated element in Soviet society, generally well accepted by the population, and hence better qualified to lead the country than the Party *apparatchiki*. Thus, he concludes, the 1980s, or more likely the 1990s, may witness a military dictatorship. See Atlantic Institute for International Affairs, 22nd Meeting, 12 June 1981, Summary of discussions on the topic of 'The Soviet Union: policies and problems', p. 5.

31 Such forces include the regular police force units (about 150,000 men and women); the special riot police troops (ZOMO), with an estimated strength of between 20,000 and 22,000; and the paramilitary forces of the Voluntary Police Reserve (ORMO) of some 350,000. All these units are directly controlled by the Ministry of Internal Affairs, which also has its own military force of one to two divisions, to be used for special purposes. See J. B. de Weydenthal, 'Anatomy of the

martial law regime: the institutions', *RFE Research*, RAD Background Report (Poland), 2 February 1982.

32 Roman Kolkowicz, 'The Military', in Skilling and Griffiths (eds), *Interest Groups in Soviet Politics*, p. 141.

33 Ilana Dimant-Kass, 'The Soviet military and Soviet policy in the Middle East', *Soviet Studies*, vol. XXVI, no. 4 (October 1974), pp. 502–21, esp. pp. 520–1.

34 Ibid., p. 512. In the quest to establish the strong role of the military in foreign policy-making one analyst goes even as far as venturing the thesis that the military has been able to turn international crises off and on so as to check trends for a reduction in defence spending: Raymond Hutchings, 'Soviet defence spending and Soviet external relations', *International Affairs* (London), vol. ILVII (1971), pp. 517–31.

35 Malcolm Mackintosh, 'The Soviet military: influence on foreign policy', *Problems of Communism*, vol. XXII, no. 5 (September–October 1973), pp. 10–11.

36 To take but one example of a contrary line of argument. One author writes that 'during the 1957 Syrian crisis, when Baghdad Pact forces threatened to invade Syria to prevent an alleged takeover by the Communist Party there, Zhukov, in an unauthorised statement over Albanian radio, declared the Soviet military's readiness "to strike at any military adventure organised by the United States near our southern borders". Almost immediately after, Khrushchev appeared unexpectedly at a Soviet–Turkish reception, announcing that the Syrian conflict should be resolved peacefully and that Marshal Zhukov had been relieved of all his posts.' Karen Dawisha, 'The Limits of the Bureaucratic Politics Model: Observations on the Soviet Case', Paper delivered to the Annual Conference of BNASEES, Cambridge, 26–8 March 1977, p. 4. Whether or not Zhukov's statement was unauthorised is a mere conjecture. On the other hand a statement like the one quoted from Zhukov's speech is not at all unusual but typical of the kind of statement that characterised the Khrushchev era. Hence, it should not be considered proof that Zhukov was pursuing an adventurous line in foreign policy.

37 Frederick C. Barghoorn, 'The Security Police', in Skilling and Griffiths (eds), *Interest Groups in Soviet Politics*, p. 96.

38 Astrid von Borcke in *Sowjetunion 1976–77*, pp. 30–2.

39 This account of the role of the KGB in foreign affairs draws on John Barron, *KGB: The Secret Work of Soviet Secret Agents* (London: Transworld Publishers/Corgi Books, 1979), pp. 27–30. Much of the information contained in Barron's book has been confirmed by Soviet defectors from the KGB, including that of Major Levchenko in Tokyo, see *Neue Zürcher Zeitung*, 14 December 1982.

40 Barron, *KGB*, pp. 29–30. Officials of the Czechoslovak intelligence service, including Ladislav Bittman and Josef Frolik (who defected to the West after the Soviet invasion of Czechoslovakia in 1968) revealed, for instance, that KGB representatives were invited by the heads of various departments of the Ministry of the Interior for 'task work' without the knowledge of the Czechoslovak leadership. See Jiri Valenta, *Soviet Intervention in Czechoslovakia 1968: Anatomy of a Decision* (Baltimore, Md: The Johns Hopkins University Press, 1979), p. 106.

41 Among Andropov's alleged qualities, according to Chernenko's 'nomination speech' to the CC on 12 November 1982, were his (Andropov's) 'passion for collective work'. Just to make sure that the point was not lost Chernenko added that in the present circumstances it was 'doubly and triply important collectively to guide the destinies of the Party'. *Pravda*, 13 November 1982.

42 This has been analysed by Hannes Adomeit, *The Soviet Union and Western Europe: Perceptions, Policies, Problems*, National Security Series, No. 3 (1979), Centre for International Relations, Queen's University, Kingston, Ont.

43   This has been shown convincingly by J. A. Emerson Vermaat, 'Moscow fronts and the European peace movement', *Problems of Communism*, vol. XXXI, no. 6 (November–December 1982), pp. 43–56.

44   The power and role of the first *obkom* Secretaries has been compared to that of the French prefects by Jerry Hough: *The Soviet Prefects* (Cambridge, Mass.: Harvard University Press, 1969). It is necessary to clarify, however, that Hough (who kindly commented on an earlier draft of this contribution) is not among those who share the 'broad agreement' concerning the role of the *obkom* Secretaries. In his view, the Secretaries are advocates of economic reform because such reform would bring more money into the *oblast*', and they would be in a position to influence its allocation.

45   See, for instance, William J. Conyngham, *Industrial Management in the Soviet Union: The Role of the CPSU in Industrial Decision-making, 1917–1970* (Stanford, Calif.: Hoover Institution, 1973), p. 285.

46   Yanov, *Détente after Brezhnev*, pp. 29–30.

47   Ibid., p. 30.

48   Von Borcke, *Sowjetunion 1976–77*.

49   Dawisha, 'The Limits of the Bureaucratic Politics Model', p. 10.

50   Stephen L. White, 'Contradiction and change in Soviet state socialism', *Soviet Studies*, vol. XXVI, no. 1 (January 1974), p. 42.

51   Brezhnev in a speech to commanding officers of the Soviet Army and Navy, *Pravda*, 28 October 1982.

52   Alexander Dallin, 'Domestic Factors Influencing Soviet Foreign Policy', in Michael Confino and Shimon Shamir (eds), *The USSR and the Middle East* (Jerusalem: Israel University Press, 1973), pp. 5–30, esp. p. 32.

53   This was expressed in the article quoted in the previous note and, more systematically, in 'Soviet foreign policy and domestic politics: a framework for analysis', *Journal of International Affairs*, vol. XXIII, no. 2 (1969), pp. 250–65 and in 'The Domestic Sources of Soviet Foreign Policy', in Seweryn Bialer (ed.), *The Domestic Context of Soviet Foreign Policy* (Boulder, Col.: Westview, 1981).

54   Vernon Aspaturian, 'Moscow's options in a changing world', *Problems of Communism*, vol. XXI, no. 4 (July–August 1962), pp. 1–20, esp. p. 6.

55   Dallin, 'Domestic Factors Influencing Soviet Foreign Policy', p. 47.

56   Victor Zorza, writing about the Politburo's problem in dealing with Sakharov. The full citation reads: 'As on every other major issue, there are differences in the Kremlin itself between hardliners and moderates on how to deal with this matter'. *International Herald Tribune*, 14 October 1975.

57   Convincing evidence to this effect is given by Uri Ra'anan, *The USSR Arms the Third World: Case Studies in Soviet Foreign Policy* (Cambridge, Mass.: The MIT Press, 1969).

58   See Hannes Adomeit, *Soviet Risk Taking and Crisis Behavior: A Theoretical and Empirical Analysis* (London: Allen & Unwin, 1982).

59   For example, by Terry McNeill in *Radio Liberty Research*, RL299/74, 20 September 1974.

60   *Frankfurter Allgemeine Zeitung*, 15 November 1982; Jerry Hough, 'Soviet succession: issues and personalities', *Problems of Communism*, vol. XXXI, no. 5 (September–October 1982), pp. 20–40, esp. p. 34.

61   See, for instance, Boris Rabbot, 'A letter to Brezhnev', in *The New York Times Magazine*, 6 November 1977, p. 55. Rabbot was a Secretary of the Social Science Section at the Presidium of the Academy of Sciences of the USSR and adviser to the Central Committee.

62   At Brezhnev's birthday celebrations in 1976: *Pravda*, 15 October 1976.

63 Hough writes in this context that Andropov was a protégé of Otto Kuusinen, a former Soviet Politburo member of Finnish extraction and a 'reformist, non-dogmatic ideologist who served as a counterpoint to the more conservative Mikhail Suslov'. When Kuusinen died, Andropov took over a reformist-minded consultative group, including such non-conformist intellectuals as Alexander Bovin, now *Izvestia* columnist, and Oleg Bogomolov, director of an institute that studies East European economic reform, and made Arbatov its head. See Jerry F. Hough, 'Who is Yuri Andropov?', *Washington Post*, 27 May 1982; Hough, 'Soviet succession: issues and personalities', *Problems of Communism*, vol. XXXI, no. 5 (September–October 1982), p. 33.

64 Eberhard Schneider, 'Die sowjetische politische Elite – ein Literaturbericht', Bundesinstitut für ostwissenschaftliche und internationale Studien (Cologne), *Berichte*, no. 21 (1981), pp. 75–9.

65 See above, note 44.

66 On the following see *Radio Liberty Research* (Munich), RL 1/78, 1 January 1978, esp. the Appendix.

Part II
The External Dimension

3

The United States Factor

Lawrence Freedman

The essential Soviet dilemma in its confrontation with the United States in Europe has long been recognised and can be simply put. On the one hand the United States is a menacing adversary and anything that weakens it, such as the collapse or serious weakening of its major alliance, is to be welcomed. On the other hand Europe has a history of turbulence and is, from a Soviet perspective, still politically fragile. The American presence can be seen as an important stabilising influence which, if removed, would open the way for more dangerous forces – especially German revanchism.

The thought that the USSR has an interest in the preservation of NATO is not one that naturally occurs to Western policy-makers although it is readily accepted by many specialists in Soviet affairs. The best bit of evidence is Brezhnev's famous Tiflis speech in May 1971 accepting the notion of force reduction talks in Europe on the eve of a crucial Senate vote on the Mansfield Amendment. It is hard to believe that Brezhnev did not realise that the prospect of multilateral arms control would immediately ease the pressure in Congress (and the British Parliament) for unilateral reductions. Moreover little was done to follow up this initiative once the immediate political effect had been achieved. For further evidence one might point to the acceptance not long after this and also after some notional opposition of North American participation in the Conference on Security and Co-operation in Europe.[1]

This may have been a moment of truth for the Soviet leaders when they were forced to confront the question of the true nature of their interests in Europe. Were they still a radical power ready to disrupt existing political arrangements in pursuit of a revolutionary creed, or were they becoming conservative in their middle age, comforted by a status quo in which they could be sure of respect and a controlling influence over that part of the world which concerned them most? In the early 1970s the logic of a détente policy, and the first rewards of that policy pointed unavoidably to the latter option. The Soviet leaders accepted that more than just tolerate the US presence, they might have to take positive steps to sustain it. The question with which this chapter is concerned is did this reflect a major and long-standing Soviet interest or just a temporary expedient? When the outcome of the détente policies were more ambiguous and relations with the USA were moving backwards rather than forwards, did a similar logic apply? Our answer must begin with an analysis of the development of toleration and even support for the US presence, before moving on to consider the factors which might have led this approach to be upset.

Up to Détente

The ability to see the US role in European affairs in a positive light depended to some extent on anxiety as to the consequences of a break-up of NATO. After all, the early 1970s was the high point of détente when Soviet foreign policy was obtaining tangible gains by way of international respectability, productive economic contact and settled borders for her allies. This was quite a lot to give up for the uncertain promise of a Western Europe in disarray – which *might* offer opportunities for some ripe pickings but might also offer an opportunity for a new political realignment centred on an insecure but assertive Germany. If the prospective benefits of the German Ostpolitik depended on Bonn feeling at ease in its own alliance, then why encourage anxiety? Moreover the acceptability of the US presence in Europe might have a *quid pro quo*. Moscow had little choice but to acknowledge the US role, but in approving this role, albeit in a rather tacit manner, it might hope to gain acceptance for its own role in other important regions of the world such as the Middle East.

Lastly, arguing in favour of the US presence was that the Americans themselves no longer looked as threatening as before. There has long been a debate in Soviet policy-making circles about whether it was possible to deal with the 'imperialists'. Malenkov's view in the immediate post-Stalin period that Soviet post-war recovery and military development was sufficient to keep the capitalist adversary at bay was criticised as being an ideological error. He was accused of failing to grasp the dynamics of the fundamental conflict between the two social systems. Actually the main criticism was that he was premature, and that Soviet strength was still insufficient to permit a substantial diversion of resources to the needs of consumers.[2] A few years later the Soviet bomb was deemed to have sobered the imperialists, while the horror of nuclear war encouraged recognition of the possibility of 'peaceful co-existence'. By the late 1950s it had become acceptable in Moscow to distinguish between the unreconstructed militarists and anti-Soviet elements within the imperialist camp, and the 'sober realists' with whom deals could be struck. The stage was set for the negotiations of 'peaceful co-existence' on the most favourable terms. Simplifying somewhat, these objectives could be understood in terms of developing sufficient contervailing power to neutralise US nuclear strength, gaining explicit American recognition of the USSR as a superpower with all the accompanying entitlements, ratifying the post-war European boundaries including ending the anomalous position of Berlin, and improving the

East's global position by the steady inclusion into the Eastern 'camp' of the victors of the latest anti-colonial struggles.

It took time before the promise of 'peaceful co-existence' could be realised. Initially it seemed as if the costs would exceed the benefits. Any dealings with the imperialists were difficult to explain to the comrades in allied countries. In China especially the toning down of the ideological attacks on the USA and the readiness to contemplate a variety of deals with the imperialists was observed with horror. Yet while these strained relations within the communist world were being endured, there was little to show in terms of improved relations with the West.

Khrushchev's boasts of imminent strategic superiority over the USA turned out to be the opposite of the truth. At the start of the 1960s the US missile programme was getting into full gear while that of the USSR was floundering.[3] Furthermore, it was no longer possible to bluff about Soviet military strength. The advent of satellite reconnaissance opened up Soviet military capabilities to a continual US gaze. Towards the end of 1961, the first year of the Kennedy Administration, Washington made known its confidence in the state of military balance.[4] Furthermore, this confidence was combined with a determined toughness in foreign policy and a curious defence doctrine that, under cover of avoiding preparations for nuclear strikes against cities, could be seen as preparations for a disarming first strike against the limited Soviet nuclear assets.

A case of strategic panic overcame Moscow. Khrushchev, rather feebly, requested from Washington acknowledgement of parity.[5] With his colleagues, he began to bluster publicly about multi-megaton weapons and orbital bombs while, privately, offensive and defensive programmes were accelerated. Most dramatic of all, there was an attempt to secrete medium-range missiles on to Cuba as a 'quick fix' to the developing problem of strategic inferiority.[6] The gamble failed to pay off. The missiles were discovered before they were operational and, in humiliating circumstances, Khrushchev was forced to withdraw. In the

USSR's weak strategic position, with a minimal capacity for power projection, the Caribbean was the last place to pick a fight with the United States.

Even in Berlin, where the local Soviet conventional position was much stronger, to the extent that the Western powers considered it indefensible,[7] Khrushchev felt unable to press home an advantage. The construction of the Berlin Wall of August 1961, while a propaganda defeat, served to stem the flow of refugees using Berlin as a convenient escape route from East to West. The NATO response indicated that, despite the formal support for the reunification of Germany, in practice they were only going to take major risks in defence of the status quo. The Soviet restraint in testing NATO's position further probably allows this point to serve as the moment when a major war over Germany became unlikely.

The defusing of the tension over Berlin, as the West accepted the trade of political stability in return for human freedom, combined with the successful management of the missile crisis of October 1962, provided an opportunity for a constructive dialogue between the two states. The exchange of letters between Kennedy and Khrushchev towards the end of the crisis opened the way for the speedy if only partial completion of the negotiations on a test ban that had been under way since 1958 but had been suspended in 1960.[8] A number of initiatives taken over the next couple of years involving outer space and reductions in military budgets and fissionable materials made this a period of effective détente.

This period came to an end in 1965 with the major escalation of the US intervention in Vietnam. This action along with the Cuban episode appears to have convinced the Soviet leadership that political clout in the modern world very much depended on military muscle and they set about trying to obtain this muscle.[9] The Soviet missile force began to grow and the Soviet Navy to expand – both quite dramatically. At this time the USSR neither expected nor received political benefits. Despite being goaded by China, the USSR stayed well clear of involvement in some of the more futile revolutionary campaigns, supporting only the most promising national liberation movements. It sought to improve its standing with the states of the Third World by currying favour with regimes of an anti-Western, rather than a specifically communist or pro-Soviet disposition. In the aftermath of the June 1967 Arab–Israeli war this brought some dividends.

Within Europe there appeared to be a trend towards a loosening of the bloc system. There were arguments in NATO over 'flexible response' in which most West European governments were combining an exaggerated view of Soviet conventional might with a sanguine view of Soviet political intentions. In 1966 France left the Integrated Military Command and, with the Vietnam War becoming a major issue, doubts were growing in a number of countries over the wisdom of alliance with the United States. However, it soon became apparent that France's example was not going to be followed and that NATO would hold together. The Soviet approach to alliance cohesion, illustrated by the invasion of Czechoslovakia in August 1968, served to unify NATO. From the Soviet point of view, Western behaviour in the aftermath of the invasion was of interest: the Brezhnev Doctrine was implicitly acknowledged in that the NATO countries offered no direct challenge to the USSR within its own 'sphere of influence'.[10]

Détente

Thus towards the end of the 1960's the political structure of Europe need no longer be understood in terms of a post-war upheaval – it had taken on a permanent form. The time was therefore ripe to acknowledge this permanence and enshrine it in treaty form. The only outstanding problem was Vietnam, which had soured US–Soviet relations in the mid-1960s. But the view was taken in the Kremlin that this problem could be contained. After all, the USA was in serious trouble in Vietnam without the USSR having had to do more than supply arms to its ally, whose success could provide confirmation that it had history on its side. Measures taken to boost the Soviet military position would ensure that the 'correlation of forces' would continue to swing in its favour.[11]

Accordingly the Kremlin felt able to begin to renew the search for détente. A certain degree of common interest had been discovered in negotiations for a Non-Proliferation Treaty, where neither the USA nor the USSR seemed worried about embarrassing its erstwhile ally (France and China respectively).[12] As the Kremlin recognised that the impact of its military build-up could be undermined if it provoked a major US response, there was willingness to begin discussions on limiting strategic arms. As this represented a consistent US objective since the early 1960s there was no trouble in getting agreement. The US view was that talks had only become possible as the USSR approached parity, and they seemed to have no trouble in accepting that one purpose of the talks would be to confirm this parity.[13] The first talks would have been held in late 1968 but were one casualty of Czechoslovakia, so they did not get under way until November 1969.

Within Europe the moves towards détente were not so much dependent on US policy as on the Federal Republic of Germany. By the late 1960s America was in no position to object to a change in German policy, whatever misgivings there may have been in Washington, when it was expanding its own contacts with Moscow. The advent of a Social Democrat/Liberal government made possible the formal acknowledgement of the permanence of the post-war division of the continent and of the Soviet hold over the Eastern portion. In the late 1960s and early 1970s a whole series of negotiations which culminated in the 1975 Final Act of the Helsinki Conference on Security and Co-operation in Europe, confirmed the territorial status quo. In this period, too, human and economic contacts between East and West improved.[14] Moscow examined whether it was possible to draw in the benefits of the West's technology without the costs of the West's ideology.

Gradually it seemed that the major sources of dispute between East and West were being sorted out and that relations could therefore move away from an adversarial plane. From the Soviet point of view a state of affairs was coming about which was as good as any that could be expected: the Soviet leaders might not see much prospect of a Westward extension of influence, but it was going to be easier to hold on to what was already theirs while still being able to obtain goods and services from their Western neighbours at favourable terms. If part of this state of affairs was the presence of the United States Army and Air Force in Europe, then so be it. In an important sense it was recognised that the two alliances depended on each other for cohesion. If NATO broke up in disarray then the resulting turbulence would soon hit the Warsaw Pact. This would threaten the strategic and ideological buffer between the USSR and the West which had been the organising concept of all Soviet regional security policies since Yalta.

Down from Détente

It was in these circumstances that Brezhnev was content to assist NATO to maintain a military balance. We must now return to our original question. Was this a reflection of a major and long-standing Soviet interest or just a temporary expedient? In the changed circumstances of the early 1980s, is the logic of the early 1970s still valid?

One part of the question concerns West Germany. This chapter addresses the part that concerns the United States, but a few observations are necessary on the German dimension. The Soviet leadership undoubtedly found it increasingly easy to do business with West Germany during the 1970s. Instead of holding a veto over détente, Bonn now appeared as an earnest and sympathetic promoter. However, and this is a point to which we will return, there is little evidence of any Soviet drive to wrest Germany away from its Alliance connections. It was more a case of encouraging Bonn to argue what are, from the Soviet point of view, relatively sensible policies within the Alliance. Furthermore, in strict strategic terms the division of Germany with one part under direct Soviet control and the other part entangled in NATO serves Soviet interests. A united and uninhibited Germany would represent a substantial and all-too-familiar threat to Moscow. The productive powers and potential of the German economy and the efficiency and size of its armed forces must worry a Soviet leadership presiding over a faltering economy and a disaffected alliance. The judgement in the Kremlin must be that if Germany for the moment appears relatively benign, then this is the product of particular circumstances. This provides an argument for sustaining those circumstances.

What then of the American part of the equation? It is clear that in the decade following the high point of détente, marked by the Brezhnev–Nixon Summit of May 1972, US–Soviet relations have deteriorated markedly. There are two sets of reasons for this deterioration. The first relates to Europe, including the USSR and its satellites. There has been disappointment on both sides as to the economic and political benefits of détente. The Soviet Union has had to accept that Western technology is no panacea for its economic problems, while for the West a decade of easy credit to the East has led to a legacy of indebtedness which is adding to the strain on the international financial system. In political terms, there has been little progress in the area of basic human freedoms in the East. This has raised doubts in the West as to the propriety of intensive contact with such disreputable regimes. To the East, expression of such doubts is tantamount to 'interference in internal political affairs'. What is not clear is the extent to which events in the military relationship here contributed to the general political decline. The upsurge in military activity in both alliances may be a symptom rather than a cause of the political decline. In addition, those Western activities to which the USSR objects most are those most closely involving the United States. Indeed it is arguable that the most controversial security issues with Europe all have something to do with the role played by the United States.

This brings us to the second set of reasons for the weakening of détente: the development of an intensifying global confrontation between the USA and the USSR. While it might be possible to portray the USSR as being a virtually status quo power in Europe, this was far less so elsewhere. We have already noticed how the sense of military inferiority engendered by the humiliation of Cuba and the American self-confidence of the first half of the 1960s led to a determination to overcome this inferiority. It was only toward the end of the 1960s that this determination began to produce results and even then it took a form that only barely alarmed the United States.

The most tangible evidence of the Soviet military build-up was in land and sea-based offensive missiles. The first reaction to the fact that the USSR was catching up and even moving ahead in this area was quite mild. At the time there was a widespread belief in the United States that once a certain point had been past – the achievement of an assured second-strike capability – then increments of new strategic power made precious little difference as it could not be turned into commensurate political advantage. Moreover, as noted above, there was every reason to believe in the early 1970s that a formal parity would be codified in the Strategic Arms Limitation Talks (SALT) which began in November 1969.

It remains a matter of great debate in the West as to whether the USSR ever saw 'parity' in this way. It is probably the case that the Soviet leaders attached more political significance to mere missile numbers than did their American counterparts, largely because of their previous experience of inferiority. There are disturbing features of Soviet military writing which suggest also an assumption of a closer relationship between the ability to prevail in war and deterrence than is common in the West.[15] However, the more alarming constructions put on Soviet military theory and practice during the 1970s were more figments of a vivid US strategic imagination than a reflection of actual Soviet plans.[16]

At any rate, after a decade of SALT the more hawkish perceptions of Soviet intentions and capabilities were on the ascendant in the USA, and those who had taken the sanguine view at the start of the decade were less confident. In part this was the fault of the negotiating process itself which encouraged tighter comparisons between the respective force structures and exaggerated the significance of any disparities. But Soviet activity itself did not help, though this could be explained as much by a belief that new military power is the basic currency in international affairs and must be nurtured with care, as by a more malign interpretation. It was unfortunate that the area in which the USSR found it easiest to build up strength – land-based missiles – was the area that the West found most disturbing. It was also unfortunate that while there were still notions in Washington that there was a 'spirit' to the 1972 SALT I agreements, the approach in Moscow was to stay very close to the letter of the law. This difference in approach led, in the mid-1970s, to a sudden flurry of charges of Soviet 'violations' of SALT.[17] Though these charges could not be sustained they led to a net loss in trust. As the USA sought to achieve, thereafter, more 'watertight' agreements there was a greater potential for high-level squabbles over low-level details.

It is of note that the categories of weapons that began to cause severe problems in the late 1970s were absent from Western concern for so long before. The USSR had been able to pose a nuclear threat to Europe before posing one to the United States. In the 1950s a large bomber force was built up, which was supplemented in the late 1960s by an equally large missile force. In part because these bombers and missiles were getting old and were not being replaced by new models,[18] and in part because so much effort was obviously going in to creating a first-class nuclear capability to take on the United States, there was a tendency to assume that the forces facing Europe were relics of a bygone age when they had been needed to keep the United States in order by threatening its allies. Khrushchev had in fact stressed this hostage status at the time of the Berlin crisis.[19] This highlighted a consistent Soviet tendency to put pressure on the United States through its allies, but it did not mean that there were not other more local reasons for the Soviet medium-range forces. There were the US 'forward-based systems' (aircraft based in Europe or on aircraft carriers near by that could hit Soviet territory) to be targeted, as well as the British and later the French nuclear forces, plus the general need to keep Europe respectful of Soviet power.

The continuing Soviet preoccupation with weapons in Europe was widened by the persistent demands in SALT for the inclusion of the US forward-based systems and the British and French systems, and also by the investment in a new bomber and missile (the Backfire and the SS-20). In Moscow the latter was explained by the former: the American refusal to include the European-based systems made it necessary to keep Soviet countervailing forces up to date. This explanation fails to account for the development programmes for the Backfire and SS-20 stretching back long before SALT and the extent to which the SS-20 seemed to have been designed with China partly in mind. It was more of a European than an American vote that had prevented the inclusion of European systems. The West European governments were prepared to forgo the opportunity to get some limits on the Soviet medium-range systems in order to prevent any interference with their nuclear connection to the United States.[20] American nuclear weapons based in Europe provided a guarantee of commitment. There was no need for a parallel pattern of deployment in the East. The anxiety then was over Europe's interests being forgotten in a superpower condominium (rather than being trampled over in a super-power confrontation). The USA was not trusted to sustain any sort of nuclear linkage with Europe if it was being enticed with major concessions elsewhere. So a major opportunity for arms control was lost. There was little point in Moscow urging the

Europeans to moderate American policy. Until well into the 1970s it was the conventional wisdom that the Europeans were far more sceptical of SALT than the United States.

As time went on it became difficult to ignore these medium-range (later rechristened 'long-range theatre' and then 'inter-mediate') nuclear forces. In SALT the Americans began to worry that the Backfire could be used to mount attacks on their terri-tory while an extra stage might be added to the SS-20 to turn it into the intercontinental SS-20. Meanwhile, the USSR observed the new cruise missiles, first to be put on aircraft, and noted their possible application on the ground in Europe. By 1977 these 'theatre' systems were part of SALT. The US Administration sought to protect the European security arrangements from being too disrupted by arms control, but it was clear that these arrangements were going to become even more complicated in further rounds of SALT.

This tendency was given a further push as NATO began to modernise its own nuclear forces. First the short-range enhanced radiation weapon or 'neutron bomb' came and went (1977–8) and then, for a variety of reasons including the debacle of the neutron bomb, the Alliance began to consider whether and how it should modernise its longer-range theatre nuclear forces. We will pick this story up later. For the moment, it is important to note the two trends of the 1970s: a growing disillusion with the procedures of strategic arms control and the increasing prominence, in both weapons plans and arms control, of so-called 'theatre nuclear forces'.

Even these problems, along with the disappointments in Europe, might have been manageable had there not been a background of growing tension in the superpowers' relations in the Third World. The Soviet desire to accumulate new military power stemmed from a belief that this power brought with it respect and influence. The United States was prepared to let the USSR accumulate military capabilities – indeed it had little alternative – but it would not accept that this brought with it any political entitlement. While in theory the Americans could recognise that the Russians were anxious for the respect that they felt due to a super-power, in practice they could rarely bring themselves to make concessions. One reason for this was that there remained genuine conflicts of interest and the Americans saw no reason to give ground unless forced to do so. Another reason was that many of the key regional powers were not particularly anxious to encourage Soviet involvement. One good example of this was the reaction of President Sadat of Egypt when it looked in the autumn of 1977 as if the USA and USSR were preparing a joint initiative on the Middle East. His dramatic trip to Israel was, in part, designed to set in motion a peace process in which the USSR would have no part.

From the Soviet perspective this was rather frustrating. Moscow had, after all, turned a blind eye to American activity in Vietnam in the run-up to the May 1972 summit. This could be taken as a recognition that there was to be no linkage between the various negotiations connected with détente and the attempts by the superpowers to maintain and improve their position in the Third World, even at each other's expense.

The only consolation to Moscow was the reluctance of the Europeans to follow the United States in the Third World. During 1973, culminating in the October War, there was a furious argument within NATO over the alleged 'regional blinkers' worn by the Europeans which made them unaware of the global threats to their security.[21] As the USSR became more active in the Third World in the second half of the 1970s, the European governments seemed more anxious over an exaggerated American response than any Soviet transgressions. It was clear that the Europeans were coming to feel that they had too much at stake in Europe to threaten relations with the USSR unless there were very good reason, and too much awkward political baggage and too little actual power to play a particularly active role outside Europe. In consequence, they acted as a drag on the more combative instincts of some American policy-makers.

In the USSR the massive investment in all types of military

capabilities and the patient pursuit of clear objectives was now beginning to pay off. By 1977 the various strands of foreign policy seemed to be coming together. It was the West's military strength that had been countered and the new parity codified in SALT, while the East was gaining access to its economic strength. The Soviet position in Europe was being ratified and stabilised. The Soviet position outside Europe was becoming even more powerful. And all this had been achieved without damage to the character of Soviet power at home. Moscow awaited a new American Administration full of détente and arms control enthusiasts.

However rumblings in the West were being heard against détente. Some rumblings had been around at the start of the process. These had largely been from Europeans who were worried about the development of some superpower condominium which would be inimical to third party interests. As time went on there was unhappiness in Europe over the lack of progress in human rights, but this was never sufficient to qualify satisfaction in an enhanced sense of security and improvements in human contacts and in East–West trade. Furthermore, while worries over the credibility of the US nuclear guarantee to Europe were hardly a novelty, the steady growth in Soviet power and the achievement of visible nuclear parity, gave these worries added point. When they were combined with anxiety over the volatility in American policy-making, there was an inevitable preference for a quiet life and a distrust of both the quality and direction of America's leadership. If things went wrong, who would suffer most?

It was in the United States that the real rumblings against détente grew. Its benefits did not seem so tangible in Washington. Only farmers were developing a real stake in détente. Otherwise the economic benefits seemed marginal. More important, the added stability brought to Europe, which was already presumed to be reasonably stable, did not compensate for the unsettling effects of the exercise of Soviet power elsewhere in the world. Even when the two superpowers were acting according to the canons of crisis management as in the October 1973 War, it was commonly assumed that the USSR was up to no good and that the object of effective diplomacy was to keep it out of effective involvement rather than to involve it in a constructive manner. The catalogue of Soviet interventions – from Angola through to Ethiopia and eventually on to Afghanistan – soon became a familiar feature of hawkish critiques of détente. According to this critique, détente and specifically arms control, had become a cover for a growth in Soviet military capabilities and an expansionist push in the Third World. The logic of this push, many suspected, was to gain control over the oil routes from the Gulf to Western Europe and the United States.

For a while it seemed as if the Carter Administration would resist these tendencies out of a desire to sustain détente, promote arms control, and to move away from the 'paranoid' preoccupation with the Soviet threat that, it was asserted, had distracted attention from the more pressing problems of North/South relations. Unfortunately, from the Soviet point of view, President Carter sought to demonstrate his liberal credentials by campaigning on the theme of human rights, and his capacity for innovations by ignoring the progress in SALT II that had been achieved by the end of 1976 in favour of a radical new proposal that combined an appeal for deep cuts with a one-sided impact in the USSR.[22] Over time it was possible to reach a modicum of understanding on both these matters but at the cost of some good will. Little could be done to stem the growing sense of a Soviet push in the Third World, particularly in the sensitive areas close to the oil routes from the Gulf to the industrialised world.

Détente hung on in the United States under increasing strain, until the last days of the 1970s when it finally broke under the weight of the Soviet invasion of Afghanistan. President Carter admitted that this event had changed his whole view of the Soviet Union. This is not the place to consider whether there are more charitable explanations of Soviet conduct, or the general developments of US–Soviet relations outside Europe. Our concern here is only to stress the importance of these events in explaining the breakdown of US–Soviet détente.

Post-Détente

The decline of the US–Soviet détente did not inevitably mean a decline of the European détente. The former reflected relationships and activities that were largely external to Europe. It soon became apparent that the West Europeans were reluctant to follow the American lead in hardening relations with the East. They shared the Soviet view of linkage – mutual agreements should serve mutual benefits and could be insulated to some extent from a conflict of interest elsewhere. The Europeans might not approve of Soviet behaviour in various parts of the world but they saw no reason to jeopardise perfectly satisfactory local arrangements in order to express their disapproval. Inevitably this attitude appeared rather craven in Washington where it was increasingly suggested that the West Europeans had succumbed to Soviet power, becoming so complacent that they failed to recognise that their own security had a global dimension.

The first years of the 1980s therefore were stormy not only in US–Soviet relations but also in relations between the USA and its allies. West Europeans began to worry about the volatility of US policy-making, intemperate overreactions and the narrow notions of national interest. Much of this concern was shared by the Soviet Union. On the basic principles of East–West trade and arms control, West Europeans found their views edging away from the United States and complementary if not identical to those of the Soviet Union, in that they shared a basis of belief in the underlying value of both of these activities.

The Atlantic divisions were to a large extent over policy toward the Soviet Union, but they were not created by the Soviet Union. The Kremlin did not offer trade and arms control only to the West Europeans and not to the United States. The most important single deals with the West were not over pipelines but over grain, and Washington found it difficult to ignore the interest of American farmers. Arms control was if anything more important in relations with the United States than with Europe. The Europeans in fact have generally shown far more interest in negotiations as a spectacle, a visible sign of East–West contact, than in the content. In London and Bonn, arms control tended to be applauded in the abstract but questioned in the detail, until it seemed that the United States had become completely disenchanted with the process. The two sides of NATO developed different views on Soviet policy because of geography. At stake for Europe was a set of regional arrangements; at stake for the United States was a global balance of power.

The Kremlin may not have created these divisions but it was certainly prepared to exploit them. Its propaganda would dwell on the differences of perception within the Alliance, applauding the Europeans when they took a stand against Washington. The greatest effort came with the attempt to disrupt NATO plans for the modernisation of its intermediate nuclear forces. The plan, approved on 12 December 1979, was to base 572 American missiles (464 cruise and 108 Pershings) in five European countries (Belgium, Britain, Germany, Holland and Italy). Much of the Soviet diplomacy over the succeeding years was designed to prevent this deployment taking place. In Soviet propaganda, and in that of the various and vociferous anti-nuclear movements that sprang up in Europe to protest at this plan, there was much stress on the fact that these were *American* missiles being inflicted on *Europe*. There was some irony in this in that the origins of the plans were European. In conception, as we have noted, this plan was to strengthen the Atlantic links by ensuring that the US nuclear arsenal was directly implicated in a land war in Europe. Rather than strengthen the links it weakened them by providing an opportunity for all sorts of anti-American sentiments to come to the fore in Europe.[23]

Many of those protesting at the new missiles in Europe were

also mistaken in their belief that the new weapons were being foisted upon them by the United States and, despite all the contrary evidence pointing to British and German initiatives in the early days of the Carter Administration, persisted with the explanation that the intent was to prepare to fight a limited nuclear war. The USSR also used this explanation, on occasions, though at other times it was suggested that the US purpose was to prepare for a first strike – a somewhat different strategy to a limited nuclear war.

Reading between the lines, and taking account of what is known about Soviet military planning, there are two distinct types of concern. First, there seems to be some worry in Moscow, focused on Pershing II, that these fast, highly accurate missiles will be directed against Soviet command and control systems as part of a much more general first strike. However, it is hard to take seriously the view that these 108 missiles by themselves could make all the difference, even accepting improved counter-force capabilities on US 1CBMs and the Western superiority in anti-submarine warfare. The suggestion that this would force the USSR to a launch-on-warning posture seems if anything to be a reverse of the truth. The fast speed of Pershing is annoying because it probably would not allow time to launch on warning.

The other concern, which is more serious, is that the new missiles cast doubt on their nuclear strategy for Europe. As far as can be discerned, Soviet planners envisage the next European war strategy with a prolonged conventional phase, during which Soviet forces would do their utmost to destroy NATO nuclear assets within Europe (with conventional forces) so that when the moment comes to move to the decisive nuclear phase, Soviet forces would face a manageable target set. This plan might be thwarted either by NATO making the first move (or preparing to do so and forcing the USSR into premature pre-emptive action), by failing to reduce NATO's local nuclear strength in the conventional phase, or by triggering an all-out nuclear exchange with the United States. Increasingly in Soviet theory and certainly in Soviet practice there is the clear suggestion that a nuclear war might indeed be limited so long as no weapons actually detonate on Soviet territory. In this sense the problem with Cruise and Pershing missiles is that they are relatively invulnerable to attack (possibly even by a nuclear barrage) and promise to bring a European war right into the Soviet homeland. This makes sanctuary status less likely and so undermines the rest of the plan. In other words, the rationale of the NATO programme might actually be warranted![24]

The Dilemma

The USSR, therefore, does have an incentive to stop the programme. It has placed some hope on the 'peace' movement in the West in this respect, although it has also indicated a readiness to make concessions in arms control negotiations. It also appears to view the peace movement as beneficial as a source of disunity within NATO. This again raises the fundamental issue in this chapter.

The USSR benefited from these divisions and tried to encourage them but it did not create them and could not fully control them. The most difficult question is how far it wanted these divisions to go: would it really have been pleased if NATO had broken up and the United States disengaged from Western Europe? The answer is still probably 'no'. One reason is that the anti-nuclear movement itself is double-edged. Its slogans and policies would if implemented threaten Soviet interests as much, if not more so, than American interests. The dissolution of the blocs, for example, would threaten domestic political management in the East far more than in the West. It might be hoped that the protest movements could be confined to the West, but that could not be guaranteed. The fear would be that the political fall-out resulting from a break-up in NATO could not but affect the Warsaw Pact. The outcome of the re-ordering of European security would be uncertain and possibly more threatening to Soviet domestic and external interests.

Secondly, the Soviet Union still has to work out some sort of relations with the United States. Looking at the basic distribution of power in the world it cannot but be impressed by the pre-eminent position of the United States and the need to come to some sort of understanding. This is brought out very clearly in an exercise conducted by the US International Communications Agency (USICA) in 1981 in which they quizzed West Europeans and Americans with regular contact with the Soviet Union on the world view of the Soviet elites. It concluded that: 'The superpower relationship remains the single most important international concern for these Soviets . . . The US is the only power that can severely damage the USSR . . . Wherever they turn, Soviets are inclined to see the hand of the United States restraining their actions, hindering their plans, and working against their interests' . . . The USA can bestow or withhold the status they require.[25] In addition, with poor grain harvests and indebtedness throughout Eastern Europe, it needs American help in problems of domestic economic management, or at least a lack of hindrance in the form of trade embargoes and restrictions. A United States in a bitter, resentful and unilateral mood could cause even more problems in terms of arms races and confrontations in various regions of the world. A United States which had fallen out with its allies would not be easier to deal with, and the problems then faced by the Soviet leadership could not be eased through even friendlier relations with Western Europe.

For the Kremlin, therefore, policy towards the United States in the European context still involves something of a dilemma. On the one hand, they are nervous about the disruptive effects of recent American initiatives to the extent that they raise the political temperature in Europe, interfere with trade and generally make life difficult. The Kremlin has always found the American nuclear presence particularly threatening and the proposed improvements make this worse. Their proposals for intermediate nuclear force reduction would eliminate this presence, at least in so far as it affects the Soviet Union. There is less worry about US nuclear threats posed to the rest of the Warsaw Pact (Hence the difference in concern with the Pershing II, which can hit the USSR, as against the Pershing I which cannot!)

On the other hand there is no indication that the Soviet leaders want to set in motion a chain of events that would cause the Americans to leave Europe. They certainly have not proposed a withdrawal themselves – for example, in the context of the conventional force reductions talks under way in Vienna. Indeed, a successful outcome at Vienna would legitimise the remaining US conventional presence. Nor have they suggested that Europe could get on perfectly well without the United States. What they have appeared to hope is that the Western Europeans offer a means of moderating American policy. When they have supported West European arguments that contradict those of the United States it is because they agree with them and not simply because they like the spectacle of argument. In this sense the shift over the past decade has been from seeing the United States' presence in Europe as a means of keeping the Germans in check, to one in which the connection provides a means by which the Europeans can keep the Americans in check.

Notes to Chapter 3

1   On the impact of the Tiflis Speech see Robin Ranger, *Arms and Politics, 1958–1978: Arms Control in a Changing Political Context* (Toronto: The Macmillan Company of Canada, 1979), p. 190.

2   H. S. Dinerstein, *War and the Soviet Union* (New York: Praeger, 1959), pp. 141–2.

3   Arnold Horelick and Myron Rush, *Strategic Power and Soviet Foreign Policy* (Chicago: University of Chicago Press, 1966).

4   That the USA was sensing its strength was made abundantly clear in a speech on 10 October 1961 by Deputy Secretary of Defense Roswell L. Gilpatric, Reprinted in *Documents on Disarmament, 1961* (Washington DC: US Arms Control and Disarmament Agency, 1962), pp. 542–50.

5   Khrushchev kept on reminding the West of the 'admission' by President Kennedy at the 1961 Vienna Summit that the two sides were 'equal'.

6   On interpretation of Soviet conduct at the time see Ray Garthoff, 'The meaning of the missiles', *Washington Quarterly*, vol. 5, no. 4 (Autumn 1982).

7   By conventional means. This was one reason why President Kennedy was reluctant to follow his instincts toward a 'no-first-use-of-nuclear-weapons' declaration.

8   Reprinted at the back of Robert Kennedy, *13 Days: The Cuban Missile Crisis October 1962* (London, Macmillan, 1969).

9   The development of Soviet nuclear forces is fully explained in Robert Berman and John C. Baker, *Soviet Strategic Forces: Requirements and Responses* (Washington, DC: The Brookings Institution, 1982).

10 See Thomas M. Franck and Edward Weisbard, *Word Politics: Verbal Strategy among the Superpowers* (New York: Oxford University Press, 1972) for an argument as to why the USA found it difficult to challenge the Brezhnev Doctrine head-on.

11 The concept of 'correlation of forces' is analysed in Chapter 1, pp. 26–35, and in Michael J. Deane, 'Soviet Perceptions of the Military Factor', in 'The Correlation of Forces' in Donald C. Daniel (ed.), *International Perceptions of the Superpower Military Balance* (New York: Praeger, 1978).

12 For background to the Non-Proliferation Treaty see William Epstein, *The Last Chance: Nuclear Proliferation and Arms Control* (New York: The Free Press, 1966).

13 John Newhouse, *Cold Dawn: The Story of SALT* (New York: Holt, Rinehart & Winston, 1973).

14 For background on East–West trade see Stephen Woolcock, *Western Policies on East–West Trade*, Chatham House Papers 15 (London: Routledge & Kegan Paul/ RIIA, 1982).

15 For a consideration of this issue see the essays collected in John Baylis and Gerald Segal (ed.), *Soviet Strategy* (London: Croom Helm, 1981).

16 Jack H. Nunn, *The Soviet First Strike Threat* (New York: Praeger, 1982); Lawrence Freedman, *US Intelligence and the Soviet Strategic Threat* (London: Macmillan, 1977).

17 John Prados, *The Soviet Estimate: US Intelligence Analysis on Russian Military Strength* (New York: The Dial Press, 1982), esp. chs 14–16.

18 Although this was not through want of trying. See Lawrence Freedman, 'The dilemma of theatre nuclear arms control', *Survival* (January/February 1981).

19 In a report on an interview with Khrushchev in September 1961, C. L. Sulzberger of the *New York Times* observed: 'Khrushchev believes absolutely that when it comes to a showdown, Britain, France and Italy would refuse to join the United States in a war over Berlin for fear of their absolute destruction. Quite blandly he asserts that these countries are, figuratively speaking, hostages to the USSR and a guarantee against war'. Horelick and Rush, *Strategic Power and Soviet Foreign Policy*, pp. 93–4.

20 Ian Smart, 'Perspectives from Europe', in Mason Willrich and John B. Rhinelander (ed.), *SALT: The Moscow Agreements and Beyond* (New York: The Free Press, 1974).

21 Henry Kissinger, *Years of Upheaval* (Boston: Little, Brown & Co., 1982), ch. 5.

22 Strobe Talbott, *Endgame: The Inside Story of SALT II* (New York: Harper & Row, 1979).

23 The issues raised by the protest movements are discussed further in Lawrence Freedman, 'Limited war, unlimited protest', *Orbis* (Spring, 1982).

24 These issues will be explored in full in a forthcoming Adelphi Paper by Steven Meyer on Soviet theatre nuclear forces and doctrine.

25 Gregory Guroff and Steven Grant, *Soviet Elites: World View and Perceptions of the US*, R-18-81 (Office of Research, International Communications Agency, United States of America, 29 September 1981), pp. 14–21.

4

The German Factor

Edwina Moreton

Germany is the linchpin of Soviet strategy in Western Europe. The division of Europe runs through Germany. And for over thirty years since the two separate German states were founded, in 1949, the Federal Republic in the west and the German Democratic Republic in the east have formed the military front line between East and West (and, since 1955, between the Warsaw Pact and NATO). That much has remained unchanged in post-war Europe. But the two German states also form the political and ideological front line. Any change in the political allegiance of either half of divided Germany would radically alter the East–West balance of power, not just in Europe, but around the globe. Hence the importance of the German problem in post-war international politics. And hence the importance of Germany in post-war Soviet strategy in Europe.

That much is clear. But how does Germany fit into Soviet strategy and how has its role in that strategy changed? Politically a great deal has changed, both behind military lines in Europe and across them. Or so it seems. The German problem – what to do about the political future of divided Germany and Berlin – had been the glowing coal at the centre of smouldering East–West tensions for over twenty-five years by the time West Germany signed the Moscow treaty with the Soviet Union in August 1970. The Moscow treaty centred on the renunciation of force in West German–Soviet relations and was followed in swift succession by the Warsaw treaty (1970), the four-power Berlin agreement (1971), the Basic treaty governing relations between the estranged German states (1972) and the Prague treaty (1973).

With that the German problem changed from being the focus of East–West tension to become a residual problem in East–West relations. West Germany had, until very recently, enjoyed a decade of as close to 'normal' relations with its neighbours to the east as could be imagined, given the post-war division of Europe into two ideologically opposing alliances. Yet the German problem had not been resolved, merely set aside. The parties to the problem – primarily East and West Germany, the Soviet Union and the Western allies – had simply agreed to disagree on some vital matters of principle concerning Germany and Berlin in order to improve their relations in other areas.

For a time, East–West relations did improve. Détente un-blocked political and economic channels clogged since the breakdown of four-power co-operation in Germany in the late 1940s. More specifically it enabled West Germany and the Soviet Union to broaden their political contacts, not just their trade and cultural relations. Correspondingly the potential for Soviet influence on West German domestic and foreign policy ex-panded rapidly, especially as Moscow still held the key to more far-reaching improvements in East–West German relations. That, after all, had been the purpose behind West Germany's new opening to the east – its *Ostpolitik* – in the 1970s.

Soviet dilemmas

There has been much speculation and no little concern among West Germany's allies at the potential political implication of this *Ostpolitik*. Was this the kind of opening to the East the Soviet Union had been waiting to exploit in the hope of drawing West Germany away from its anchorage in the West? Possibly. Yet one of the conclusions of this chapter will be that, if anything, détente in Europe posed even more complex problems for Soviet strategy towards West Germany. Holding the West Germans at arm's length, as enemy number one, in the 1950s and 1960s had allowed the Soviet Union to sidestep some of the most difficult problems which have since arisen within its own camp over the permissible degree of contact between East and West – the ideologically correct and politically safe balance between competition and co-existence.

The element of competition is still there. But after 1970 the element of co-existence was greatly strengthened. Although relations between West Germany and the Soviet Union have improved considerably and this has opened up a new dimension to Soviet foreign policy in Europe, change has had a reciprocal impact. Friendship – even just the diplomatic sort – opens up opportunities and imposes costs on both sides. West Germany has not just been influenced by but has itself also influenced Soviet foreign policy as a result. And West Germany's impact on East Germany and the rest of the Soviet alliance has been particularly noticeable.

Perhaps more than at any time since the Second World War, the past decade or so has confronted Soviet policy-makers with a basic dilemma: are Soviet interests in Europe in practice best served by a policy aimed at relative political stability across the familiar and relatively stable East–West divide, or is there more to be gained by a policy of exploiting divisions within the Western Alliance and encouraging basic changes of alignment among the allies of the Soviet Union's chief rival, the United States? (The dilemma is a familiar one to Western policy-makers thinking about Eastern Europe.)

Simply to state the question in those terms already cuts across that body of Western opinion that assumes a single-minded pursuit of Soviet political-cum-military domination in Europe, whether the image used is skittles, dominoes or salami tactics. The argument here will not be that such goals have never figured in Soviet thinking about Western Europe – rolling back the frontiers of capitalism is bound to have some appeal in the Kremlin. Rather it will focus on the competing priorities in Soviet policy in Europe – and in Germany in particular – and the conflict between short- and long-term goals.

For example, are long-term Soviet interests best served by a united or a divided Germany? In the shorter term can the Soviet Union entice West Germany away from the Western Alliance while still keeping a firm grip on East Germany? Or in the Soviet calculation must the presumed price of a West German realignment be so high as to cause political instability in East Germany or elsewhere in Eastern Europe? And if so, is it worth it? Is the Soviet aim so to loosen the bonds between West Germany and the Western Alliance that the American political and military commitment to the defence of Europe is seriously weakened? Or is the Soviet Union more concerned at the prospect of a militarily and economically strong West Germany cut loose from the straitjacket of NATO security policy? None of these questions has a simple answer.

The problem is complicated for Soviet policy-makers – as indeed it is for their Western counterparts – by the fact that just as the German problem is part of a wider East–West division in Europe, so increasingly in the past decade, as the German problem was partly defused, the conflict in Europe has come to be seen by both superpowers as only one of several possible theatres of tension and confrontation. On the other hand, although nobody expects the spark of a future East–West conflict necessarily to be struck in Europe, there is still enough dry tinder there to be ignited from outside. So the region continues to be central to the balance of power around the world, if only because so much military might on both sides meets in the centre of Europe.

If European politics could have been frozen somewhere back in the early 1960s, with West Germany as the most junior of America's junior allies in Europe, the problem of Germany might look very different today in both East and West. But European politics have not stood still. West Germany's economic, political and military weight within the Western Alliance has increased enormously. Its army now forms the main supporting pillar of NATO on the European mainland. Its economic stability has been of vital importance within the EEC. The Federal Republic's anchor in the Western Alliance has always been – and still is – the guarantee of West German security. But in the 1980s a good case can be made that, vice versa, the security and cohesion of the Western Alliance is now very much dependent on the continued stability and support of a strong and loyal West German state.

As West Germany's importance to the Western Alliance has grown, so the country has assumed increased weight in Soviet strategy towards Western Europe. If the Soviet Union is ever to snap the link that binds the United States to the defence of Europe and binds Europe to a larger Western political, economic and ideological alliance, then West Germany is the place where Soviet pressure must tell. And the Soviet Union knows it. That is where the unresolved German problem fits in.

As East–West relations have soured in the 1980s, West Germany's attempts to protect the gains of its *Ostpolitik* have opened up a surface crack in the Western Alliance. This in turn has created opportunities for Soviet mischief-making, which the Kremlin has not been slow to exploit. But exploiting West Germany's disappointment at the fading of détente does not itself amount to a strategy. If the Soviet Union and the United States has been engaged these past thirty years in a simple tug-of-war over the political allegiance of West Germany, Soviet strategy would need little elucidation and would have caused fewer headaches for the makers of Soviet foreign policy.

So what have been the dominant drives of Soviet policy towards West Germany and the German problem? The period since the Second World War divides roughly into three, possibly, four, phases in which there has been a remarkable underlying consistency in Soviet policy, but in which it is possible to trace the effects of some of the competing priorities outlined above.

114

The Confusion of the Early Years

The war years had left the Red Army and therefore the Soviet Union in control of much of Eastern Europe – a *fait accompli* later to be regretted by Stalin's wartime allies in the West. By the end of the war a divided Europe was, at least in retrospect, a foregone conclusion. Both Stalin and Churchill saw the process clearly in the rest of Europe.[1] But what of Germany?

At least for the first few years after the war, the issue of Germany and the process of its division was treated separately in Soviet policy from the division of Europe. This was in part because Stalin was unclear about his own long-term objectives in Germany and, as a consequence, even less clear about the strategy he should follow, beyond insisting on punitive reparations against the wartime invader of Soviet territory. The solution of all concrete issues, such as the all-important border settlements, had been left by the Allies to await a final peace treaty to be signed with an all-German government, although there was no indication of when or how such a government was to be formed. Not surprisingly, as relations between the Allies soured, the fate of Germany became closely linked to the policies of the four powers in other fields.[2]

Adding to his side of the muddle, Stalin seemed to have no clear idea whether Soviet interests would be best served by a divided Germany, with the Soviet Union in direct control of a separate East German state, or by a united, neutral Germany with the prospect of gaining the allegiance of the whole of Germany at some future date. For example, the Communist Party in the Eastern zone, under its leader, Walter Ulbricht, was given the go-ahead to begin the reconstruction of political life in the Soviet zone. Yet other parties were soon licensed too – presumably in part so that, under strict control, they could fight subsequent all-German elections.[3]

The catalyst which clarified Soviet policy in Germany was the decision by the Western Allies, foreshadowed as early as 1946, to bypass four-power administration, which was by now badly stalled over Soviet demands for high reparations, and to initiate the fusion of the Western zones into what was to become a separate West German state. In 1948, the Western Allies introduced a currency reform in their own zones aimed at reviving the German economy. The proposal to extend the reform to the Western sectors of Berlin, which was likewise under four-power administration, was met with the Soviet blockade of Berlin.

As an aggressive attempt to defend the status quo in Germany Stalin's blockade was badly thought out and badly handled and produced the worst possible outcome for Soviet policy in Europe.[4] At a time when the American military presence in Europe had been reduced after the war, the blockade elevated the American political, military and economic commitment to Berlin, Western Germany and Western Europe to a symbol of the defence of democracy around the globe. It also hastened the division of Germany and encouraged the speediest possible integration of the new West German state into the Western political, economic and military alliance. The deep suspicion of Soviet motives engendered by the blockade scotched any further hopes for a settlement of the German problem for at least another two decades, including consideration of Stalin's 'peace note' of 1952, which offered German reunification in return for German neutrality.[5]

Much of Soviet policy toward West Germany after Stalin's death in 1953 was devoted to trying to undo the harm done to Soviet interests by the blockade. Having failed to delay the division of Germany, the Soviet Union made repeated attempts to revive the issue and put it back on the agenda of four-power discussion, but with increasingly little expectation of success.

The Two-State Theory

The event which switched Soviet policy firmly behind the division of Germany was the inclusion of West Germany in the

NATO military alliance in 1955. The creation of two separate German states in 1949 had altered the timescale for the 'resolution' of the German problem; but as far as Soviet policy was concerned, the formal incorporation of the two Germanies into their respective military alliances in 1955 (East Germany was actually not admitted as a full member of the Warsaw Pact until 1956) ruled out the possibility of reunification in any form. Henceforth the Soviet Union was to insist that recognition of the division must be the basis for any European settlement and that the German problem could only be resolved within this wider European framework. The policy of peaceful co-existence enunciated by Khrushchev in 1956 allowed for the peaceful existence side by side of states with differing social systems. There was no place in this theory for reunification.

In 1955 the two German states each attained sovereignty, although in each case legal restrictions still applied by virtue of continuing, if ambiguous, four-power responsibility for 'Germany as a whole' enjoyed by the Western Allies and the Soviet Union respectively. Now both German states had a legitimate say in their own future. Yet neither German state was able to take upon itself the political responsibility for resolving the German problem. West Germany was happy enough to accept the restrictions of Germany's continuing four-power status, since the West German government maintained the goal of eventual national reunification under Western auspices and on that based its claim to the right to speak for all Germans, including those in the East. The division of Germany was to West Germany an abnormal state.

The East German government chafed at the rein the Soviet Union still held on its political autonomy. Being the smaller German state and with little confidence in the enduring affections of its population, the division of Germany and Soviet support for a separate East German state was a political lifeline for the SED regime. Yet any formal restriction on GDR sovereignty was a reminder of the fragility of SED power. The Ulbricht regime had some cause for celebration, however. Until

1955 any Soviet initiative on Germany had threatened to succeed only at East Germany's expense. After 1955 the picture changed in important ways.

From 1955 until the government of Willy Brandt came to power in West Germany in 1969, Western policy laboured under a fundamental paradox. Having taken a conscious decision to create a separate West German state, the Western powers and successive West German governments pledged their steadfast support for the aim of German reunification. But by that time the Soviet Union was happy to settle for a divided country. West Germany missed the point.

After 1955 the Soviet stake in East Germany increased enormously. East Germany became the Soviet Union's most important trading partner in Comecon; its armed forces were closely integrated into the Warsaw Pact and were placed effectively under Soviet command;[6] ideologically and politically the East German regime earned the reputation of being Moscow's most loyal supporter in Eastern Europe. Increasingly from the mid-1950s onwards the issue for the Soviet Union was no longer one of East German expendability in the search for a united Germany drawn away from the West. What was at stake in East Germany's relations with its allies throughout the coming decades was the degree of influence the GDR might exercise over the details of Soviet Germany policy, as against the degree to which East Germany's leaders have been obliged to conform to unwelcome Soviet initiatives within the framework of a divided Germany. In short, in the three-cornered relationship between the Soviet Union, East Germany and West Germany, the Soviet–East German axis was by now clearly the most important to Soviet security.

Yet the Soviet Union was involved in the German problem at several different levels. It was and still is the GDR's major ally, and for many years, due to the successful international isolation of East Germany by West Germany, was the channel through which the East German regime was obliged to conduct its relations with the outside world. Yet the Soviet Union is also one of the four powers with continuing responsibilities for 'Germany as a whole'. This gives it a useful political lever against West Germany and ensures a continuing Soviet involvement in the political development of the Western Alliance. At the same time, the Soviet Union is a global power with interests to promote and defend well beyond the confines of Germany or Europe. More broadly, in Soviet eyes a West Germany integrated into the Western security alliance represented the spearhead of American military power in Europe. For that reason, if for no other, the Soviet Union would have been determined to keep a toe-hold in Germany. The unresolved German problem has provided excellent footing.

Having now accepted a divided Germany, Soviet objectives in Europe became much clearer. From this point onwards the Soviet Union was determined to prevent a solution of the German problem on West German terms and to limit West German influence in Eastern Europe until such time as West Germany, too, accepted the division. By contrast the West German strategy for reunification – the Hallstein doctrine, which sought to isolate the GDR by threatening sanctions against any state which established diplomatic relations with the GDR – was interpreted as a threat to the status quo in Europe and hence as a threat to European security and Soviet security interests.

Soviet Pressure on West Germany

The second Berlin crisis, lasting intermittently from 1958 until the building of the Berlin Wall in August 1961, was a Soviet attempt to force formal acceptance of this status quo on the West. The conventional wisdom has it that Khrushchev, like Stalin before him, gambled on using the vulnerability of the Western position in Berlin to force a change in Western policy and that, also like Stalin, he lost. Khrushchev threatened to sign a separate peace treaty with East Germany, which would have meant abandoning four-power control in Germany, and to turn Berlin into a 'free' city, forcing the Allies to negotiate any access to the city with a 'sovereign' East German state. Yet instead of levering the Western allies out of Berlin and cutting West Berlin off from its ties to the West, Khrushchev was forced to build a wall across Berlin to cut off an increasingly weakened East Germany and East Berlin from the destabilising influence of an open border to the west in West Berlin. The wall was indeed an embarrassing necessity – as the crisis deepened the flow of refugees across the one remaining open border inside Germany became a flood.[7]

Yet, much to the annoyance of the Ulbricht regime in East Germany,[8] Khrushchev in the end was prepared to settle for a much smaller prize than Western capitulation. Not that he would have been sad to see the Western Allies pack their bags and leave Berlin to its fate. But contrary to the conventional wisdom, Khrushchev probably got what he realistically might have hoped for: the crisis jolted the Western powers into *de facto* acceptance of the status quo in Germany and forced them in practice to limit their support of West German aspirations in Berlin to the defence of 'three essentials': Western presence in the city, Western access to the city and the continued economic viability of West Berlin.[9]

Khrushchev had successfully demonstrated the vulnerability of the Western presence in the city and the West German claim to sole representation of the German nation. East Germany's disappointment at the final outcome of the crisis – Soviet back-pedalling over a separate peace treaty and the still ambiguous status of Berlin – sowed the seeds of later rows between East Germany and the Soviet Union over whether full recognition of East Germany by the West should be made a precondition of all further progress in East–West relations. But it also started the chain of political reconsiderations that led eventually to West German recognition of the separate existence of East Germany.[10]

In the meantime the Soviet Union switched the focus of its

attack from the Allied presence in the city to the West German presence as part of a counter-campaign to isolate West Germany as the only state actively committed to changing the status quo. The underlying aim was the same: to wring out of West Germany recognition of post-war boundaries in Europe. This underlying strategy – based on the premise of two German states – remained constant. From then on what varied was Soviet expectation of success.

The Soviet-Inspired Rejectionist Front

The West German government, however, was determined to keep the goal of reunification alive by continuing to ignore and where possible isolate the GDR and persuade even its closest allies in Eastern Europe to put economic self-interest above fraternal solidarity. For West Germany, a growing economic giant but a political dwarf, trade was the only real weapon it had against the East. It was used where possible as a continuation of politics by other means. There was no lack of interest in trade relations with West Germany and the policy met with some success. A trade offensive launched at Eastern Europe, beginning in 1962, by the West German foreign minister, Gerhard Schroeder, and part of a strategy known as the 'policy of movement' achieved a series of trade agreements: with Poland (March 1963); Romania (October 1963); Hungary (November 1963); and Bulgaria (March 1964). Each of the agreements included West Berlin, which East Germany insisted was beyond West German jurisdiction. Only direct Soviet pressure on Czechoslovakia prevented the completion of the ring of agreements, which deliberately excluded the GDR. Romania and West Germany later established full diplomatic relations in January 1967.

Paradoxically, West Germany's trade offensive had helped bolster the Soviet Union's two-states theory since all the East European states recognised East Germany, but at the same time it had exposed a serious weakness in fraternal support for the GDR's demand from its allies in the Warsaw Pact for backing in its claim to full West German recognition. The offensive ground to a halt because in the final analysis, whatever the benefits of trade with West Germany, the Soviet Union was not prepared to see West Germany succeed and extend its influence in Eastern Europe at East Germany's expense. The fate of the 'policy of movement' held an important lesson for West Germany: that the key to a successful policy toward its Eastern neighbours lay after all in Moscow. Similarly, although West Germany was not directly involved in the crisis in Czechoslovakia in 1968 (despite Soviet propaganda efforts to find a scapegoat after the fact), the reassertion of Soviet control in the bloc, marked by the invasion in August 1968, was in retrospect a precondition for the pursuit of an active Soviet *Westpolitik* in response to Brandt's *Ostpolitik*.

In the meantime the Soviet Union did not sit idly on its hands waiting for the light to dawn in the chancellery in Bonn. This second, long phase in Soviet German policy saw a deliberate effort to encourage oppositional tendencies and heretical thoughts about official West German policy within the West German opposition party, the Social Democrats. As early as 1964, at the end of the Khrushchev era, much to Ulbricht's annoyance, the Soviet Union had begun to revise its negative assessment of West German Social Democracy.[11] In the spring of 1966 a speakers' exchange tentatively arranged between the West German Social Democrats and the East German SED was aborted only after it became clear that the Social Democrats were not prepared to renounce the framework of official policy on the German question.[12] Later the same year, the Soviet Union cautiously welcomed Social Democratic participation in the new West German government, the Grand Coalition of Christian Democrats and Social Democrats, led by Kiesinger (CDU) as chancellor and Brandt (SPD) as foreign minister.

The consistency of Soviet German policy was underlined following the formation of the new government. Recognising the block put on its policy towards the East by its previous rigidity over the German question, the new Kiesinger–Brandt government offered to conclude renunciation of force agreements which, while not specifically including the GDR, would take account of 'Germany's division'; promised that contacts beneath the level of formal inter-state contacts with East Germany would be encouraged; and recognised Poland's desire to live in a state with 'secure borders' (even if it was still not prepared to recognise the borders themselves). But the new tone in Bonn was not matched by any movement on the central issue of West Germany's claim to sole representation of the German people and its refusal to recognise the existence of a separate East German state. Consequently the change of tone in Bonn brought no change of heart in Moscow. The Soviet Union and East Germany worked closely together to block any further progress in West Germany's relationship with Eastern Europe until after the Czechoslovak crisis in 1968.

But it was within the West German Social Democratic party that the ultimate futility of maintaining the claim to sole representation was recognised. The new approach accepted that the policy pursued by successive West German governments since 1949 had been highly successful in integrating West Germany into the Western Alliance, but had failed to address in any practical way the problem of Germany's physical division. The culmination of a re-thinking process which went back at least to the second Berlin crisis was expressed in a new concept of 'change through rapprochement' outlined by Herbert Wehner and officially adopted in policy form at the SPD Party Congress in April 1969. It meant acceptance of East Germany as a separate state within one German nation, in the hope that a more realistic policy on Germany's division would open up new possibilities for overcoming the practical effects the division had caused. It also meant the pursuit of a compromise formula with Poland. The new SPD proposals stopped short of East Germany's demand for the full diplomatic recognition of East Germany by West Germany. However, the impact of the Social Democrats' changed approach was immediate. Gomulka in Poland immediately proposed talks on the new basis. And in the run-up to the West German elections held later in the year the Soviet foreign minister, Andrei Gromyko, in July offered to re-open four-power talks on Berlin. When SPD Party policy became the official policy of a new Social Democrat–Free Democrat coalition government in October, the stampede of its allies, with Soviet blessing, to begin settlement of bilateral relations with West Germany left East Germany bruised and sulking.

Two States, One Nation, and *Ostpolitik*

In short, it was West Germany not the Soviet Union that under-took a fundamental reassessment of its German policy and ushered in the third major phase of post-war Soviet German policy.[13] In a matter of months the diplomatic, economic and political channels which had been blocked for years began to unclog. West Germany had not simply caved in all down the line. The Brandt government fought through its insistence that, although there were two German states, there was still only one German nation. And it set itself the task of lowering the political and social barriers that held the people of Germany apart. Neither the Moscow treaty of 1970 nor those that followed, including the Basic treaty signed with bad grace by East Germany in 1973, compromised Brandt's contention that the principle of German reunification be upheld, even though its practical impossibility for the foreseeable future was recog-nised. The Berlin agreement, too, secured the future of West Berlin to the extent possible given the conflicting interpret-ations of the city's status. Indeed, the wording of the agreement was devised precisely to skate around those conflicting views.

Still, the Soviet Union had the greater cause for self-congratulation as the era of confrontation softened into the era of negotiation in the 1970s. Aside from any beneficial spin-offs from East–West relations, such as increased trade and the like,[14] this partial settlement of the German problem left the Soviet

Union holding several useful cards. It had managed a significant improvement in its political relations with West Germany while retaining its grip on a none-too-happy East Germany. It had unblocked economic channels – or at least removed political blockages – without conceding any of West Germany's earlier political goals over the national question. And it had chaperoned a settlement of sorts of intra-German relations without apparently losing any of its own influence either in Eastern Europe or in central Europe, where it still held on to those ambiguous four-power responsibilities for 'Germany as a whole' and Berlin. Finally, because of the nature of East German–Soviet relations and the continued political dependence of East Germany on the Soviet Union, the key to any further improvement in East–West German relations – the motivation for Brandt's radical re-think of *Ostpolitik* – still lay in Soviet hands.

But where to go from here? The increasing normalisation of relations with West Germany only added to West Germany's importance to Soviet policy in Europe and in East–West relations in general. In some ways – for example, in trade – relations became more prosaic. But a 'special relationship' with Bonn – a term beloved of the Soviet Union but always rejected in rhetoric and in practice by West Germany – also lit up new political horizons darkened since Stalin lost the political initiative on Germany in 1948.

As a key member of the Western Alliance West Germany was now an important communication channel for Moscow on everything from arms control to trade. But the relationship with West Germany was also a potential lever the Soviet Union might some day hope to use to exploit any differences inside NATO. And finally, there was always the prospect that an increasingly 'normal' and politically profitable relationship with the Soviet Union might encourage West Germany to drag its anchor and drift further from its moorings in the Western Alliance. Although the change in West German policy and the prospect of some movement in East–West relations stirred anew old

125

thoughts in Soviet strategy towards Germany, the possibilities were far from endless.

West Germany's self-liberation from political adolescence did not imply a simultaneous desire to liberate itself from its alliance with the West. As a result the Soviet Union was confronted with a set of conflicting priorities. Although undoubtedly a concession in some ways to Soviet demands, the Brandt government's decision to accept the status quo in Europe brought West German policy more comfortably into line with that of its allies in NATO. Indeed, Brandt stressed at the time that West Germany's new *Ostpolitik* could only succeed on the basis of a secure *Westpolitik*.

Paradoxically it was the Soviet Union and East Germany that first experienced the political wake of *Ostpolitik*. First, there was the problem of persuading the East Germans to go along at all with a policy that neatly dovetailed with the Soviet objective of normalising relations with West Germany but that overlooked the East German demand for full diplomatic recognition by West Germany. In the event the two agreements that particularly concerned East Germany, the Basic treaty and the four-power Berlin agreement, were the best East Germany could have hoped for short of that objective. In both the two sides agreed to disagree on important points of principle, leaving plenty of room for ambiguity and for East Germany to continue to insist that four-power responsibility applied only to West Germany and West Berlin.

The cost, though, was a major crisis of confidence in East German–Soviet relations which reached its high point in the winter of 1970 and the spring of 1971, as pressure mounted on the East German regime not to obstruct Soviet policy. The row was a major factor, though not the only one, in the replacement of Ulbricht by Erich Honecker as leader of the SED.[15] Honecker was prepared to go along with the Soviet deal on Berlin and intra-German relations, but since then has been no less energetic than Ulbricht was before him in defending East German ground against West German or Soviet encroachment.[16] Since any new concession by the Soviet Union to West Germany on the German question can only succeed at East Germany's expense, the issue can be expected to re-surface whenever the Soviet Union attempts to use its leverage in the German problem in support of its foreign policy goals in Europe.

East German opposition to the West German interpretation of intra-German relations has also put a considerable damper on West Germany's original hopes for détente in Germany. Just as Brandt's *Ostpolitik* fell short of Honecker's expectations as regards diplomatic recognition of East Germany by West Germany, so Honecker has made certain that progress in intra-German relations has fallen short of West Germany's expectations. What was supposed to be a process of *'Wandel durch Annäherung'* has become for the East German regime *'Wandel durch Abgrenzung'* – meaning the strict delimitation of East Germany from West Germany and the separate development of the East German state. To aid that separate development, in October 1980 East Germany insisted on erecting a money wall, imposing additional heavy exchange requirements on visitors to East Germany from West Germany.[17]

Secondly, for all its greater pragmatism, the Brandt government had recognised the separate existence of East Germany precisely in order to initiate a more normal state-to-state relationship, improve contacts between Germans on both sides of the iron curtain and so help bridge the growing gulf between them. However it is dressed up, the aim was still internal change in East Germany as a step towards eventual reunification. To the extent that West Germany succeeded in its goal, however long term that goal may be, this could only impair Soviet security, which rests on the stability and loyalty of East Germany.

Similarly, the *Ostpolitik* was only part of a broader pattern of improved East–West relations, culminating in the signing of the Helsinki accords in 1975. This new pattern of East–West relations brought some unanticipated problems for the Soviet Union and several of its allies. The Soviet Union had pushed hard for the Helsinki agreement as a formal, multilateral seal on acceptance by the West of the status quo in Europe. But borders may be inviolable and unalterable by force – as agreed at Helsinki – without being impermeable to East–West communication and the flow of ideas. Of the three baskets of proposals adopted at Helsinki and the follow-up conferences, trade and security were of greatest interest to the Soviet Union. But the third – greater contact between East and West and the freer flow of information – was to prove more important in many ways as a considerable embarrassment.

In East Germany alone, within a few months of the publication of the Helsinki documents, over 100,000 people are reported to have applied for exit visas to West Germany, citing the Helsinki accords and the UN declaration on human rights. East Germany's German problem was clearly not yet dead. A wave of dissent rippled through the rest of Eastern Europe and the Soviet Union, the effects of which are still taxing the security police to this day. In East Germany's case, however, the impact of Helsinki was magnified by the massive upsurge in visitors allowed in from West Germany and West Berlin as part of the new intra-German relationship. Trade, too, if it has any political impact at all, has over the years in East Germany's case reinforced the preoccupation of East Germans with the standard of living and material wealth of their neighbours in West Germany – all of which can happily be viewed by most East Germans by tuning in to West German television. Only the vigilance of the East German regime has prevented such developments from becoming major destabilising factors, as opposed to irritants. At the same time the undoubted attraction of West Germany for many East Germans has helped the East German regime put a brake on Soviet–West German relations where there is a danger of putting East German stability at risk.

The Benefits of the Status Quo

Despite obvious Soviet moves to cultivate closer contacts with

West Germany, to the extent that détente was an alliance-wide phenomenon, improved relations with West Germany flowed naturally enough from and fed into an improvement in East–West relations in general. It was therefore difficult to disentangle Soviet German policy from the wider Soviet purpose in détente. However, some points are worth making about this third phase of Soviet German policy.

First, although the German problem and its political possibilities remained central to the Soviet conception of détente, for much of the 1970s the Soviet Union was able to enjoy the diplomatic, economic and political dividends of a general improvement in East–West relations. In particular, the Soviet Union could use its improved political relations with the leader of the Western Alliance, the United States, to advance its claim to strategic and political parity as a superpower. Although American–Soviet trade never lived up to its early promise, for the Soviet Union arms control talks, summitry and crisis-management were among the fruits of détente. As long as this wider détente continued, in some ways the Kremlin had potentially more to gain from dealing with West Germany as a member – albeit an especially important one – of the NATO alliance than from encouraging West Germany to push beyond the alliance consensus and so run into conflict with its allies. That is not to argue that Soviet policy-makers lost sight of the long-term political potential in West German–Soviet relations. But it is to suggest that considerations of short- and medium-term gain set the general framework of policy towards Germany in the détente era.

The second point in part bears out the first. For years, the Soviet Union had refused to consider American participation in any European security framework and indeed had always made a point to offer Europe the prospect of improved relations, perhaps along the lines of the Franco–Soviet special relationship, in return for the exclusion of American influence and the American military presence from Europe and a recognition of the status quo. Paradoxically this was also the period when the

Soviet Union saw least practical possibility of that happening. In a sense, galling though it was, the American presence in Europe solved one of the Soviet Union's potential security dilemmas – what to do about West Germany. Yet as West German policy towards East Germany changed in the period from 1969 onwards, so did Soviet policy towards European security. Opposition to United States and Canadian participation was dropped and both states were signatories to the Helsinki accords. Not that the Soviet Union ceased to worry about NATO as a military alliance, but in the improved climate of the mid-1970s security in Europe was a goal to be achieved by negotiation rather than confrontation.

Rapallo Re-visited?

Only when East–West relations soured badly following the Soviet invasion of Afghanistan did the focus of Soviet policy in Europe begin to shift and each element of Soviet German policy was thrown into sharper relief. In the good times the increasingly warm relationship between Leonid Brezhnev and Chancellor Brandt, then later Chancellor Schmidt, had been a handy back-channel for East–West message-passing; after Afghanistan it was to become the Soviet Union's only channel for talking directly to a major Western government. Before Afghanistan West Germany might have been seen in the Kremlin over the long term as a potential lever to exert some Soviet influence in NATO discussions on a wide range of issues. Suddenly the need for leverage – over arms control in Europe, East–West trade and NATO sanctions policy – had become urgent. So, had the long-term goal of prising West Germany away from the Western Alliance now taken on a new operational meaning as tensions rose between East and West?

The opportunities – or at least some of them – are there. Despite the Soviet invasion of Afghanistan and despite the imposition of martial law in Poland – the two events which have most radically transformed Soviet–American relations for the worse – West Germany, along with several of its West European allies, has been reluctant to translate its condemnation of Soviet actions and threats into extensive trade embargoes. The split that opened within the Western Alliance was between Europe and America, not West Germany and the rest. Yet in the resulting row within NATO it was West Germany's motives that were most closely questioned. The reason is simple: after a decade of détente it is West Germany that has the largest legacy to protect: not just the 300,000 or so jobs tied up in trade with the East, but also improved political relations with East Germany and the Soviet Union, increased contacts between East and West Germans (though these have suffered as East–West relations have cooled) and the continued relaxation of tensions surrounding Berlin. It is no accident, but rather a political statement from the East, that the new low in East–West relations in general has not been marked, as had usually happened in the past, by Soviet or East German proddings at West Berlin.

There is no doubt that West Germany is a 'marked' country in Soviet foreign policy. President Brezhnev's visit to Bonn in November 1981 was not only his last visit to a Western country; West Germany was probably the only Western country in which he would have been welcome. Already in the late 1970s the Soviet Union had set up an International Information Department attached to the Communist Party's Central Committee, whose job it was to influence public opinion in Western Europe but particularly, it seems, in West Germany. The new department was headed by Leonid Zamyatin with Valentin Falin as his deputy until January 1983. Falin, as a former Soviet ambassador to Bonn, is a formidable expert on Germany.

Despite a certain cooling of relations between the East and West German governments (due mainly to the unilateral raising of foreign exchange requirements by the East Germans), high-level contacts were none the less encouraged on both sides. When martial law was declared in Poland Chancellor Schmidt was in East Germany on an official visit, which had been delayed

131

by a previous convulsion in the long-running Polish crisis. Despite the prolongation of martial law and despite the change of government in Bonn in October 1982, a return visit by Honecker to West Germany is still in prospect.

Specific reasons for this focus on West Germany are not hard to find. As the debate heated up within Europe over the NATO decision to deploy new medium-range nuclear weapons to offset the perceived threat from the Soviet SS-20 arsenal, West Germany – the key country in NATO deployment plans – was peppered with visits by senior Soviet officials. The East German government had its part to play here too. Repeated East German anti-NATO and anti-nuclear propaganda barrages were aimed at the West German peace movement, appealing wherever possible to all-German sentiments and portraying NATO as the main threat to peace and to Germany. These were matched by barely veiled threats to the West German government, suggesting that the missile issue was the 'acid test' of Bonn's desire for genuinely improved relations with East Germany.[18] (Although the 'peace' propaganda had a boomerang effect: 1981 saw the beginnings of an unofficial East German peace movement prepared to question not only NATO nuclear weapons but also Warsaw Pact nuclear strategy in Europe.)

Was the assiduous attention paid to West Germany softening up on the Soviet part for a new Rapallo treaty sixty years on?[19] A move, perhaps, to bind West Germany into a web of increasing political and economic commitment to the East at the expense of its alliance with the West? Certainly, by 1982, the Soviet Union had little left to lose in its relations with the United States, which were at their coolest possibly since the Cuban missile crisis of October 1962 – and therefore little to gain from maintaining its cautious line in its policy towards America's allies in Europe.

During 1982 and early 1983 there is no doubt that the Soviet Union was concentrating its attention on salvaging what was left of the benefits of détente in Europe, while doing its best to exacerbate the evident strains within the Western Alliance over the NATO missiles, the Siberian gas pipeline contracts and the rest. But Rapallo was a government-to-government agreement for which no amount of enticement to Europe's businessmen and anti-nuclear campaigners could substitute. And although any West German government – not just a leftward tilting Social Democratic one but also a Christian Democrat-led coalition – would be loath to lose the political and social, as much as economic, benefits détente has brought to Germany, in reality the Soviet Union can have little real hope of using simply the maintenance of those still meagre ties to lever West Germany out of alignment with the West.

Unlike at the time of Rapallo in 1922, there are now two German states. And when the chips are down East Germany is still the most important of the two to the Soviet Union. Short of surrendering up East Germany – something which would cut across the entire grain of Soviet foreign policy since the death of Stalin – there is little the Soviet Union could offer a dissatisfied West German government that would compensate for the loss of power and influence which cutting the Western anchor would entail. Beyond a certain point, quite simply the Soviet Union can only pursue its relations with one German state at the expense of the other.

There were no illusions in the Schmidt government or the Kohl government which succeeded it about the practical prospects for formal reunification. Nor are there any illusions in East Germany that any West German government, whatever its complexion, could be encouraged to give up the theoretical possibility of reunification at some later date. Although East Germany was clearly disappointed at the fall of the Schmidt government in October 1982, and responded bitterly to new accents on the *Ostpolitik* of Kohl's Christian Democrat-led coalition in Bonn, they could hardly have expected much more in practical terms out of the previous government. Where the East German reaction was sharp, the initial Soviet reaction was cautious but still downbeat.

All the same, in the immediate future, short of a rapid and unexpected warming of Soviet–American relations by the

Andropov regime in Moscow, the Soviet Union is likely to continue to focus its attention sharply on the European end of the NATO trans-Atlantic alliance. And inevitably West Germany will remain central to Soviet strategy. There has anyway long been a body of opinion in the Soviet Union advocating closer economic ties with Europe rather than with the United States for technical, not just for political reasons.[20] The sensitivity of the nuclear issue in Europe during 1983 adds major security and political issues to the scales as well. Following the visit to Moscow in January 1983 by the new leader of the Social Democratic Party, Hans-Jochen Vogel, the Soviet press left its readers in East and West in no doubt that when it came to security issues it would much prefer to see a Social Democrat government returned in West Germany.[21]

Yet how far the Soviet Union could or would want to draw such a government out of the Western security framework – even if only to deepen the divisions within NATO, not to offer the prospect of German reunification – remains in doubt. The Soviet Union would still not welcome a more militarily self-assertive West Germany on its doorstep and would be unlikely to want to encourage the sort of political and military disintegration of NATO that might produce such a result.

For its part, West Germany has sometimes been accused of aspiring to the role of 'interpreter' between East and West in order to further its own goals in *Ostpolitik*. The charge was flatly rejected by Helmut Schmidt, at whom it was first levelled. The problem was put graphically by his successor, Helmut Kohl:

> I am not talking about détente in a vacuum: there isn't any water between us and the Soviet Russians. In a few hours' travel by tank from this room [in Bonn] you will meet the first Soviet tank division. We are not in a well-equipped interpreter's cabin, we are in the direct line of fire of world politics.[22]

So far that basic sentiment has been shared by all the major West

German political parties. Although prepared to defend the practical gains of the *Ostpolitik*, particularly the expanded if still limited ties with East Germany, West Germany has so far recognised that integration in the Western Alliance is not only the guarantee of West German security, but also the prerequisite for wielding influence in defence of its own conception of *Ost-* and *Deutschlandpolitik* in the East. At times in the past four years West Germany has advanced further in its *Ostpolitik* than its allies were prepared to follow – but only to the point of causing irritation in the Alliance, not to the point of rupturing it.

Moreover, in the bad times as in the good, the relationship with the other superpower, the United States, will remain the most deep-seated preoccupation of the Kremlin leadership precisely because of its implications for Soviet security. Attempts to use West Germany to prise apart the American commitment to Europe are themselves a confirmation of that fact. The division of Germany and the continuing German problem offer the Soviet Union a handy lever.

There are many ways in which the Soviet Union can seek to exploit West Germany's continuing commitment to one German nation, especially if the splits in the Western Alliance widen and the West German political system hits a bout of turbulence – as it well might – in the 1980s. However, Soviet actions so far suggest that the idea of a reunified and powerful Germany in the heart of Europe is no more welcome a prospect in the 1980s and 1990s than it was in the 1950s. The German problem remains unsolved and for the foreseeable future insoluble because West Germany lacks the leverage to solve it and because the Soviet Union lacks the political will.

Notes to Chapter 4

1   In a speech at Fulton, Missouri, in March 1946, Churchill had spoken of an 'iron curtain' cutting Europe in two and warned his audience of the dangers of Soviet influence in Eastern Europe. For Stalin's determination to hang on to the territories his armies had won see Milovan Djilas, *Conversations with Stalin* (London: Penguin, 1970), p. 93.

2 Philip Windsor, *German Reunification* (London: Elek Books, 1969), p. 14.
3 The 'Gruppe Ulbricht' had been flown into the Soviet zone of Germany in April 1945, to begin the construction of a 'socialist' administration in the zone. After Ulbricht's Communist Party's poor electoral showing, in 1946 the Communist Party and the Social Democratic Party were merged in the Soviet zone to form the Socialist Unity Party (SED). An account of these years is given in Carola Stern, *Ulbricht. A Political Biography* (London: Pall Mall Press, 1965), ch. 4.
4 Hannes Adomeit, *Soviet Risk-Taking and Crisis Behaviour* (London: Allen & Unwin, 1982), ch. 6.
5 N. Edwina Moreton, *East Germany and the Warsaw Alliance: the Politics of Détente* (Boulder, Colorado: Westview Press, 1978), pp. 14–16. In 1953 and again in 1956–8 the Soviet Union appeared to put some pressure on the Ulbricht regime to moderate its policies, perhaps in 1953 with a view to a possible new diplomatic initiative on the German question. A similar, unexplained flurry of Soviet activity came in 1964, just before Khrushchev fell from power. See N. Edwina Moreton, 'The Impact of Détente on Relations between the Member States of the Warsaw Pact: Efforts to Resolve the German Problem and their Implications for East Germany's Role in Eastern Europe, 1967–1972', Ph.D dissertation, Glasgow University, 1977, pp. 41–5.
6 Although this close relationship was not necessarily always to be taken as a mark of trust or confidence on either side. Moreton, 'The Impact of Détente' pp. 34–5.
7 Figures in Moreton, 'The Impact of Détente', App. A, p. 355.
8 Moreton, 'The Impact of Détente', pp. 80–93, for a discussion of East German–Soviet differences during the second Berlin crisis.
9 Moreton, 'The Impact of Détente', p. 92.
10 For a detailed account of the second Berlin crisis see Adomeit, *Soviet Risk-Taking*, chs 11–15.
11 Moreton, 'The Impact of Détente' p. 97.
12 Ibid.
13 This is a point often overlooked in analyses of Soviet foreign policy, the assumption being that the Soviet Union would have responded to the earlier Kiesinger overtures but for the crisis in Eastern Europe in 1968, and if the West Germans had offered an attractive enough economic package as a sweetener. This author disputes that interpretation. See Moreton, 'The Impact of Détente' ch. 3 and the comparison of the Kiesinger and Brandt policy statements in App. F, p. 360.
14 The upsurge in Soviet–West German trade after 1970 and the economic obstacles in its path are documented in Angela Stent, *From Embargo to Ostpolitik* (Cambridge: Cambridge University Press, 1981), pp. 179–207.
15 Moreton, *East Germany and the Warsaw Alliance*, pp. 182–90.
16 Two examples are East German obstruction of West German – Czechoslovak negotiations in 1973 and East German opposition in 1974 to a proposed Soviet–West German energy deal that was to include Berlin. Moreton, *East Germany and the Warsaw Alliance*, pp. 221–5.
17 Between November 1967 and October 1972 6.3m. West Germans visited the GDR and East Berlin (excluding day trips to East Berlin) – i.e. a monthly average of 105,500; between November 1972 and December 1979 the figure was 22.3m. – i.e. a monthly average of 259,000 and an increase of 246 per cent. *Facts and Figures*, Press and Information Office of the Federal Government, 1981. Immediately after the new currency regulations were imposed the figures dropped by almost half and have not yet recovered. The economic cost of improved contacts has been high. Between 1970 and 1980 West Germany and West Berlin made hard currency

payments to East Germany estimated at DM6.8 billion – for improved roads, communications etc.

18 Quotation taken from Werner Otto, 'A Faltering Start', *Kommentare*, p. 3 – an undated publication of the East German foreign press agency distributed in October 1982. The campaign, which had begun while Helmut Schmidt was still West German chancellor, continued with renewed vigour against the CDU-led government of Helmut Kohl in the run-up to the federal elections, due to be held in March 1983. See also the Tass statement issued following the Brezhnev–Honecker meeting in the Crimea, reported in the *Financial Times*, 12 August 1982.

19 The Rapallo treaty of 1922 between Germany and Russia allowed for co-operation in the military sphere which enabled Germany to circumvent the restrictions placed on it after the First World War. The signing of a German–Soviet treaty was interpreted in the West as a German rebuff to Western interests.

20 Erik P. Hoffmann and Robin F. Laird, *The Politics of Economic Modernization in the Soviet Union* (Ithaca, New York: Cornell University Press, 1982), pt 3.

21 *Pravda*, 14 January 1983, attacked the Kohl government directly over its support for United States defence policy.

22 Interview in *The Economist*, 18 December 1982.

5

The China Factor

Gerald Segal

Why have a chapter on China in a book on the Soviet Union and Western Europe? The reply is only partially encapsulated in Alexander Haig's comment that China is the sixteenth member of NATO. China, as the world's third most important power after the USA and the Soviet Union, is relevant to any consideration of the superpowers' basic interests. Europe is the crucial zone of East–West contention, and as such the impact that China has on the superpowers affects Europe as well.

How is one to assess China's influence on Soviet policy towards Western Europe? To restrict the analysis merely to the military sphere as inherent in Haig's quip, would not do justice to the China factor. The following analysis will begin with an assessment of the way in which China has influenced Soviet ideological interests, both in international and Euro-communist areas. Then the broader political effect of China, including the impact of the great power triangle,[1] will be studied. Thirdly, Peking's potential effect on Moscow's economic interests in Europe will be analysed, and finally the problems caused by China in the military sphere. Clearly these categories are not mutually exclusive nor necessarily comprehensive. But they should help organise our thoughts about the China factor for Soviet strategy in Western Europe, and hopefully justify the need for this chapter.

One major caveat must be issued before proceeding to the

main text. Although the analysis often suggests that the Soviet point of view changes, some might still obtain the impression that 'the Soviet point of view' is unified. This would be an error. The existence of divergences in Soviet foreign policy is fully accepted. This is especially valid for such complex issues as a great power triangle where the possible policy options are more numerous. For example, Soviet attitudes toward US arms sales to China or American attempts to 'play the China card' have provoked less than unanimous reactions from Kremlin decision-makers.[2] But for the sake of brevity and simplicity, the analysis emphasises the consensus that generally governs Soviet foreign policy at any one time. The consensus may shift in response to the numerous cross-cutting cleavages that make up the policy process, but the outcome is generally consistent, even if it is conservative.[3]

The Ideological Realm

Despite the current 'realist' fashion to denigrate ideology as a crucial factor in communists' foreign policy, it is clear that for the Soviet Union and China, the battle over ideological values has only marginally lost some of its urgency. As regards Soviet strategy in Western Europe, ideology is relevant both in global terms, as well as in relation to Europe.

The impact of the China factor for Soviet ideology has been most potent on the global level. So long as the Sino–Soviet alliance held firmly together in the most chilling portions of the cold war, Moscow could get on with fighting the main enemy in US capitalism. Then the equation of global power was simple, although the relatively tight bipolarity of the 1950s did not allow for many Soviet ideological gains. Toward the late 1950s the emerging Sino–Soviet split shattered not only the cosy bipolar daydreams of the superpowers, but more importantly shattered the myth of unity in the communist world. The question remains, was this positive or negative for Soviet strategy in Western Europe?

Since the Sino–Soviet split developed in part because of Moscow's pursuit of détente with the West, the implications of the communist rift were at first positive for the Soviet Union in Western Europe. The West was more disposed toward the Soviet case because Moscow was seen as the moderate and reasonable wing of a revolutionary movement. Khrushchev's efforts to sell himself as a more friendly Russian bear than suggested in cold war cartoons, was aided by the emergence of a more radical China carping at Moscow from the left. The West was also less concerned about dealing with the Soviet Union when it appeared that the Kremlin had deep problems of its own, and thus was less likely to pose a threat to Europe. Many Western leaders appreciated in the early 1960s that since the tearing noise of the once whole cloth of international communism could be heard around the world, then Moscow's ideological appeal would never again hold the same attraction for unsatisfied revolutionary forces. The cloth might conceivably be stitched together again, but it would never be as strong as the original.

In the 1960s, China's descent into the Cultural Revolution only enhanced the Soviet Union's image as the moderate communist power. While Soviet ideology had not changed, the simple comparison to China put the Kremlin in a favourable light. Even with the end of the Cultural Revolution, this ideological balance did not change. Despite Sino–American détente based on a reassessment of the global balance of power, Chinese ideology remained more radical than that of Moscow, albeit often confused. Chairman Mao had to die before the extremism could fade away.

The defeat of radical forces in China following Mao's death and the open declaration by Chinese leaders of greater pragmatism in domestic and foreign policy, finally altered the image of Peking's position on the radical wing of communism. Western Europe now saw the Soviet Union as the radical, revolutionary and more dangerous ideological challenge. France and China supported the same side in Zaire's conflicts of the late

1970s and Britain and China ended up supporting Mugabe in Zimbabwe. Around the world, China was linked to West European interests against Moscow and the full implications of the Sino–Soviet rift were now apparent. Many in the West continued to be wary of China's supposed change in ideological line but, especially after the Soviet invasion of Afghanistan, the harder definition of communism in Moscow was seen as the main challenge to Europe. At the same time, China was seen to soft-pedal its ideology at home by proclaiming the necessity to 'seek truth from facts' and to engage in joint ventures with Western capitalism.

Moscow was not pleased. The Soviets were now perceived in Western Europe as the radical communists and thus appealed less than ever to the Europeans. Whereas China used to be perceived as the global ideological crusader, now the Soviet Union was cast in that role. But what of the specific impact of the China factor on Soviet ideology in Europe? Did Peking do as much damage there as it did on a global scale?

The China factor's main ideological impact in Europe in the 1950s was restricted to the continent's eastern portion.[4] Peking's posture on events in Poland and Hungary in particular was important, but by no means crucial to Moscow's resolution of the delicate ideological dilemmas inherent in its allies seeking more diversity in the alliance structure. However, the leading ideological challenges in Europe in the 1950s came from the Yugoslavs, and here China had even less impact. In fact, Peking was on the Soviet side of that issue, badgering from the left for less tolerance of Tito's independent line. The open Sino-Soviet split in the early 1960s provided only somewhat more for an important China factor in ideological matters when Peking obtained tacit support from Romania in Sino–Soviet polemics. But China was used more by Bucharest for its own purposes, rather than Peking being able to manipulate the Romanians. China's only real friend in Europe was the atypical Albania; hardly an ideological force to be reckoned with in either part of the continent.

In Western Europe the Chinese split from the Soviet Union had a similarly low-key impact.[5] Some European communists, pre-eminently in Italy, saw the rift as a time to make a stand against Khrushchev's desire for rigid opposition to China. As in dissident East Europe, these West Europeans were using China to help make their own independent stand against Moscow, but even this secondary use of the China factor could not have been pleasing to the Soviet Union.

Not until the death of Mao Zedong did China fully capitalise on this potential opening in Western Europe. For the first fifteen years of the Sino–Soviet rift China had been on the opposite side of the communist spectrum from the Eurocommunists. But in a remarkable turnabout after Mao's death, China forged new links with Eurocommunism on precisely the issue that separated them both from Moscow: the question of Soviet control of international communism.[6] The Eurocommunists had been cultivating this issue for quite some time, but in the late 1970s China jumped on the bandwagon as part of Peking's anti-Soviet drive. China's interest in moderate East European economic models at the same time further reinforced the links on ideological grounds with moderate European communism.

A myriad differences continue to separate the Euro-communists and the Chinese Communist Party, but their perceived unity on the basis of anti-Sovietism is of growing concern to the Soviet Union. The linking of its two main ideological opponents by 1980–1, along with increasing success for independent ideological paths in East Europe and especially Poland, no doubt has made Moscow even more wary of the China factor on ideological matters in Europe.[7] The trend toward diversity, in the face of the Soviet Union's desire to hold on to its definition of unity, is a long-standing dilemma for the Kremlin in European ideological matters. Moscow's increasing loss of control of the ideology that it sees as its own is now more apparent than ever, and Soviet strategy in Western Europe is more complicated and less persuasive as a result.

The Political Realm

Arguably the two most devastating defeats for Soviet foreign policy in the post-Second World War period were the Sino–Soviet split in the early 1960s, and the nascent Sino–American détente of the early 1970s. Moscow's 'loss' of China was felt in almost all areas of Soviet foreign policy, including Europe.

At first the Sino–Soviet rift had its clear political advantages for Moscow in Western Europe. Khrushchev was seen to differ from Mao on a wide range of issues, but few were as important as the Soviet willingness to engage in détente with the West. The West Europeans were pleased to see moderation in Moscow, for it validated their argument with Washington that the cold war could be modestly moderated. The 1963 Partial Test Ban Treaty was both a symbol of this new détente, as well as the salient symbol of Soviet perfidy as far as China was concerned. The China factor, at this stage, served Soviet interests.

However, the Sino–Soviet split was far from favourable to Moscow in the wider perspective. The period prior to the open polemics in 1963, as well as the few years following, was one of acute complications for the Kremlin. The Soviet leaders attempted to maintain the position of the pivot power in the great power triangle by balancing the pressures from the Chinese Charybdis against those from the American Scylla. Moscow sought to avoid making any hard choices between either of the extremes and an analysis of Soviet foreign policy at this time shows relatively increased caution and confusion.[8] In Western Europe in particular, the Soviets found it difficult to pursue détente openly, for fear of driving Peking further away and deepening division in international communism.

The Europeans, for their part, continued their attempts to entice Moscow into closer contacts.[9] Not that the Europeans were rabidly anti-Chinese, but they saw the need for an overall reduction in international tension far more than did their American allies. Indeed, the West Europeans were also at the forefront of the movement to improve ties with China when the

143

USA was calling for containment of 'Peking's adventurism'. Thus Moscow was not able, even if it so desired, to build an anti-China coalition in Europe. The Europeans were not willing to be embroiled in the Sino–Soviet conflict and, if anything, their dual desire for détente with Moscow and Peking only added to the Soviet Union's predicament in Europe.

The Kremlin's dilemma did not ease when they removed Khrushchev in October 1964. The Moscow-initiated campaign for 'united action' with China against the USA in Vietnam was largely barren, but what was worse was the fact that the Vietnam War made détente with the West even less likely. Moscow had neither détente nor good relations with China and felt the pivotal pressures of the great power triangle even more intensely than ever. Matters went from bad to worse in 1969 with the simultaneous Soviet-orchestrated Berlin crisis and the spontaneous combustion along the Sino–Soviet border.[10] Following so soon on the heels of the invasion of Czechoslovakia and the Brezhnev Doctrine in 1968, the Soviet position in Europe had gone from bad to worse. China was now more than ever linked to Soviet problems in Europe because Peking could make common cause with Europeans concerned about the growth of Soviet power.[11]

This new unity of anti-Soviet forces was at first slow in developing as China moved cautiously in casting off its legacy of anti-Americanism. But if the Kremlin felt that the 1970s were going to be a gloomy decade, they should have been cheered by the fundamental moderation and caution in West European foreign policies. Just as Europe was unwilling to acquiesce in a vicious anti-Chinese policy while pursuing détente in the 1960s, so they were unwilling to acquiesce in a vicious anti-Soviet policy while pursuing détente with China in the 1970s.

Moscow's most persuasive position in these debates was its geography. The Soviet Union was a European power while China was not, for in the words of the Chinese aphorism, 'distant waters do not quench fires'. The West Europeans never lost sight of the fact that come what may, they had to get along with the Soviet Union. This was their motive for East–West détente in the 1960s, and it had lost none of its relevance despite China's increasingly strident warnings about the Soviet threat in Europe. It is important to note that in the early 1970s it was Western Europe that was in the forefront of economic and military deals with China, but by the end of the decade the USA had taken the lead, and thus drew the main Soviet criticism.[12] European sensitivity to Soviet sensibilities was no doubt a major factor in this reduction in their relative relations with China.

This new type of China factor in the 1970s (and early 1980s) was clearly more worrying to the Soviet Union than the 1960s variant of pressure from the radical left. But Moscow did not have to make the point to the Europeans that they could not afford to fight to the last European on behalf of China. Western Europe already fully appreciated this reality. However, the Soviet fear of a Sino–European alliance based on anti-Sovietism remains prominent. Such acts as the invasion of Afghanistan, a state symbolically one step removed from both Chinese and European national security interests, does not ease Moscow's problem and is grist for the anti-Soviet campaigners' mill.

This is not to suggest that the Soviet Union has a uniform view of the China factor in Western Europe.[13] Moscow has clear preferences. West Germany, which consistently puts its European and Soviet ties first and avoids arms sales to China, is a Kremlin favourite. Bonn is also the most important European actor for the Soviet Union, so the Soviets' approval is qualitatively more important. Britain is on the opposite end of the spectrum. This is not merely because of the great involvement in military deals with China, but also because of London's harder line on the Soviet Union, especially under Thatcher. France with Giscard d'Estaing in control was more on the German end of the spectrum, although doubts over arms sales to China were of concern. France under Mitterand is relatively unknown, but the French socialist had particularly close ties to China in the years prior to his 1981 election triumph.

The Soviet Union now seems more resigned than ever to

accepting a certain degree of influence for the China factor in Western Europe. For example, Hua Guofeng's 1979 tour of Western Europe was criticised not on the grounds of China's right to be concerned with Europe, but rather on the nature of his anti-Soviet remarks.[14] This acceptance of great power realities is something the Kremlin already appreciates, in that it has long granted tacit acceptance to US influence on the continent. But like the US presence, Moscow is not pleased with China's shadow, and the Soviets continually attempt to mini- mise and reduce these 'outside' forces. The cry of 'Europe for the Europeans' has long been the Soviet Union's most effective weapon in splitting the USA from its allies, and it is even more likely to keep the China factor under control.

China will probably continue to have an effect on Soviet–West European relations, but the potential for growth in this realm in part depends upon the subtlety with which Moscow manages its policy. Apart from Moscow and Peking improving their own bilateral relations, there are few new tactics the Soviets might usefully consider. To cry wolf about Sino–European anti- Sovietism is counter-productive, if only because it provides the Europeans and the Americans with room for leverage. The Kremlin openly acknowledges its neuralgia on China and thereby provides scope for those who would play on that weakness. West Europeans know only too well how firmly you can pull the bear's tail before it swings angrily in response. Both the Soviet Union and the West Europeans have a vested interest in limiting the China factor, but like the US factor in Europe, the complexities and sensitivities of the actors make it plain that there are no simple solutions.

The Economic Realm

Has China affected the Soviet Union's economic relations with Western Europe? Upon first reflection, such issues as the grant- ing of Most Favoured Nations (MFN) status to China and not the

146

Soviet Union by the EEC might suggest a positive reply, but a more detailed analysis suggests a limited role for the China factor.

In 1949 the Western industrial nations formed the Co-ordinating Committee (COCOM) on technology transfers to the communist world. China obtained special treatment, of a negative kind, as it was covered by the China Committee (CHINCOM) which imposed more severe restrictions. The anti-China bias was lifted in 1957 with the abolition of CHINCOM and from then until the present, both communist powers were treated the same. In the mid-1970s it appeared that a new 'China differential' would be established in COCOM procedures that favoured Peking over Moscow.[15] However, the Europeans who at first favoured this change as they were in the forefront of the China trade, soon changed their minds. It soon became clear that the USA and not the Europeans would pick up the new contracts in its mad dash to play 'China cards' against the Soviet Union. Thus, despite shifts of opinion in COCOM, the USSR has not suffered as a result of the China factor. If there is any bias at present in Peking's favour, it has more to do with the fact that the kinds of technology no longer embargoed are of greater use to China than to the USSR, if only because of the relatively retarded state of China's economy. It is however obvious that while this bias may harm the Soviet Union's sense of relative power re-garding China, it does no harm to Soviet economic relations with Western Europe.

The more specific issue of trade relations with European economies is somewhat more complex. China clearly has better formal ties with the European Economic Community, although this is a recent phenomenon. China recognised the EEC in 1975 and obtained MFN status in 1979, while Moscow took longer in providing quasi-legal recognition of the EEC and still does not have MFN status.[16] However, one should not be misled by form. In essence the Soviet Union negotiated with the EEC, especially after the 1973 regulation that all trade agreements should be channelled through the EEC Commission. More importantly, a detailed analysis of Soviet and Chinese trade patterns since 1970 when Peking first seriously entered European trade, shows that far from having suffered with the advent of the China factor, Soviet–EEC trade has increased even faster.

Chinese exports to the EEC have risen just less than 10 per cent in the decade since 1970, while Soviet exports are up somewhat more than 10 per cent (see Table 5.1).[17] China's trade remains less than 1 per cent of total EEC trade while the Soviet total alone is closer to 7 per cent. In the early 1970s China's exports to the EEC were closer to 30 per cent of the Soviet total, and now they have dropped to under 20 per cent. The growth in Soviet trade has been as gradual as that of China, but has managed to maintain a higher pace than Peking could muster, even during the 'boom times' in Sino–European trade. By no twist of the statistics can one argue that the Soviet Union has lost out with the growth of China's economic ties with Western Europe.

In this same ten-year period, Soviet and Chinese imports have shown a far less steady pace with Chinese imports fluctuating between 13 per cent and 34 per cent of the Soviet total, with no apparent pattern. Chinese imports are roughly 10 per cent higher than its exports as a percentage of the Soviet totals, but the figure tells you little about the importance of the China factor. Unlike the communist powers' exports to the EEC, in imports they are not in competition with each other. The Soviet Union has little cause to be upset with somewhat higher Chinese imports other than in the more general sense of opposing Western support for the Chinese economy. With Soviet imports 70 per cent higher than those of China, Moscow's complaints have no basis in fact.

If these figures of exports to, and imports from the EEC are broken down into their SITC categories, the above conclusions are reinforced. Table 5.2 shows clearly that in only one of the five main categories of Soviet and Chinese exports do the two powers trade in the same sort of goods. Groups 0, 3 and 8 are widely divergent and group 6 is becoming more so after having

Table 5.1 *EEC Imports from and Exports to China and the USSR (Millions $ US)*

	1970	1971	1972	1973	1974	1975	1976	1977	1978	1979	1980
EEC imports from China	254 −5%	282 +10%	363 +22%	666 +45%	819 +19%	804 −2%	949 +16%	994 +5%	1,211 +18%	1,830 +34%	2,598 +30%
EEC imports from the USSR	962 +5%	1,092 +12%	1,221 +11%	2,357 +48%	3,753 +37%	4,285 +12%	6,129 +31%	6,950 +12%	7,528 +8%	10,543 +29%	14,350 +27%
EEC exports to China	349 +15%	335 −6%	328 −2%	733 +55%	939 +22%	1,428 +34%	1,310 −9%	901 −45%	1,884 +53%	2,853 +34%	2,362 −21%
EEC exports to the USSR	1,103 −4%	1,125 +2%	1,471 +24%	2,658 +45%	3,974 +33%	6,095 +35%	5,759 −6%	6,881 +2%	7,027 +2%	8,452 +17%	10,304 +18%
EEC imports from China as a % of EEC imports from the USSR	26	26	30	28	22	19	15	14	16	17	18
EEC exports to China as a % of EEC exports to the USSR	32	30	22	28	24	23	23	13	27	34	23

Note: In 1973 the EEC expanded by three members. Without the additions the rise in trade would have continued, but less sharply.

Table 5.2   *Leading SITC Categories' Percentage of the EEC's Imports from the USSR and China*

EEC imports from China	Group 0	Group 2	Group 3	Group 6	Group 8
1980	18	22	6	21	20
1978	18	29	.5	23	20
1976	19	28	.2	23	14
1974	20	28	.4	24	11
1972	24	36	.2	21	9
1970	16	46	0	21	6
EEC imports from the USSR					
1980	.7	10	74	6	.4
1978	1	14	62	8	2
1976	1	19	56	13	.5
1974	2	26	46	14	.8
1972	4	28	41	15	.7
1970	5	29	40	15	.6

been an area of relative competition in the past. Group 2 goods comprise relatively similar portions of Soviet and Chinese exports to the EEC, but even here, if the category is broken down into its components, the two communist powers trade in different goods. So even if the earlier figures might have suggested a pattern of rising Chinese exports and falling Soviet ones, it is clear that the two states trade in different goods and so can hardly be in competition with each other for West European trade.

Table 5.3 shows something very different, but nothing that contradicts the previous argument. Here it is plain that China and the Soviet Union import overwhelmingly in the same three SITC categories from the EEC. China used to import more than the Soviet Union in group 6 and less in group 7, but now that relationship is reversed. What this shows is not competition between the two powers, for Europe would happily export more to both if it could. Rather it shows similar needs for finished high quality goods and Western technology. Thus Moscow can hardly criticise Peking for dealing with the West,

150

Table 5.3   *Leading SITC Categories' Percentage of EEC Exports to the USSR and China*

EEC exports to China	Group 5	Group 6	Group 7
1980	25	19	47
1978	12	35	43
1976	14	32	50
1974	16	37	40
1972	22	45	29
1970	29	37	25
EEC exports to the USSR			
1980	16	32	30
1978	18	52	22
1976	10	36	43
1974	12	43	35
1972	11	33	42
1970	11	31	45

for it does so in the same categories and in higher numbers. Neither can Moscow criticise the West Europeans for shoring up the Chinese, for they seek the same benefits and to a greater extent.

If these figures are broken down into the main West European nations trading with China and the Soviet Union, the pattern is the same. The Federal Republic of Germany is clearly the main trader with both Peking and Moscow and in our ten-year survey period has always remained in trade surplus. Like general EEC trade, German imports from China as a percentage of imports from the Soviet Union has fallen, but it also has been generally more stable than the EEC totals. The salience of Germany in the trading relationship for the USSR makes it all the more important that Moscow is more pleased with Bonn than with any other West European state. The Kremlin has little about which to complain.

Britain is at the opposite end of the spectrum from Germany in its trading patterns. London is the most erratic of the leading traders, but even the percentage of its imports from China never rose above 38 per cent of imports from the Soviet Union. British

Table 5.4 Percentage of Imports and Exports from Selected European States and China and the USSR

	1970	1971	1972	1973	1974	1975	1976	1977	1978	1979	1980
FRG imports from China as a % of imports from the USSR	25	26	25	21	16	17	16	16	15	14	20
FRG exports to China as a % of exports to the USSR	40	30	23	26	23	19	23	18	30	41	26
UK imports from China as a % of imports from the USSR	27	26	31	31	22	24	13	13	23	28	38
UK exports to China as a % of exports to the USSR	43	30	34	83	56	38	28	17	24	62	39

France imports from China as % of imports from the USSR	34	27	36	34	31	22	21	17	18	18	13
France exports to China as a % of exports to the USSR	30	43	18	16	24	32	31	6	14	17	12
Italy imports from China as % of imports from the USSR	22	22	26	29	15	14	11	14	13	20	15
Italy exports to China as a % of exports to the USSR	19	20	29	22	17	14	12	6	17	23	20

exports to the powers fluctuate even more, and the occasionally high percentage (often in sensitive goods) may in part explain Britain's reputation for criticism from Moscow for allowing China excessive influence.

Between the German and British models, lies France and Italy. Although Italian trade in absolute numbers is less than that of Germany, it is more stable. What is more, the Soviet Union can be particularly pleased that Italian imports from China have been some of the lowest in the EEC. The French also have a relatively positive mix from the Soviet point of view, and in keeping with the EEC pattern, trade with Moscow has increased faster than it has with China.

In sum, the Soviet Union has a poor case in complaining about the China factor in the economic realm. While Moscow may not like West European exports to China, especially in the much commented upon joint ventures, the Soviets have long received similar treatment, and on a larger scale. Now that there are cut-backs even in these joint ventures, Moscow's concern must be even less. More generally, there is virtually no evidence that China's economic relations have hurt the Soviet Union. Moscow may lament China's special treatment from the EEC, but the evidence does not support any serious Soviet complaints. If there is to be a massive increase in Chinese trade, it may well have to come with closer co-operation between Moscow and Peking. Their evidently greater economic compatibility than with Western Europe might well be an important spur for Sino–Soviet relations in general. But this is another question, and one which provides the Soviet Union with little reason to be upset with EEC economic relations.

The Military Realm

The fourth and final realm of potential influence for the China factor is the most important, for all states must be paramountly concerned with national security. A Soviet analysis of China as a military force in Western Europe would quickly reveal no primary role for Peking. Unlike the superpowers, China lacks the ability to project military power (aside from nuclear weapons) far beyond its regional base. China now appears to be developing a blue-water navy, but it is still a long way from being a match for the superpowers' forces. Thus on this basic level, the Chinese military has no role to play in Europe.

However, military force and strategy is more complex than merely those primary national security threats. Three secondary problems involving the Chinese military in Western Europe can be identified. First, there is the Soviet concern about fighting a two-front conventional war; one against Europe and another against China. There are clearly some important opportunity costs when Moscow feels forced to spend heavily in defence against a perceived Chinese threat. The build-up of Soviet forces on the Sino–Soviet frontier since the 1960s has been dramatic, accounting for 80 per cent of the total increase in Soviet military spending between 1968 and 1979. There are 100,000 more Soviet troops on the border with China than there are in Eastern Europe. Roughly one quarter of all Soviet military spending concerns China and these costs have grown at twice the rate as for the rest of the Soviet armed forces. In recent years the Soviet increase has continued with impressive force modernisation along the frontier with China.[18] These costly programmes do not necessarily mean that all the spending would have been allocated to the Western front if it were not for China, but somewhat more resources could now be facing the West Europeans. Defending on two fronts rather than one is obviously less preferable from the Soviet point of view and raises deeply felt fears of global encirclement.

This Chinese military factor is not so much one that exists as part of the European military problem, but they are clearly related. There does not need to be collusion between China and the Europeans (and there probably isn't any) for the Soviet Union to feel that at least in a secondary way, China affects the European balance. These feelings tend to become perceived facts in Moscow when Chinese military men exchange lengthy visits with European counterparts and attend NATO manoeuvres. A great deal of good military strategy is concerned with potential use of force and therefore the Clausewitzian connection between military and politics becomes crucial.

For those who prefer to study capabilities rather than intentions, it is also possible to see this secondary Chinese military factor as an implicit problem in the MBFR talks. If these discussions should reach some sort of agreement, will the withdrawn Soviet forces merely be transferred to other parts of the Soviet Union, including the Sino–Soviet frontier? If so, it might merely lessen Moscow's costs in building up its Asian military and would only add to pressure already exerted on China, a state the West considers some sort of friend. MBFR can also be affected if Moscow and Peking manage some sort of border disengagement pact. Where would the forces withdrawn from the Chinese border go, and would they add to the perceived threat in Western Europe? These implicit links between the Chinese and European theatres can no longer be overlooked in arms control discussions. Some sort of account needs to be taken of geographic problems, for the transfer of military force from one theatre to another is illusory arms control. Just how these problems are overcome is another issue, but it is clear that from the Soviet point of view, there is an important connection between military problems in the Chinese and European theatres.

Similar problems are evident when looking at the second area of Soviet military concern with China and Europe – the strategic nuclear forces. The China factor played a minimal role in SALT,[19] but in the prelude to possible SALT III negotiations Moscow made it increasingly clear that China's third force would have to be included in discussions of weapons totals.[20] Western analysts tended to focus on the independent French and British nuclear forces, but for the Soviet Union, the Chinese third force was a greater worry than the European units. The contemporary discussions about strategic arms reduction talks

(START) will surely bring these problems to the fore. Moscow has argued that it needs an ability above and beyond that to cope with the USA, in order to meet a potential Chinese threat. If START is to make massive reductions, then it will quickly meet this higher Soviet level deemed necessary to deter China. The Europeans, who are especially interested in successful arms control between the superpowers, might well have to accept a different sort of pact if Moscow is to be satisfied about China. The Kremlin's concern with third forces of nuclear weapons is therefore another area that links Europe and China in military policy.

A related problem is nuclear weapons in Europe and the new discussions on limitations of forces in this theatre.[21] The Soviets' SS-20 mobile system which is the focus of so much debate in the European area, was apparently developed for use against China and not the West.[22] The dynamics of weapons research and development are beyond the scope of this paper, but the China factor in military affairs apparently has also affected this realm. More importantly, the problem of how to limit these SS-20s cannot escape a consideration of the China factor. One third of the missiles are aimed at China, another third against Europe, and a final third are capable of 'swinging' between one theatre and the other. A deeply difficult problem for those seeking arms control of nuclear weapons in Europe, will be how to control these SS-20s that because of their range and mobility can be swiftly switched from one area to another. For example, if you pursue a 'zero-option' that will eliminate all land-based theatre missiles (including the SS-20), will that mean all Soviet forces capable of hitting China as well, or will Moscow be able to simply shift the weapons eastward? One possible solution might be to broaden the negotiations to include China, but Peking shows no sign of accepting superpower-defined nuclear arms control procedures. Another possible solution would be to limit forces in each geographic area, but that would encourage the development of forces with longer range and mobility and further confuse the already complex procedure of counting nuclear forces. What is more, there is no certainty that China would play along, and as it seems that Peking is now in a new phase of nuclear weapons development, it is possible that China's actions might torpedo the talks by 'forcing' the Soviet Union to request higher ceilings in Asia. It used to be said that Moscow earned a 'China dividend' from arms control because it limited the arms race with the West and thereby allowed greater spending against China. This no longer seems to be the case, for the China factor has made European arms control even more complex. Even if the problems of technology can be overcome, the talk of ceilings for geographic zones means no future dividend for Moscow. The most logical alternative, the involvement of China in talks, both in MBFR and nuclear forces, seems most unlikely. Therefore it is difficult to be optimistic about these negotiations (and for other reasons as well) because the China factor on military issues raises major complications.

The third area of the China factor in military affairs in Europe concerns the problem of arms sales by the West to China.[23] To a certain extent this is linked with the problem of Moscow's perception of a two-front threat. As G. Arbatov said in 1978, 'what sense would it make for us to agree to reduce armaments in Europe if armaments are simply to be channeled by the West to the Eastern front? . . . You cannot reconcile detente with attempts to make China some sort of military ally of the North Atlantic Treaty Organization . . .'[24] On this issue the Soviet Union has had less complaint with China, and more with the Europeans who might sell weapons to Peking.[25]

The problem remains important for Moscow in that it sees arms sales as a symbol of a state's friendship with the Soviet Union. Any deeper Soviet concerns about the Chinese military threat being affected by such sales are largely confined to the longer term. But in the short term Moscow was especially pleased with German refusal to sell arms to China, and especially displeased with British and to a lesser extent French and Italian decisions to undertake such deals. In the medium term it is obvious to Moscow and indeed the rest of the world that China is not going to make the large-scale arms purchases that many feared, and in any case the Chinese economy cannot even bear the massive costs of an indigenous military modernisation. Thus arms sales to China remain worrying to Moscow as an aspect of its fear of a two-front war, but as a military factor on its own, Moscow does not view this Sino–European link as a major dimension.

In sum, there is a military realm to Soviet analysis of the China factor, but it is not one of a direct Sino–European connection. China's military force remains a regional concern. However, the dimensions of the problem related to a two-front war, both on the conventional and nuclear levels of power, illustrate that China does have an important impact on the way Moscow views military issues in Western Europe. These problems are likely to grow in the future, as arms control cuts closer to the bone (hopefully) and China continues to develop its power. These military dimensions may be less direct than some of the ideological and political roles for China in Western Europe, but the importance of the military dimension may well make these military issues more important in the long run.

Conclusions

This chapter began with a question and will conclude with the summary of a possible answer. The role of China in the Soviet approach to Western Europe unfortunately did not emerge as a simple one. That there is an important China factor for Soviet policy is hopefully now not in doubt, but the precise nature of that importance is less certain.

Two realms of policy stand out as being most affected by the China factor. First, Soviet military policy towards Europe has been deeply affected by China, albeit not in a direct fashion. The concern with a two-front war has created problems for the Kremlin far beyond the relatively simplistic days of the cold war confrontation in Europe. In the future, many dimensions of

Moscow's military concerns in Western Europe, from conventional to nuclear forces, will be affected as a result.

Secondly, the split in the communist world has done deep damage to the Soviet Union's ultimate objective of obtaining world revolution. The tear in the ideological cloth, despite twenty years of sewing classes, has not been repaired. Without the appeal of the well-made ideological cloth, Moscow's basic policy objective of persuading capitalism in the European case of the error of its ways, is made all the more difficult.

The Soviet problems in the political realm, unlike in the military and ideological areas, were seen to be important, but to a certain extent creations of Moscow's own errors. The centrality of the 'Europe for the Europeans' argument still meant that the West Europeans never allowed the China factor to get out of hand. Following the trail of money in the economic realm illustrated this view. West European economic relations with China did grow in the 1970s, but not as fast and never at the expense of relations with the far more important Soviet Union.

Moscow's super-sensitivity resulting in at least a declaratory 'persecution complex' (cries of anti-Sovietism at every turn), may well be a result of deeply held fears of encirclement and pressure in the military and ideological realms. To a certain extent the Soviet Union can lessen the role of the China factor in Western Europe, by merely recognising and separating the important from the less important realms of policy. But in the end the China factor in Western Europe is likely to endure in some real fashion. The only development that could alter such pessimism for the Kremlin, lies to a certain extent within Soviet control – an improvement in Sino–Soviet relations. Perhaps the Soviet Union might be wise to pay somewhat more attention to détente in the East and not merely to détente in the West.

Notes to Chapter 5

1 Gerald Segal (ed.), *The China Factor* (London: Croom Helm, 1982); and Gerald Segal, *The Great Power Triangle* (London: Macmillan, 1982).

2   Gerald Segal, 'The Soviet Union and the Great Power Triangle' in Segal (ed.), *China Factor*.

3   Karen Dawisha, 'The limits of the bureaucratic politics model', *Studies in Comparative Communism*, vol. 13, no. 4 (Winter, 1980); Uri Ra'anan, 'Soviet decision-making and international relations', *Problems of Communism*, vol. 19, no. 6 (November–December 1980).

4   Edwina Moreton, 'The Triangle in Eastern Europe' in Segal (ed.), *China Factor*.

5   Lawrence Freedman, 'The Triangle in Western Europe' in Segal (ed.), *China Factor*.

6   Kevin Devlin, 'The Challenge of the "New Internationalism"', paper presented to the conference on The Sino–Soviet Conflict: The Seventies and Beyond, Seattle, September 1980; Elizabeth Teague, 'The "New Internationalism" in the PCI in Practice', *Radio Free Europe Research*, RAD/230, 2 October 1980.

7   Segal, 'The Soviet Union and the Triangle'.

8   Segal, *Great Power Triangle*.

9   See generally articles by Richard Harris, Francois Fetjo and Heinrich Berchtoldt in A. M. Halpern (ed.), *Policies Toward China: View from Six Continents* (New York: McGraw Hill, 1965).

10 Edwina Moreton, *East Germany and the Warsaw Alliance: The Politics of Detente* (Boulder, Colorado: Westview Press, 1978).

11 Morris Rothenberg, *Whither China: The View From the Kremlin* (Miami: Center for Advanced International Studies, 1978).

12 Lawrence Freedman, *The West and Modernization of China* (London: Chatham House Papers No. 1, RIIA, 1979); Douglas Stuart, 'Prospects for Sino–European Security Cooperation', *Orbis*, vol. 26, no. 3 (Fall 1982).

13 For example, S. Yurkov, 'China and Western Europe', *Far Eastern Affairs*, no. 4, 1979; G. Apalin, 'Peking, the West and detente', *International Affairs* (Moscow) April 1978; A. Larin, 'Britain in China's foreign policy', *Far Eastern Affairs*, no. 3, 1979; also *Soviet News*, 24 June 1980.

14 Yurkov, 'China and Western Europe'; also BBC/SWB/SU/6255/A3/1; No. 6258/A3/2; No. 6259/A3/1, for reports on the trip.

15 A. Doak Barnett, *China's Economy in Global Perspective* (Washington: The Brookings Institution, 1981), Section 2.

16 Christopher Binns, 'The development of the Soviet policy response to the EEC', *Co-existence*, vol. 14, no. 2 (October 1977).

17 All trade data is based on the annual volumes of trade statistics published by the Organization of Economic Cooperation and Development. In 1981 the pattern continued to show that in Sino–EEC trade, the most important rival was the USA, not the USSR: *Daily Telegraph*, 14 November 1981.

18 Testimony to the Subcommittee on Priorities and Economy in Government of the Joint Economic Committee, 95th Congress, 2nd Session, 26 June, 14 July 1978; *Allocation of Resources in the Soviet Union and China – 1978*; also *International Herald Tribune*, 23 May 1980.

19 Michael Pillsbury, *Soviet Apprehensions About Sino–American Relations, 1971–4* (Santa Monica: The Rand Corp., P-5459, June 1975); and Segal, 'The Soviet Union and the Triangle'.

20 *The Threat to Europe* (Moscow: Progress Publishers, 1981); William Garner, 'SALT II: China's advice and dissent'; *Asian Survey*, vol. 19, no. 12 (December 1980).

21 Lawrence Freedman, *Arms Control in Europe* (London: Chatham House Papers No. 11, RIIA, 1981).

22 Freedman, 'Triangle in Western Europe'; and Lawrence Freedman, 'The dilemma of theatre nuclear arms control', *Survival*, vol. 18, no. 1 (January–February 1981).

23   V. Baburov 'China and disarmament', *International Affairs*, no. 5 (May 1981); Yurkov, 'China and Western Europe'; N. Kapchenko, 'Beijing policy: calculation and miscalculation', *International Affairs* (July 1979), and 'The threat to peace from Peking's hegemonistic policy', *International Affairs* (February 1980).
24   *Observer* (London), 12 November 1978.
25   Gerald Segal, 'China's strategic posture and the great power triangle', *Pacific Affairs*, vol. 53, no. 4 (Winter, 1980–81); also Lucian Pye, 'Dilemmas for America in China's modernization', *International Security*, vol. 4, no. 1 (Summer 1979); Freedman, *The West and Modernization of China*.

Part III

Soviet Strategies

6
Military Strategy

R. A. Mason

In 1948, when the Soviet Union began to exert military pressure on the Western enclave in Berlin, estimates of the strength of Soviet forces ranged from 2.5 to 4 million men under arms. Malcolm Mackintosh, for example, usually a reliable source, suggested that there were about 1 million Soviet troops in Europe.[1] French, British and American forces in Europe at that time comprised only some ten under-strength divisions employed on garrison duties. In the sinking temperatures of the cold war, Western Europe began to feel itself threatened by Soviet military power and a resurgent communist ideology. Then there was no U2 reconnaissance aircraft, no SR-71 and no satellite to locate and quantify the armoured divisions, the airfield, and the widespread infrastructure of the Soviet forces. The threat was amorphous, yet, to Western Europe undoubtedly ominous and pervasive.

Thirty-four years later, 'The Military Balance' of the International Institute for Strategic Studies could confidently state the size, organisational structure and principal employment of all arms of the Soviet forces, and while both sides still found it impossible to agree on identical figures when meeting for arms control negotiations, the disparity was now reckoned in tens of thousands and even that disparity owed something to differences in organisational definitions. And yet despite much greater reliability in identification of the size and scope of Soviet forces, and those of its Warsaw Pact allies, and despite the fact that by 1983 they possessed many times the strength of their post-war predecessors, the exact nature of their roles in Soviet strategy toward Western Europe remained a source of extensive debate.

On the one hand stood the maximisers, those who traced a consistent Soviet search for hegemony over not just Western Europe but as far as its military power could reach. At the other end of the scale were those who saw the Soviet Union as the prisoner of its own history and ideology, obsessed with the fear of Western imperialist attack, ever mindful of the counter-revolutionary invasions, the disasters and deprivations of the Great Patriotic War and subsequently of the occasional calls in the West for 'pre-emptive' nuclear attack on the Russian motherland. Both images, the aggressive, revisionist, proselytising Soviet Union and the status quo, defensive, underconfident Russia can be amply substantiated, as indeed can several others.

The arguments of both maximisers and minimisers have been presented and analysed in considerable depth on both sides of the Atlantic,[2] yet there can be little debate about the fact of a strong Soviet military dimension in its strategy toward Western Europe. Indeed, since 1945 the Soviet Union has been in no position to exert economic pressure and any spread of Marxist–Leninist ideology has taken place despite its example rather than in its emulation. Apart from perennial encouragement of internal divisive and disruptive elements it is self-evident that military strength has been a primary instrument of Soviet diplomacy toward Western Europe. How has it been applied? What has been its impact? What is its extent at the threshold of the 1980s and what is its likely evolution?

Precedents

Actual occurrences of direct military action by the Soviet Union against the West have been infrequent since 1945. In 1946 two unarmed American transport planes were shot down over Yugoslavia, prompting a speedy deployment of six B-29 long-range bombers to Frankfurt from where, in November, they flew along the borders of Soviet-occupied territory and 'surveyed airfields to determine their suitability for B-29 operations'[3]. There is now considerable doubt whether those B-29 aircraft did in fact have the capability to deliver atomic weapons, but they were the same type which only the previous year had attacked Hiroshima and Nagasaki and the threat they offered to the Soviet Union must have seemed very real. When eighteen months later the Soviets halted all Western road and rail transport to Berlin, the harassment of Western aircraft was again followed in July 1948 by the deployment of two further squadrons of the 301st Bombardment Group to Western Germany. But whether their presence actually deterred Stalin from increasing military pressure or whether the Berlin blockade was simply a gesture by a cautious, strong-nerved but comparatively impecunious military poker player is impossible to say until the Soviets introduce their own 'Freedom of Information Act'. Indeed, the Berlin airlift confrontation epitomised the perennial problem of assessing the comparative importance of Western resolve or Soviet determination in situations when military force has been brandished. Even after the lifting of the blockade, Western aircraft were occasionally harassed.[4] In the skies over central Europe there was not the same rigid territorial boundary nor the same risk of instant escalation which was present when ground forces faced each other across the then intangible 'iron curtain'.

It was inevitable, therefore, that when ground forces did come face-to-face in Berlin in 1961 the crisis should assume far more serious proportions. NATO was now twelve years old, tactical nuclear weapons had been deployed in Europe by both sides and in August the USA deployed 1,500 troops to West Berlin to supplement the tri-national garrison now encircled by two Soviet divisions[5]. Yet even the apparently overt Soviet threat of military force to change the status quo in Berlin may have been motivated in part by Soviet domestic politics or even by misunderstandings.[6] What however is not in dispute is that military pressure was initiated by the Soviet Union, was met by positive Western military response and declared resolve, and the pressure was withdrawn after an unusual example of communist lateral thinking had produced the Berlin Wall to check the East German population exodus.

The direct threat in 1956 of nuclear attack, on the other hand, contained in the letter from Bulganin to London, Paris and Tel Aviv at the time of the Suez crisis, falls into a very different category. It was made only after the three nations were manifestly not being supported by the USA and the Western partners were themselves nationally divided over the adventure. But the threat was apparently given serious consideration and it did win widespread political approval in the Arab world even if suspected by Arab leaders to be devoid of substance.[7] Again, it is impossible to say how far the threat would have been substantiated if Britain and France had not withheld their forces and if the USA had not raised the level of military alert in some of its strategic air command and maritime units. Nevertheless, the fact was that an extremely serious military threat had been used by a nuclear power against two countries which did not at that time possess the ability to respond in kind against the Soviet Union.

After 1961 there was no major incident in Western Europe involving Warsaw Pact and NATO forces and no specific threat of military force, as opposed to the frequent indeterminate declamations such as those delivered by Mr Brezhnev in October 1982. After the trauma of the Cuban crisis, Western Europe lived through a period marked more by *Ostpolitik*, SALT, MBFR and Helsinki than by sustained or intermittent military pressure from the East. Yet by 1983 there was a widespread unease in Western Europe about the military balance or lack of it which was shared by all shades in the political spectrum, albeit manifested in different ways. The left wing tended to concentrate on alleged US bellicosity and proposed deployment of nuclear weapons such as Pershing II,

Cruise missiles and MX. A greater number acknowledged the comparative peace and stability enjoyed in Europe for thirty-seven years, pointed to the considerable all-round increase in Soviet military strength which had begun in the period of détente and was showing no sign of slackening in pace, reflected uneasily on the use of force directly by the Soviet Union in Czechoslovakia and Afghanistan and at long range in Africa and the Middle East, and noted that the traditional Soviet dedication to military strength as an instrument of policy had not been rescinded. Moreover, the achievements of that military instrument in Soviet strategy toward Western Europe were by 1983 considerable.

The Balance Sheet

Eastern Europe was clearly defined as a Soviet sphere of influence. The private agreements at Potsdam and Yalta had been publicly codified by Brezhnev. However desperately Poles, Hungarians or Czechs might react to the extent of Soviet control, they had become aware that they could expect no military assistance from the West. The Soviet Union had constructed a military pact, bilateral treaties, and economic infrastructure on foundations laid by the Russian armies of occupation. Their continued presence not only encouraged internal conformity but ensured that Western military strength would not be used to upset the new status quo. By comparison, British, French, Dutch and Belgian armed forces had been used in many other areas of the world between 1945 and the mid-1970s in support of national or friendly interests. The first and permanent value of Soviet military strength had been to inhibit such actions, regardless of their contemplation, by Western European countries in Europe itself. The influence of Soviet military force on Western Europe, however, was far more positive than simply as a deterrent to action, which in any event would have been highly problematical. The aligned Western

countries felt compelled to allocate extensive national resources to provide defence against what was seen as a perpetual
threat from the Soviet Union. And at least until the late 1970s it
was the threat from Soviet conventional forces which loomed
large over Western Europe.

As early as 1947 the United States Joint Chiefs of Staff had
formally acknowledged the conventional weakness of the
Western Allies:

> The allies do not have the capability of mobilizing or trans-
> porting in the early stages of the war, ground and tactical air
> forces of sufficient strength to destroy the Soviet Armed
> Forces which would have to be encountered in depth along
> any of the avenues of approach which lead to the heart of
> Russia . . .[8]

Despite repeated analyses of Soviet conventional superiority
and proposals for improved defences to meet it, very little was
actually achieved to narrow the gap. From the earliest dispatch
of the B-29s in 1946 the disparity was overcome first by the
introduction into the theatre of nuclear weapons and then by
the presentation of a seamless deterrence posture which incorporated a limited conventional defence at one end and the
intercontinental nuclear forces of the United States at the other.
Alliance members allocated more resources to defence for a
longer period of peace than at any time in European history, but
because of constraints of competing domestic priorities and
indeed because of the very system of national values which
the defences were designed to protect, the resources were
frequently big enough to prompt internal criticism but never
enough to provide adequate conventional defence. Whether
the resources could have been allocated to better effect[9] is
relevant to an examination of the overall military balance but
not to the impact of Soviet military strength on Western
European resource allocation.

It may be argued, therefore, that without any economic

pressure of its own, the Soviet Union forced Western Europe into habits of government expenditure very difficult in degree if not in kind from those of earlier generations. Nor were the implications only economic. Politically, Western Europe was drawn into a very different relationship with the United States, despite the positive independence of France and the special relationship of the United Kingdom. Military dependence as reflected in the substance of the nuclear guarantee and in the contribution of United States conventional forces to the Alliance, did not sit well with traditions of Western European independence of action developed over 1,000 years. Therefore the many problems associated with American 'leadership' of what is otherwise an almost exclusively Western European grouping also have their roots in the military confrontation on the continent. It is now simply a matter for speculation as to how far an alternative European 'third force' had been precluded by the existence of an 'Atlantic' organisation and how far European inability to provide adequate defence for itself has been the product of an assumption of perennial nuclear protection by the United States.

The third indirect product of Soviet military strategy toward Western Europe has been the increasingly divisive, if incoherent, movement for nuclear disarmament. Whatever the possible fate of alternative strategies, with their own various social and economic implications, and whatever the degree of manipulation of protest movements by those with less altruistic motives, the spring of this movement lies in that same Western response to Soviet military pressure which sought the quick and effective threat of nuclear retaliation. Protest identifies proposals to increase the effectiveness of nuclear weapons deployed in Western Europe but seldom traces the problem to its roots in the pressure of Soviet conventional military strength and the failure, from whatever reason, of Western Europe to meet it without recourse to those nuclear weapons.

The perceptions and response of the USA to Soviet military strategy are, strictly speaking, outside the limits of this study, but in passing it may be observed that the fact that the USA is virtually invulnerable to either Soviet conventional forces or to short-range nuclear weapons must inevitably influence its strategic priorities. Even the usurpation of the adjective 'strategic' to mean 'intercontinental between the United States and the Soviet Union', while equating 'tactical' with 'theatre', indicates a breadth of interpretation by the United States which would not be shared by everyone in the defence ministries of London, Bonn and Paris.

Finally, Soviet military pressure has forced Western differences of opinion about how to respond to her activities beyond Western Europe. Until the mid-1960s, indirect pressure was exercised in the Third World by the Soviet Union primarily by encouragement of dissidence and instability in old colonial territories and other one-time spheres of Western influence. In June 1967, however, in the immediate aftermath of the Arab–Israeli conflict, the London *Economist* observed:

> The combination of an offensive ideology with a defensive strategy is apt to produce diplomatic defeats. To avoid more Cubas and Sinais the Russians will have either to resist the temptation to take on commitments in the third world (which includes encouraging 'wars of liberation'), or else to acquire the military capacity this sort of policy calls for. This means building aircraft carriers and acquiring staging posts for airborne troops. It will be a bad omen for East–West relations if there are signs that they have chosen this second way out of their dilemma.[10]

Less than ten years after that prescient article Soviet military power had been projected down to the Himalayas, across the Red Sea, into the Horn of Africa and deep into Southern territories of the continent. Again analysts disagreed about Soviet motives, but West European governments perceived an additional threat to energy and raw materials resources on which their economies heavily depended, even though they could not agree how best to respond to it.

It is, however, possible to argue that in many respects the application of the military instrument, or even simply its brandishing, has been counter-productive to the Soviet Union in its relations with Western Europe. It prompted the return of United States armed forces to Europe and the subsequent formalisation of their presence within the NATO agreement. It provoked against itself the formation and maintenance of the strongest and best organised peacetime coalition the world has ever seen. By maintaining far more conventional land forces than any traditional defensive strategy could ever demand, the Soviet Union provoked the deployment of a short- and medium-range nuclear weapon potential riposte which offers the shortest possible warning time and hence the greatest danger to the Soviet motherland and its allies. The accumulated impact of the permanent proximity of overwhelming Soviet military power was to submerge traditional Western European sources of conflict in a common cause. Even when potentially fratricidal violence broke out on both northern and southern flanks it could be contained within the North Atlantic Treaty Organisation. A measure of that common cause is not the fact that Greek and Turk could occasionally still disagree, but that for the first time in many centuries the disagreement had not provoked serious conflict.

In sum, therefore, the evolution of Western Europe since 1945 has been influenced by many factors, but relationships between the countries themselves, between themselves and the USA and between themselves and the Eastern bloc have been consciously maintained in the shadow of Soviet military strength. Domestically, the most effective way to provide a defensive response to that strength has frequently and increasingly stimulated political controversy in several Western governments. By 1983 the Soviet Union enjoyed a presence in, and pretension to influence over the European Sub-Continent greater than at any time in European history. Its government permitted the Novosti Press to seek to influence the NATO defence ministers and their democratic electorates by threats of instant, launch-on-warning response even to accidental firings of medium-range NATO nuclear weapons.[11] Such bluster reflected the fact that while it was many times stronger militarily than it had been in 1945, the Soviet Union was in some respects far more vulnerable. Moreover, there was no guarantee that as the decade progressed its military strength would become a more effective instrument of policy.

Perception and the Military Instrument

The utility of military force as an instrument of policy lies in its ability to create more favourable circumstances for the diplomat to exploit. On several occasions since 1945 Soviet force was actually employed, for example in Hungary, Czechoslovakia, Afghanistan and indirectly in Africa. Towards Western Europe, however, except for the isolated instances noted earlier, it has been the presence, the potential for employment, which has exercised the influence. Whereas employment is recognisable and ultimately quantifiable, potential can only be measured by perception. Perception assesses the capability of the military force were it to be applied. If perception also identifies hostile motivation, intent and precedent, then a neutral military instrument becomes identified as 'a threat'. Hence the commonplace expression in Western Europe which prompts so much irritable denunciation by Soviet commentators and cartoonists.

A Western military assessment or 'appreciation' of the Soviet military instrument tends to concentrate on capability but cannot ignore both precedent and the fact that the greater the military capability, the wider ranging the options for its use and the greater its possible influence on motivation and intent. Any such assessment must take great care neither to underestimate the opposition, which could clearly prove disastrous should conflict occur, nor to be over-pessimistic, which could invest an opposition with invincibility, reduce the morale of one's own forces and induce a disproportionate diversion of resources for one's own defence. Moreover, while it is possible for the purposes of analysis to dissect the Soviet military instrument and examine the strengths and weaknesses of its components, in practice the reciprocity between them prompts caution in the search for exact quantification of each.

The Permanent Advantages

Nevertheless, even with such caveats it is possible to identify several advantages which Soviet armed forces would enjoy over their Western counterparts if they were to be employed in a European conflict and which, therefore, influence Western perception in peacetime.

The first group of advantages which have remained constant since 1945 are those which are readily identifiable by a glance at a map of Europe. Numbers of course have changed over the years but in 1982 the nineteen Tank and Motor Rifle Divisions of the Soviet group of forces in Germany, which could be expected to spearhead any attack across the inner German border, were located only 300 miles away from the sixty-nine divisions of the Soviet armies in the European military districts of Russia.[12] A large proportion of the latter divisions was maintained at a high state of combat readiness and, using the highly developed road and rail network of Eastern Europe, could reach a combat zone near the inner German border in two or three days. Moreover, the Warsaw Pact forces as a whole have the advantage of interior lines. For example, the divisions in East Germany could also be swiftly reinforced from the further eleven Soviet and thirty-seven[13] allied divisions from elsewhere in Eastern Europe. All had the further geographical advantage in that with the exception of a front in Northern Norway, the pressure points in Central Europe are contiguous: from the Baltic coast down to the Balkans.

The asymmetric influence of geography may be summarised

175

by noting that the forty-five armoured and mechanised divisions of NATO, plus the thirty-nine others[14] (amphibious, infantry, etc.) are deployed in Europe in areas separated by the Baltic, the Channel, the Alps, the territories of Switzerland, Austria and Yugoslavia, the Adriatic and the Aegean. They could be swiftly reinforced by a further sixteen divisions but thereafter would depend on mobilisation of reserves and the arrival of a further eight divisions from the USA across an air or sea bridge of 3,000 miles.[15]

The final geographic element in the appraisal is that a large proportion of combat-ready Warsaw Pact forces are deployed close enough to the inner German border to give very little warning by their movement of an impending attack on the West. On the other hand, several NATO divisions, for example the Belgian and Dutch, are located in peacetime several hundred miles away from their defensive combat positions, while the bulk of the United States ground forces are deployed to the south of the major access routes across the North German plain.

So, even if there were no disagreements about the relative size and quality of the Soviet military instrument, there could be no doubt that European geography considerably enhances it. Similarly, it undoubtedly benefits from its monolithic nature.

It is not just that the voluntary NATO organisation would require a consensus for military action which the Soviet-dominated Warsaw Pact could take for granted. The implications of monolithic control extend downwards into standardised equipment, doctrine, tactics and communications to a degree that is frequently the envy of Western professional soldiers. NATO standardisation of equipment, despite progressive improvements and a fund of good will, is inhibited by the national desire of fully independent members to safeguard their own industries. That independence is epitomised by the presence in the Alliance of different kinds of main battle tank, artillery, small arms, aircraft and weapons. The Warsaw Pact on the other hand is equipped almost entirely by Soviet built T64 and T72 tanks, BMP mechanised infantry combat vehicles, self-propelled or wheeled artillery and the Mikoyan and Sukhoi families of aircraft. Such basic and widespread standardisation facilitates extensive inter-operability between formations and regions to an extent not yet enjoyed by NATO units.

That uniformity of equipment is harnessed to a common tactical doctrine recently summarised by an authoritative British observer as:

> based on the philosophy of offensive operations taking place within the context of a short campaign. This doctrine is characterised by the employment of two main principles, namely fire power and manoeuvrability. The principles of war for the Soviet ground forces might be listed as follows: advance and consolidation, morale, offensive action, adequate reserve, surprise and deception, concentration, economy of force, manoeuvre and initiative, combined arms and annihilation.
>
> These principles lead to a concept of operations in which the stress is laid upon concentrating vastly superior forces on to a particular sector in order to make a decisive break-through.[16]

Conformity to these principles would in conflict be imposed by a military communications net increasingly duplicated and hardened for protection against physical attack, designed to ensure that Soviet control would be exercised over all Warsaw Pact formations on land and in the air.

The final permanent advantage accruing to the Soviet military instrument is the freedom it enjoys from any public questioning about its priority or utility. There have been debates within the Soviet Union on several occasions about priorities to be afforded to industry or to agriculture. There is, however, no record of any suggestion that resources allocated to the armed forces, or their traditional roles as an instrument of policy, should be reconsidered. Indeed on 27 October 1982 in one of his last reported speeches, Mr Brezhnev reassured Soviet army and navy commanders that however national funds were re-allocated the armed forces would always have a top priority claim on national resources.[17]

The Sharpening of the Weapon

These inherent military advantages have endowed Soviet foreign policy toward Western Europe since 1945, but several developments in the 1970s reinforced them and proportionately heightened Western military concern. The instrument was sharpened by a consistent and extensive conventional re-equipment programme, by re-organisation to increase tactical and strategic combat effectiveness, and finally by a dramatic and widely publicised increase in theatre nuclear capability.

Soviet ground forces and increasingly those of their Warsaw Pact allies have acquired greatly increased firepower and mobility in the last decade as a result of the introduction of the T72 tank, increase in personnel in both tank and mechanised rifle divisions, increase and modernisation of artillery units and deployment of more accurate, more mobile and longer-range battlefield nuclear artillery and surface-to-surface nuclear missiles. Command, control and communications between the whole have been improved by large-scale introduction of automated systems.

It is, however, a relatively unpublicised improvement in Soviet air power which has threatened the greatest disturbance of what was hitherto referred to as the 'military balance'. For twenty years after the Second World War, the Soviet air forces were largely defensive and short-range in character. Soviet fighters, for example, were numerically superior to their NATO counterparts but were largely unable to operate at night or in bad weather whilst fighter bombers could carry only light bombloads over much shorter ranges than those of the Western air forces. The Western assessment of the longer-range manned bomber threat was clearly reflected in the rundown of British and United States national air defences in the 1960s. In almost every respect – aircraft performance, navigational and other instruments and weapons – the West enjoyed a technical superiority which more than offset Soviet numerical advantages.

The implications of such advantages were extremely important in a period when NATO moved from its previous 'tripwire' strategic posture in 1967 to its present declaratory position of forward defence and flexible 'appropriate' response. To counter the persistent Soviet strategic advantages already described, rapid Western reinforcement and redeployment in a time of tension would be essential. Before the outbreak of conflict airlift would deliver the first and swiftest reinforcements both within the European theatre and from beyond it. Should deterrence fail and conflict actually occur, Western fighter bombers would be called upon to attack invading Soviet armour, deny Warsaw Pact reinforcements, protect NATO's own ground forces from Soviet air attack, destroy Soviet aircraft and Warsaw Pact airfields and protect the ever increasing flow of reinforcements and supplies moving across the Atlantic by sea and air and passing through European ports and airfields. Finally, a proportion of SACEUR's aircraft could be called upon to deliver nuclear weapons should such a political decision be taken. By 1982, however, improvements to Soviet aircraft and ground-to-air defences had made all these tasks much more complicated

The improvement in Soviet combat aircraft could be measured in several ways, for example by a three-fold increase in pay-load or by the extension of range to such an extent that the United Kingdom itself could be threatened by conventional air attack by SU24 fighter bombers based in Poland or by TU22 Backfire bombers looping around the islands to attack from the north-west. NATO airfields, communications, reinforcements, re-supply areas, headquarters, all became vulnerable to Soviet aircraft which themselves could increasingly deliver stand-off weapons in all weather by night and day. In 1982 there were unconfirmed reports that yet another new close air support aircraft, the SU25, was being added to the Soviet inventory in Eastern Europe after combat 'trials' in Afghanistan. Indeed, the Afghanistan campaign, despite the obvious differences in terrain, climate and opposition, provided an increasing number of Soviet aircrew with combat experience which could only enhance their basic skills in Europe. Nor did the Soviet Union see fit to publicise the fact that the majority of 'third generation' combat aircraft deployed in Eastern Europe were also able to deliver nuclear weapons.

Used widely in Afghanistan and of particular significance in Europe when deployed alongside the major Warsaw Pact ground formations, was an assault and close support force of heavily armed helicopters. The helicopter compared to fixed-wing aircraft tends to be vulnerable and relatively restricted in range but is an ideal weapon system for use when it can be deployed near to its designated combat area, to provide heavy close air support to rapidly advancing forces or to place airborne troops on keypoints ahead of them. Indeed, by 1982 Soviet helicopter quality, and complexity of tactical operations, were prompting considerable examination by NATO staffs.

Less dramatic in appearance than the new generation of fixed-wing combat aeroplanes and helicopters, but conferring a further important enhancement of Soviet military options, was the increase in airlift capacity and range during this same period. By 1982 the Bear could fly and carry a great deal a long way from his lair. The speed and efficiency of the enhanced airlift was seen first in the invasion of Czechoslovakia in 1968, then again in the swift assistance provided to Syria and Egypt in 1973, and latterly in the Afghanistan invasion of 1979. The older, medium-range unpressurised AN12 Cubs of Soviet Military Transport Aviation were first supplemented by fifty heavy-lift long-range AN22 and now are steadily being replaced by IL76 4-jet transports which can theoretically lift twice the Cubs' payload five times as far.[18] These aircraft can be supported by Cubs, IL76s and over 1,000 medium- and long-range transports of the

Soviet State Airline Aeroflot. For example, twice yearly troop rotation takes place between Eastern Europe and the Soviet Union. Only a decade ago it was carried out almost entirely by surface transport, now almost entirely by air. The implications for Soviet reinforcement in Europe, and for rapid long-range projection of force elsewhere, are self-evident.

Close co-ordination between Aeroflot and Soviet Military Transport Aviation ensures a flexible tactical and strategic application of airlift resources, and there was further evidence by 1982 that other branches of the Soviet air forces were being re-organised to enhance their own effectiveness. For example, the command structure of medium- and longer-range bomber units was modified to allow them to take greater operational advantage of their increased range and pay-load. Helicopters, on the other hand, were closely integrated with tactical army units with corresponding potential increases in locally responsive concentrated firepower. The air defences of the Eastern European satellites were incorporated into a comprehensive system which stretched from the inner German border back into the Soviet heartland. In these ways the Soviet Union sought to combine the flexibility conveyed by centralised control of airpower assets with the need to provide swift local response to tactical situations.

In 1945, when the Soviet Union had transported several hundred Germany military scientists back to Russia, a variety of experimental and development anti-aircraft weapons had also been taken. Subsequently it invested considerable resources in the development of surface-to-air defences to complement its manned interceptor fighters. In 1960 the dramatic destruction of Gary Powers's U-2 reconnaissance aircraft near Sverdlosk by a SA-2 ground-launch missile marked the end of the invulnerability of the high-flying aircraft. The facts subsequently disclosed by Penkovsky that thirteen missiles had been fired at the aircraft of which eleven had missed, one had shot down a MIG fighter seeking to intercept and finally one had been successful, were at the time less significant than the political capital which

Khrushchev was able to make out of the discomfiture of the United States government. By 1983 a dozen different kinds of low-, medium- and high-level surface-to-air missile, supplemented by radar-laid anti-aircraft guns, were deployed across Eastern Europe and Western Russia. They were supported by and integrated with a network of several thousand early warning and missile control radars. When one remembers the extremely important offensive roles demanded of Western aircraft by NATO strategy, the significance of these defensive systems is obvious. Moreover their increasing effectiveness allowed the Warsaw Pact to divert more of its own fighters and fighter bombers to offensive roles, thereby complicating the tasks of Western air defences even further.

Therefore, even if the military instrument had been sharpened only in its ground and air force elements, the effects would have been formidable, but Western Europe was not only vulnerable to pressure directly from the East: it could be threatened with isolation from its North American partners and denial of its access to the raw materials required not just to maintain its military strength but for its basic peacetime economic viability. Consequently, the rapid expansion of the Soviet Navy under the leadership of Admiral Ghorshkov understandably prompted considerable Western concern. In the early 1960s the Soviet Navy was a 'white water' service, seldom venturing beyond coastal waters and regarded as the Cinderella of the Soviet armed forces. By 1983 it was fully equipped to project Soviet power across the globe by a balanced fleet of light aircraft carriers, cruisers, destroyers, frigates, submarines and auxiliary vessels second only in strength to the United States Navy.[19] Supported by a modernised naval aviation arm which included long-range, nuclear-equipped bombers, anti-submarine and reconnaissance aircraft, and short-range offensive support fixed-wing aircraft and anti-submarine helicopters, it could not only threaten NATO's Atlantic umbilical cord but bring indirect pressure to bear on countries in the Third World whose continued good will was essential to Western Europe.

The Alliance could draw a little consolation from the fact that in maritime operations geography favoured the West. It would be very difficult for the Soviet Union either to concentrate the combined power of its Northern, Baltic, Black Sea and Far East fleets on any one theatre of operations at a time, or to co-ordinate the timing of large-scale naval aggression with an offensive in Central Europe. Nevertheless, the quantum change in Soviet naval strength added a completely new dimension to its military power *vis-à-vis* Western Europe.

The progress of Western European conventional weapon development in the same decade is on the public record, readily traced through the annual editions of the IISS, 'The Military Balance'. Sufficient here to observe that until 1979, defence expenditure in real terms declined and major re-equipment programmes were typified by the interceptor and short-range fighter bomber aircraft such as F15 and F16. Although NATO's strategic posture was officially modified in 1967, provision of the increased manpower, weapons, aircraft, armour, communications and reserves demanded by the strategy of flexible response was affected first by the diversion of United States emphasis to South-east Asia and then by the increasing difficulties faced by the Western European economies after the oil crisis of 1973. So much so, that in 1979 in the face of the quite obvious increase in Soviet military strength, the Alliance members finally pledged a 3 per cent increase in their defence provisioning to seek to match it.

However, in the same uneasy decade a further and funda-mental change in the military relationship between the two blocs took place. In 1946 the United States enjoyed a nuclear monopoly; in the 1950s and 1960s the Western Alliance still enjoyed a perceived superiority in both intercontinental and short-range nuclear weapons over the Soviet Union. The strategic shift taken in 1967 tacitly acknowledged the decline in that superiority as the Soviet Union deployed its own ICBMs and shorter-range missiles in Eastern Europe and Western Russia. In the 1970s it progressively re-equipped its tactical and strategic rocket forces with weapons of improved mobility, increased range, greater accuracy and more efficient warheads.[20] Then, in 1977, it deployed a completely new missile which at once was perceived to tip the nuclear balance in Europe. The SS-20 is highly mobile, its three very accurate warheads can be independently targeted, it can be rapidly re-loaded and from locations in Western Russia on either side of the Urals it can threaten any target in Western Europe without fear of retaliation or pre-emption from any European-based surface-to-surface or air-to-surface weapon. The esoteric and arcane complexities of nuclear confrontation, the impact upon it of this new deployment, the resulting implications for both Western deterrence and for the Soviet military instrument have been extensively analysed in great detail,[21] but the central issue is, for Western Europe, unpleasantly simple. It may be expressed in the form of a question.

Is the bedrock of Western deterrence since 1945 – the strategic and tactical underwriting of Western European military security by indeterminate threat of a possible nuclear riposte, even to a conventional attack – still credible in the face of Soviet intercontinental nuclear parity and perceived theatre superiority? The question is straightforward; the answer depends, and hopefully will continue to depend, on perception. Hence the uncertainty and controversy about the exact extent of Soviet military power and its utility as a political instrument for use in Soviet foreign policy against Western Europe.

Soviet Perceptions

For thirty-six years Western Europe has perceived an overwhelming complex military threat from the East, but how, one wonders, has the Soviet government assessed the potential utility of its own military instrument? There is no shortage of evidence of how it views the role of military force generally, or rather the role of socialist military force. One of the best known summaries was written by Colonel Doctor of Historical Sciences V. M. Kulish in 1972:

> The Soviet Union and other socialist countries, by virtue of their increasing military potential, are changing the correlation of military forces in the international arena in favour of the forces of peace and socialism. This is exerting a very sobering effect on extremist circles in imperialist states and is creating favourable conditions for achieving Soviet foreign policy goals in the international arena, based upon the principles of peaceful co-existence.[22]

Nor does the Soviet Union lose any opportunity to emphasise the extent of her military might, whether on the occasion of the twice-yearly Red Square parades or by periodic well-publicised speeches or articles by senior military commanders.[23]

Unlike Western countries she does not casually use commercial journals to discuss the problems and deficiencies associated with new equipment or lapses in morale among the armed forces, or difficulties in meeting defence budgets, or tactical mal-deployments – a practice which must make the job of Soviet Military Attachés in the West close to a sinecure. Nevertheless, the many military advantages possessed by the Soviet Union and her Warsaw Pact allies are tempered by weaknesses and dilemmas which must influence their own assessment of the instrument's practical utility. Indeed, not the least consummate skill of recent Soviet leaders has been the ability to derive the maximum possible political and diplomatic impact from occasionally over-exaggerated military effectiveness.[24]

If there are reservations in the Kremlin about the employment of the military instrument against Western Europe, they might stem from three considerations. One might be the fear of unacceptable nuclear damage to the Soviet heartland resulting from either escalation of a conventional conflict or swift retaliatory Western response to large-scale conventional

Warsaw Pact attack. Secondly, there could be doubts about the Pact's actual ability to achieve the desired extent of military success in an operation against Western Europe. Thirdly, there could be concern about the implications for the Soviet Union should its armies suffer heavy defeat in such operations. Each of the considerations could be based on a number of complex, and occasionally contradictory, factors.

The first – Soviet fear of nuclear devastation of the motherland – is a basic assumption in the Western nuclear deterrence posture. Some American analysts have argued on the other hand that the Soviet civil defence programme[25] and some aspects of its military doctrine indicate a willingness to fight and to win a war which could well include intercontinental nuclear exchange. The two points of view are not incompatible. To a certain extent the Soviet government is a prisoner of its own ideology. It has professed to believe in traditional Marxist-Leninist interpretation of international conflict which predicates imperialist aggression against the Soviet Union. Published strategic thought usually assumes an attack on the Soviet Union or its allies which is swiftly followed by a counter-offensive prepared to operate with both nuclear and conventional weapons. For example, in an article in *Red Star* on 30 October 1970 General-Lieutenant I. G. Zav'yalov, a distinguished contributor to the evolution of modern Soviet strategic thought, observed:

> The art of conducting military actions involving the use of nuclear weapons and the art of conducting combat actions with conventional weapons has many fundamental differences. But they are not in opposition to one another and are not mutually exclusive or isolated one from the other. On the contrary, they are closely inter-related and are developed as an integrated whole.[26]

Indeed, a considerable amount of recent Soviet analysis has focused on 'The Scientific-Technical Revolution in Military

Affairs' or, more simply, the impact of nuclear weapons on traditional Soviet military strategy. However, if such weapons are to be wholly integrated and if the potential opposition rather unsportingly refuses to distinguish clearly between conventional and nuclear response, and even worse prepares to blur the boundaries of tactical and strategic nuclear counterattack by placing nuclear weapons in Western Europe which could reach Central Russia, then a Soviet war-fighting strategy could have unwelcome repercussions. Expressed more simply, Soviet declaratory war-fighting strategy could be said to actually enhance the West's deliberately imprecise, nuclear deterrence posture. As long, that is, as the West maintains obvious linkage between tactical and longer-range weapons capable of actually reaching Central Russia.

Those who are particularly concerned about a Soviet willingness to risk a nuclear encounter also point to its well-recognised custom of fostering memories of the horrendous Russian losses and sacrifices in the Great Patriotic War and suggest that a nation which has lost 20 million dead in one war will be prepared the more easily to accept similar casualties in a nuclear exchange. It is obviously impossible to refute this argument, but there are other more obvious reasons for the constant remembrance. Henry IV on his deathbed advised the young Prince Hal, 'Be it thy cause to busy giddy minds with foreign quarrels'. In similar manner it is good practical politics for the government in the Kremlin to foster folk memories of foreign invasion, thereby justifying continued extensive defence expenditure, the privileged position enjoyed in Soviet society by military cadres and the legitimacy of the government itself, as the bastion against a perpetual threat of imperialist aggression. If such a policy should also prepare the Russian peoples to sustain the horrors of a Third World War, so much the better. The construction of a civil defence programme is part of this general ambience and a further example of that element of Soviet strategic thought which appears to believe that war with imperialism is still inevitable, and that should it occur, the Soviet state must be the

187

one to survive. There is, however, considerable evidence to suggest that despite the extensive theoretical analysis of the impact of nuclear weapons on Marxist-Leninist military philosophy, there has been no resolution of the basic dilemma: how far can military force still be a viable instrument of policy if it risks the physical destruction of the Soviet centre of government and large areas of Mother Russia? But it should not be forgotten that the conventional strength of the Russian armed forces, padded by the territories and troops of the Warsaw Pact, ensures that such a penalty for aggression against Western Europe could only be exacted by long-range nuclear weapons.

Prospects of Success

But suppose some Soviet government, for whatever reason, did decide that the deterrence posture of Western Europe was no longer credible; that the risk of nuclear retaliation against the heartland was so low that its military instrument could be employed. Even possessing the military advantages already summarised above, the Soviet Union could not be absolutely certain that a military offensive would in fact be successful, even against NATO's thinly-stretched defences. The Soviet General Staff would need to resolve a few problems before advising its masters that conventional success could be guaranteed. These problems might well involve a decision about the timing and exact nature of an attack on the West, and a sober assessment of the difficulties that could arise after such an attack had been launched.

The well known essential ingredients of Soviet military strategy are surprise, exploited by the momentum of concentrated force applied at high and continuous speed. These ingredients, however, might now be a little more difficult to blend. In recent years, while the in-position strength of Soviet forces in Central Europe has increased considerably, so has the

West's ability to monitor their activities. Large-scale exercises which could, like the Egyptian example of 1973, be used to mask a surprise attack are now by formal agreement notified in advance to NATO, thereby allowing safeguards to be taken if such be considered appropriate. Satellite and other surveillance systems can detect abnormal Warsaw Pact activity such as increased signals traffic, troop deployment, issue of weapons and fuel stocks etc., far more effectively than even at the time of the Czechoslovak invasion of 1968. If, therefore, the Soviet forces sought to amass the overwhelming force necessary to guarantee conventional success, there would be an attendant risk of giving the West additional warning time in which to adjust defence deployments and to rapidly reinforce by air, unimpeded by hostile action. Furthermore, if the Soviet generals really were captives of their own propaganda, they might believe that such warning of attack could be used by the West to deliver some kind of pre-emptive strike of their own.

On the other hand, a Soviet attack without warning from current, unreinforced positions would perhaps in Soviet eyes lack the overwhelming force favoured by Soviet generals in the Second World War and expounded in subsequent strategic analysis. Even that broad dilemma might be further complicated by the fact that as a matter of peacetime routine the twice-yearly arrival of new conscripts to the Soviet front lines obviously dilutes quality still further and might, in the eyes of cautious Russian generals, restrict the windows of opportunity still further.

If, however, the Warsaw Pact did decide upon an optimum timetable of attack which permitted the advantages of limited reinforcement to outweigh the disadvantages of increased warning time, there could still be no guarantee of success. For a start, the graduates of the various Russian staff colleges might recall a text from their studies of Clausewitz:

Only one more element is needed to make war a gamble – chance: the very last thing that war lacks. No other human

189

activity is so continuously or universally bound up with chance. And through the element of chance, guesswork and luck come to play a great part in war.[27]

Even if that caution were to be overtaken by confidence in a favourable 'correlation of forces', there is no shortage in published Soviet training manuals of a hearty respect for Western military technology. For example, Western ground and air delivered precision-guided anti-armour munitions are still superior to those of the Warsaw Pact. NATO commanders publicly express concern at their lack of quantity, but even their limited presence, deployed for example among the sprawling and expanding suburban villages of North Germany, could present Soviet tank commanders with far greater problems than those faced across the broad expanse of Western Russia in 1944. But perhaps most threatening of all to the Soviet tactical requirement for sustained momentum is the potential contribution of NATO air forces. Soviet peacetime exercises suggest heavy dependence on pre-planned, carefully structured and closely integrated combined armed movements. By definition, an offensive so predicated is vulnerable to disruption, dislocation and delay of its many parts and of paralysis of command and control systems. That vulnerability could be compounded by failure to encourage initiative among junior ranks. The perceived ability of Western airpower therefore to isolate forward echelons from their immediate support, to slow down or divert reinforcing units and to cut lines of communication might in some circumstances seem to the Warsaw Pact High Command a greater impediment to success than an ability simply to destroy armour. An assumption might be that the Soviet Union could replace armoured units faster than the West, with its comparatively limited conventional weapon stocks, could destroy them. Loss of momentum, on the other hand, would give time for Western defence to be strengthened and, perhaps most ominously from the point of view of the invading forces, by delaying success would increase the risks of prompting that very nuclear escalation which had been discounted at the outset.

Such speculation must inevitably be cloudy. The Soviet Union could, for example, be so confident of its own nuclear strength that it might itself strike Western airfields or troop concentrations with small yield weapons producing limited collateral damage. Or it might take advantage of its overwhelming chemical weapon superiority to attack similar targets without fear of retribution in kind. Indeed, a surprise chemical attack could be so advantageous that its possibility and the lack of any viable Western deterrent in kind prompts frequent NATO expressions of unease. If, however, for whatever reason it was considering a purely conventional attack, respect for Western military technology and especially for the quality of Western airpower might induce restraint.

Whether its assessment of the reliability of its Warsaw Pact allies would add to the restraint remains a matter for conjecture. It now exercises extensive control, directly or indirectly, by Soviet commanders on non-Soviet Warsaw Pact units. One is reminded of Frederick II of Prussia who placed NCOs behind his infantry platoons with the task of shooting those soldiers who wavered or turned tail in the face of the enemy. Eastern European nationalism, dislike of Russia, memories of Soviet repression in 1953, 1956 and 1968 and increasing awareness of the realities of life in Western Europe must impinge upon assumptions of unqualified loyalty to the Soviet Union, but there is nothing in the attitude of professional non-Soviet soldiers and airmen to lead the West to count on their unreliability. How their Soviet comrades regard them, however, may be a different matter. The attitude of Poland, especially, sitting athwart the major reinforcement routes from European Russia is probably a source of some concern to the Soviet High Command.

Loss of the Military Instrument

Indeed, Poland might figure in the third set of considerations affecting a Soviet decision to use force against Western Europe. What would be the implications for the Soviet Union if the Soviet armies suffered heavy defeat, even if the heartland remained inviolate to nuclear attack?

It is interesting to recall that the Bolshevik Revolution of 1917 followed hard upon the defeat and disintegration of the Tsarist armies in Europe. Since then, the roles of the Red Army have comprised protection of the inheritance of the Revolution within Russia; the instrument of control of the satellite comrades of Eastern Europe; defence of socialism in Afghanistan; custody of the disputed boundaries with China;[28] primary conduit of foreign policy projection elsewhere, and indeed perhaps the ultimate sanction of the Soviet government itself. What therefore would the implications be for that Soviet government of large-scale military disaster? Russian commanders have frequently been profligate with the lives of their soldiers and the campaigns of the Second World War were no exception. Indeed, current Soviet military doctrine suggests a willingness to accept heavy losses in the pursuit of victory. But could any Soviet leadership approve a foreign adventure in Western Europe if there remained any possibility of decimation of the Red Army without recognisable and proportionate success.

The Contemporary Nuclear Issues

From this last reflection, it is possible to speculate about Soviet responses to a Western increase in conventional strength which might permit the occasion to be delayed when NATO commanders would be compelled to have recourse to battlefield or short-range nuclear weapons. Expressing the problem in a different way, one can summarise the military disadvantages which would accrue to the West if such a policy were to be followed without it being accompanied, not just by a reduction in Soviet weapons of a similar nature, but by a reduction in Soviet in-position conventional forces.

The reliance by the West for many years on nuclear weaponry to offset a perceived conventional disadvantage has already been traced. If nuclear weapons comprise the Queens of the battlefield, their mutual removal would enhance the military potential of the conventional Rooks, Bishops, Knights and Pawns. Such a situation could only strengthen the position of the Warsaw Pact. Pursuing the analogy, the minor pieces could be concentrated without fear of their decimation. Concentration of force as required by Soviet strategy even in an age of greatly enhanced firepower per soldier still demands large-scale concentrations of armies which in turn increases their vulnerability to attack by nuclear weapons. Removal of that vulnerability would free Warsaw Pact staff officers to plan much more confidently on securing the initial mass required to sustain the momentum of an offensive.

Further, the greater the delay in Western use of nuclear weapons, the longer the opportunity for Warsaw Pact conventional forces to neutralise NATO's theatre nuclear systems: particularly missile sites and airfields housing dual capable aircraft, which are well publicised targets for Soviet air and airborne forces. After such neutralisation, Western Europe could become vulnerable not only to the Warsaw Pact armoured divisions but to the Soviet Union's own relatively invulnerable theatre nuclear arsenal and in particular to the SS-20s. At the same time the imprecise but strongly emphasised link in NATO strategy between conventional and nuclear response would be weakened and the risk of escalation which could envelop the Western Soviet Union proportionately reduced. One extremely important strand in the tapestry of Western deterrent strategy would be frayed if not destroyed altogether.

It is difficult therefore to see how the Soviet Union could perceive anything other than its advantage from a Western unilateral decision to reduce dependence on nuclear weapons, unless such reduction was accompanied by negotiated Warsaw

Pact conventional force reductions or, alternatively, by considerably enhanced Western conventional defences. Even the briefest of summaries indicates the additional problems for the West which such enhancement would involve. Assuming no change in the fundamental West German position that the concession of large tracts of territory to invading forces – buying time by space – would be unacceptable, enhanced conventional defences would demand heavy Alliance spending on more and highly mobile Anti-Tank Guided Weapon (ATGW) teams, more ATGW helicopters, more fixed-wing close air support aircraft, more longer-range all-weather interdiction aircraft, more highly mobile SAM systems, increased weapon stocks, more manpower, and large-scale peacetime redeployment of ground forces nearer to the inner German border. Moreover, such forward redeployment could very easily be construed or represented by the Soviet Union as a threatening act in itself and in terms of lowering tension actually be counter-productive. An alternative strategy based on fixed forward defences such as nuclear or conventional minefields would remain vulnerable to outflanking by sea via the Baltic, by land through Austria or by air via the airborne divisions; quite apart from the additional political complications inherent in deployment of more not fewer nuclear weapons. Ironically, a third possibility of removing Western nuclear weapons from the central region but retaining an ability to bring them to bear from positions further in the rear would imply, in the shorter term at least, increasing their peacetime deployment in areas such as the United Kingdom and introducing them into Spain. The political implications in those countries of such a geographical parallel to the deployment of the SS-20s in the Soviet Union needs no further embellishment in 1983.

In sum, any reduction of dependence on nuclear weapons by NATO would replace one set of military problems by another and would pose complicated questions of defence appropriations to member nations. It might reduce the chances of the early use of nuclear weapons in a European conflict but would certainly facilitate the implementation of the Soviet Union's own military doctrine. It is probable, therefore, that the raising of the nuclear threshold, unless it were to be accompanied by Warsaw Pact conventional arms reduction, would strengthen the military element in Soviet policy toward Western Europe.

Such speculation about Soviet perceptions of a nuclear threshold revision is complicated by the contemporary evolution of the debate involving the SS-20, ground launch Cruise missile and Pershing II. Since 1979 the USSR has had the constant objective of stopping deployment of both GLCM and Pershing II. The advent of Mr Andropov was marked by an increase in diplomatic activity with the additional ingredient of an offer to reduce SS-20 deployments in Europe. The diplomatic offensive may well have sought also to encourage disagreement and fears within the Western Alliance about a further and possibly destabilising extension of a nuclear arms race, but there is a recognisable logic in the military rationale behind the Soviet objectives.

First, however, it is important to recall the differences between the two kinds of weapon: GLCM and the Pershing ballistic rocket. GLCM is very small, sub-sonic and very low flying. From potential sites in Western Europe it would take approximately three hours to reach Western Russia. It is relatively cheap to construct, easily mobile and once launched extremely difficult to intercept. The Pershing II ballistic missile, on the other hand, would take between four and six minutes to reach Soviet territory from sites in Western Germany, it carries a more destructive pay-load than GLCM and could only be intercepted by an exceptionally fast reacting anti-ballistic warning and active defensive system. It is politically convenient for the Soviet Union to bracket them together in diplomatic offensives but the threats they present differ considerably and moreover those differences are well perceived in Moscow.

It is highly improbable that the Soviet Union has any fear of GLCM being used in a pre-emptive counter-force attack by the West. Its launch would be readily detectable by several routine

Warsaw Pact intelligence courses and its three-hour flight time to targets in Russia would permit the Soviet government to choose from a variety of responses, including a nuclear counter or simply redeployment of its own missiles such as the SS-20. Because of its telemetric terrain-matching guidance system GLCM can follow a devious track to its target, but it cannot go looking for a target which has moved. Knowledgeable Soviet analysts when pressed to explain their exaggerated fears of a GLCM pre-emptive attack have been known to be very vague or to change the subject because they must otherwise acknowledge its improbability[29]. In fact, the threat from GLCM is actually perceived by them to be far more complex and in some aspects far more serious.

It is theoretically possible to intercept a low-flying cruise missile by extremely rapid reacting surface-to-air missiles such as the current Russian SA-10, but only if the SAM is so located that its guidance system can acquire its target in what is almost line of sight. The basic laws of physics are strongly in favour of a small manoeuvrable cruise missile flying at only 50 feet above the earth's contours at some 500 miles per hour. Moreover, if the interceptor should itself trigger the nuclear warhead of the attacking missile, interception close to the target would be counter-productive. When one considers the vast extent of Soviet territory, the difficulties of intercepting the missile earlier on its route are apparent. Nor could the Soviet Union be over-optimistic about the ability in the near future of fighter aircraft equipped with 'look down, shoot down' weapons systems to be very successful. It is one thing to look down on and to see a tiny low-flying object, it is quite another to devise an air-to-air missile whether heat-seeking or radar guided, which could guarantee a high kill probability. Moreover, rapid advances in computer micro-miniaturisation are already making it possible to equip a cruise missile with its own electronic counter-measures, which will increase the tasks of the defence even more.

It is not, therefore, the destabilising threat of a pre-emptive counter-force strike, but the enormous cost, complexity and diversion of very scarce resources to provide a defence against GLCM which causes the greatest Soviet concern. Indeed, Soviet defence analysts have professed to believe that the real objective of the USA in deploying GLCM is to force the USSR into bankruptcy by having to provide a defence against it.[30] Soviet military perception of GLCM deployment may well be not one of great concern for its short-term impact on combat in Europe, but its longer-term implications for the demand for a whole new generation of air defence provision for the Soviet Union itself.

Pershing II on the other hand is in Soviet eyes militarily de-stabilising; not in its increased accuracy, mobility or pay-load, but in its range, which unlike Pershing I can reach Soviet territory. In theory it could destroy not only Warsaw Pact targets in Eastern Europe but Soviet SS-20 batteries or any other Soviet missiles on the ground. Moreover, because of its very short flight time it could make even a launch-on-warning counter strategy very problematical. In theory it could, like any ballistic missile with an exo-atmospheric trajectory, be vulnerable to an ABM system, but the provision of such a system would also be extremely expensive and very complex. In Soviet eyes Pershing II is too well suited to a NATO strategy of flexible response for it to be allowed to be deployed without strenuous opposition. The fact that the many times more numerous, much longer range and triple war-headed SS-20s present a far greater threat to Western Europe than Pershing II does to the Soviet Union is of course not acknowledged in Moscow.

Thus either GLCM or Pershing II deployment would greatly enhance the Western deterrent posture, present the Soviet Union with very serious defensive problems and complicate, albeit in different ways, their calculations about the efficacy of their own military instrument toward Western Europe. In the early months of 1983 it was possible to discern some Soviet uncertainty about how best to prevent the deployment of both. In his speech to the 26th Party Congress in February 1981

Mr Brezhnev had offered a moritorium on the deployment of all medium-range missiles (including SS-20s) in Europe. In November 1981 the Reagan Administration's counter-proposals to refrain from deploying GLCM and Pershing II in Europe in return for the dismantling of all SS-4s, SS-5s and SS-20s was rejected out of hand by Moscow. In December 1982, Mr Andropov in turn offered negotiations on a reduction in intermediate range systems which would include not only his European-based medium-range missiles but also the British and French independent forces and American 'forward base' systems such as dual capable aircraft and aircraft carriers in European waters.

Subsequently, while on a visit to Bonn, Mr Andrei Gromyko announced at a State dinner on 18 January that 'the Soviet Union is ready to reduce its medium-range nuclear missiles to the combined total of British and French nuclear forces and to remove those above this figure behind a line in Siberia from where they would be unable to reach Western Europe', and that the Russians 'were also ready to limit the number of tactical weapons with a range of less than 1,000 kilometres to the number deployed by the West.[31] The proposals were accompanied by the warning that 'the Russians would do whatever was necessary to ensure their own security. If the West deployed the [GLCM and Pershing II] weapons, equilibrium would be maintained but at a higher level and this (he said) would make peace more precarious and lessen the security of nations.'[32]

The Gromyko address, like its predecessors, assiduously encouraged the politicians and peace groups in the FRG and Western Europe who were campaigning for unilateral renunciation of both GLCM and Pershing II. Moreover, not only was it diplomatically well timed if heavy-handed, it was from a Soviet military point of view extremely practical. In January 1983 British and French nuclear missiles excluding weapons carried by aircraft totalled 162[33] while total SS-20 deployment on both sides of the Urals was probably less than 340 of which rather more than 200 might be targeted against Western Europe. If therefore the British/French force level was to be accepted as a baseline for Eastern European SS-20s, the practical result would be a virtual freeze, not a reduction on their deployment in the theatre, while SS-20 deployment elsewhere could proceed apace. Moreover, some 480 SS-20 warheads would remain targeted against Western Europe; British and French 'independent' nuclear missiles would have been formally accepted as 'theatre' nuclear forces – a position steadfastly denied hitherto by both countries and by the USA – while finally the deployment of GLCM and Pershing II would have been forestalled. All in all, not a bad evening's work by the Russian Foreign Minister.

In fact, this well publicised 'initiative', carried in person to the heart of West Germany, was little more than a repeat of one of Mr Andropov's own speeches in Moscow made two months previously. It conveniently ignored the fact that negotiations on intermediate nuclear forces had begun in Geneva in 1981 and were still continuing, and the Western position had always been that the negotiations should concentrate on those intermediate systems of most concern to both sides, i.e. SS-4, SS-5, SS-20, cruise and Pershing II. The French and UK systems were not included because the negotiations were bilateral and concerned with superpower parity.

Nevertheless, the Gromyko speech could exert considerable diplomatic pressure on Western governments without any weakening of the Soviet instrument. Moreover, if the proposals were to be accepted by the West, the longer-term result would be that instead of the threat from 2–300 warheads of the obsolete slow-reacting SS-4s and -5s, Western Europe would face the 480 much more accurate and much more responsive SS-20 warheads. That consideration would probably influence Western military reaction.

It may, however, have been significant that Soviet proposals at the end of 1982 and the beginning of 1983 were accelerating in number and increasing in stridency if not in practical concession. That trend may have owed something to the assumption of power by Mr Andropov, but it could also have been influenced by Soviet perceptions of limitations to its diplomatic opportunities. Diplomatic leverage on this occasion was depending not on the Soviet military instrument including the SS-20, but on the exploitation of Western domestic opposition to the deployment of GLCM and Pershing II. The success of its strategy would therefore, in the last resort, depend on factors beyond its own military control: a situation hitherto, as in its rejection of the theory of Mutual Assured Destruction, quite unacceptable to any Soviet government. If, for example, the Western peace movement was to dissipate in the manner of its predecessor twenty years previously, perhaps this time as a result of a determined, well co-ordinated Western domestic political counter-offensive, the Soviet Union would have received a serious diplomatic reverse. Moreover, any proposals which threatened the enforced relocation of the bulk of the 'third generation' offensive elements of the Soviet air forces would not be favourably received by the Soviet General Staff. Indeed, it was probable that in the debate over theatre nuclear strategy as a whole, both the response to GLCM and Pershing II and to the possibility of disruption and redeployment of powerful dual capable assets, the influence of the Soviet military would again be decisive.

The Future

Nor should such an outcome be surprising. Clausewitz observed that in war one should identify the enemy's 'centre of gravity . . . the hub of all power and movement, on which everything depends. That is the point against which all our energies should be directed.'[34] If he had been able to survey Soviet power since 1945 he might have concluded that its centre of gravity lay not in the inertia of a Soviet population imbued with patriotism, immured in generations of physical hardship and acceptance of rigid political control, nor in an industrial infrastructure scattered across a continent, nor even in a party bureaucracy woven through all levels of society, but indeed in the Soviet armed forces themselves. A corollary of the dependence of the Soviet government on the military instrument could be its nakedness if the instrument were ever to be dashed from its grasp. There are therefore many constraints on its use in Soviet strategy toward Western Europe and, in the foreseeable future, it is not too difficult to predict the steps which it might take to reduce them.

It would seek to remove the threat of escalation to nuclear attack on Russia from conflict in Central Europe by disconnecting the United States's nuclear guarantee from the Western European Allies. It would seek to prevent, or to remove, alternative nuclear threats to its heartland from independent nuclear forces such as those of France and Britain. It would seek to prevent the location or deployment by the United States in Western Europe or its surrounding oceans of theatre nuclear weapons which could also reach Russian territory. It would seek to remove short-range nuclear weapons from Central Europe itself to reduce the threat of mass destruction of its own ground forces. It would pursue policies of arms limitation which maximised its advantages of geographical proximity to Western Europe and its conventional numerical in-place superiority. It would seek to secure its rear by removing, or at least assuaging, sources of military tension with China. It would seek by every means at its disposal to close the weapon technology gap between itself and NATO, especially in airpower.

A survey of contemporary Soviet activities[35] and statements reveals just how far these steps are already·in train. Their scale and effectiveness will no doubt be influenced by further imponderable factors; perhaps the most likely being the continued solidarity and credibility of the Western deterrence posture and the least likely the impact of internal Soviet economic difficulties on its defence procurement. Overall, in its relations with Western Europe the Soviet Union is likely to continue to prefer the traditional and least expensive method of employing the military instrument: that of simply brandishing it.

Certainly a bankrupt ideology and threadbare economy are likely to inhibit alternative instruments of policy. Under what circumstances the threats would be translated into action is likely to depend on the assessment by the Soviet government of the possible costs of the enterprise. At present those costs probably seem much too high.

Therefore, any unilateral Western response to the threat which deliberately or inadvertently reduced the costs of the instrument without at the same time reducing its effectiveness, might actually encourage greater, not less Soviet dependence on the military dimension in its policy toward Western Europe.

DISCLAIMER

The opinions expressed in this chapter are those of the author alone and do not necessarily reflect the views of the British Ministry of Defence or any other department of Her Majesty's Government.

Notes to Chapter 6

1   M. Mackintosh, *Juggernaut: The Russian Forces 1918–1966* (London: Macmillan, 1967) p. 271.
2   See, for example, a recent extensive European analysis in *Soviet Strategy*, ed. John Baylis and Gerald Segal (London: Croom Helm, 1981).
3   R. A. Mason and M. J. Armitage, *Airpower in the Nuclear Age, Theory and Practice* (London: Macmillan, 1983) p. 180.
4   Stephen S. Kaplan, *Diplomacy of Power* (Washington: Brookings Institution, 1981), p. 120.
5   For a summary of these events see Kaplan, *Diplomacy of Power*, p. 128.
6   Kaplan, *Diplomacy of Power*, p. 129.
7   Kaplan, *Diplomacy of Power*, p. 155.
8   As reported in Walter Millis (ed.), 'The Forestal Diaries', quoted in Mason and Armitage, *Airpower in the Nuclear Age*.
9   See, for example, the contributions of David Greenwood, Director of the Defence Studies Institute at the University of Aberdeen, during 1981 and 1982.
10 *Economist*, 13 June 1967, p. 10.
11 As reported in *The Times*, 1 December 1982.
12 IISS, 'The Military Balance 1982–1983' (London: International Institute for Strategic Studies), pp. 14–15.
13 IISS, 'The Military Balance', p. 132.
14 ibid.

15 IISS, 'The Military Balance', p. 6.
16 J. Hemsley, in *Soviet Military Power and Performance*, ed. J. Erickson and E. Feuchtwanger (London: Macmillan, 1979), p. 48.
17 As reported by the *Financial Times* on 29 October 1982.
18 *Soviet Military Power* (US Government Printing Office, 1982), p. 36.
19 *Soviet Military Power*, pp. 39–51.
20 In 1982, many of these weapons were reported to be fitted with chemical warheads (*Soviet Military Power*, pp. 37–8). A German viewpoint, suggesting that the Soviet Union possessed 350,000 tons of conventional chemical agents and 700,000 tons for use in binary weapons, as opposed to a United States quantity of only some 10 per cent of those totals was expressed by H. Stelzmüller in 'NBC Defence, A German Viewpoint', *International Defence Review*, vol. 15, no. 11, 1982, p. 1,571.
21 See, for example, Lawrence Freedman, *The Evolution of Nuclear Strategy* (London: Macmillan, 1981).
22 Extract from V. M. Kulish, *Military Power and International Relations*, Moscow: International Relations Publishing House, 1972), quoted in *Soviet Military Thought*, vol. 11, *Selected Soviet Military Writings 1970–75* (United States Government Printing Office, 1976), p. 30.
23 See, for example, *The Soviet Armed Forces, the Dependable Guard of Socialist Achievements* by Marshal of the Soviet Union A. A. Grechko, translated in *Soviet Military Thought*, vol. 11 (United States Government Printing Office, 1976), pp. 165–84.
24 The most dramatic example occurred at the time of the launching of Sputnik in 1957, but Soviet annual air displays have frequently been used to suggest a military capability for airpower which was potential rather than contemporary.
25 Fully described in the 374-page (translated) volume· *Civil Defence* from the publishing house for Higher Education, Moscow 1970, published as Vol. no. 10 in the *Soviet Military Thought* series by the United States Government Printing Office.
26 *The New Weapon and Military Art*, translated in *Selected Soviet Military Writings 1970–1975: A Soviet View* published by United States Government Printing Office, as Vol. 11 in *Soviet Military Thought*, p. 210.
27 Clausewitz, *On War*, ed. M. Howard and P. Paret (Princeton: Princeton University Press, 1976), p. 85.
28 Approximately 35–40 per cent of Soviet land and air forces are usually estimated to be deployed in the Far-Eastern territories but with greatly improved airlift many could be transferred to Europe very quickly. The precedent of the Great Patriotic War, when the Soviet Union secured its rear against Japan by traditional diplomacy after a short military campaign, is one which could theoretically be repeated in the event of a proposed European adventure. In 1945 the successful Red Armies were redeployed to defeat the Japanese Manchurian forces. In the future, however, the Soviet Union may not wish to gamble on such an outcome against the Chinese army after a stern conflict in Central Europe.
29 Such views were expressed to the author in conversations with senior Soviet defence analysts in the Institute of United States and Canada and in the Institute of World Economy and International Relations in Moscow in March 1981.
30 Ibid.
31 As reported in *The Times*, 17 January 1983, p. 1.
32 Ibid.
33 As summarised in IISS, 'The Military Balance', pp. 112–17.
34 Clausewitz, *On War*, pp. 595–6.
35 See IISS, 'The Military Balance', pp. 11–13, for a summary of current trends in Soviet military procurement.

7
Economic Strategy

Angela Stent

The USSR has always pursued a dual policy toward economic relations with Western Europe: on the one hand, it has traded with the West to acquire technology for modernising its economy; on the other hand, it has attempted to use this trade for political purposes, to gain influence over Western Europe and to separate Europe from the United States. Today Soviet economic relations with Western Europe are a central aspect of its strategy toward the West. The economic aspects of Soviet *Westpolitik* have become more important since the late 1960s, particularly after the prospects for Soviet–American technology trade diminished in the mid-1970s. Moreover, the USSR has reaped unexpected political dividends from its economic ties with Western Europe largely because of American actions which it does not determine, but which have caused major disputes within the Western alliance. The Kremlin has arguably secured as many political as economic gains from its commercial ties with Western Europe. This chapter will examine Soviet economic and political expectations of economic détente with Western Europe,[1] discuss how the Kremlin evaluates the results of its economic *Westpolitik* and elaborate on future possibilities for Soviet economic strategy toward Europe.

The Background: History and Economics

Russian economic involvement with Western Europe has always

been episodic, with periods of intense contact followed by withdrawal. In the last century, and prior to détente, there were two major periods of Russian economic interest in Western Europe as a source of technology for modernisation. Both before and after the Revolution, Russia's trade patterns with Europe were those of an underdeveloped country exporting raw materials in exchange for the developed West's machinery. Count Sergei Witte's strategy for industrialisation in the 1890s involved a major drive to gain foreign capital and machinery. After the Bolshevik revolution, Lenin sought to attract foreign capital in the NEP period, but the most concerted attempt to use Western machinery for modernisation came during the period of the First Five-Year Plan.[2] Thereafter, the USSR returned to autarky, promoting national independence from foreign economic ties until the end of Stalin's life. Russia always sought to limit its dependence on the West at the same time as it strove to catch up with Europe militarily.

The first sign that the USSR was interested in changing the Stalinist pattern of autarky came in 1952, when the Soviets organised the International Economic Conference in Moscow whose theme was 'peaceful co-existence through trade', and which was attended by Western European delegations. The motivation was both economic and political: the USSR sensed that Western businessmen were becoming more interested in restoring traditional trade links with Russia; and it also perceived an opportunity to gain political dividends by playing different capitalist countries off against each other. In particular, it sought to persuade West European businessmen that the US-inspired strategic embargo imposed by CoCom (the Paris-based co-ordinating committee, founded in 1949, that administered export controls toward the communist nations) was counter-productive to their economic interests.[3]

Although Khrushchev tried to encourage greater economic intercourse with Western Europe, he was only partially successful, because of European political and economic reservations. It was only after his removal that the Stalinist policy of autarky was significantly modified, and a concerted attempt was made to utilise Western machinery and technology resources to accelerate the growth and modernisation of the Soviet economy. The 1966 contract with the Italian Fiat company to construct an automobile factory in the Volga Valley was the first major co-operation agreement of this new policy, and was followed by several more with other West European nations.[4] In this period, most Soviet officials stressed that the main reason for pursuing closer economic ties with Europe was political, because these ties would improve relations between the USSR and the West.

Despite the USSR's reluctance to admit the economic reasons for its increased interest in closer commercial ties with Western Europe, there are many indications that economic factors were one of the major motivations behind the decision to embark on a policy of détente with the West after the Soviet invasion of Czechoslovakia. The Stalinist economic system, although it proved highly effective in industrialising the USSR and enabling it to become a viable military power, was nevertheless unsuited for meeting the needs of consumers as well as those of the military. Khrushchev's erratic economic reforms failed to solve the problem. More importantly, the Kosygin reforms of 1965 were also inadequate for overcoming the major problems of inefficiency and lack of innovation. These decentralising reforms were never fully implemented because their political implications proved to be too threatening for Soviet bureaucrats with a vested interest in centralisation.[5] There is considerable evidence that a major decision was taken in 1968–9 to seek increased imports of Western technology to increase the productivity of the Soviet economy, bolster growth rates, and avoid the necessity for potentially destabilising domestic economic reform.[6] Although Brezhnev's decision to improve relations with Western Europe and the USA was motivated by a variety of political considerations, economic factors also played a crucial role. In 1969, the USSR hoped that the United States would become its major Western economic partner, but it was also interested in closer ties with Western Europe.

Since 1969, Soviet authors have become more open in their discussions of the Soviet economic need for closer commercial relations with the West, instead of focusing exclusively on the West's need for these economic ties, as they did in the past. There are indications that a debate about the economic advantages and disadvantages of détente has been waged within the Soviet leadership for some time, and parallels the political discussions about the advisability of the USSR becoming too involved with the capitalist world. The more traditionalist-minded politicians argued against too great an involvement with the economies of Western Europe, because this might create undesirable dependence on capitalist countries and compromise the USSR's sovereignty.[7] The 'modernisers', on the other hand, stressed the economic value of closer East–West economic ties. As a recent book put it:

But there is also an objective foundation for improving economic relations between socialist and capitalist states. The new stage in the development of productive forces connected with the scientific and technological revolution contributes to the further internationalization of all economic life and the ever greater vitalization of the international division of labour . . . Although each social system proceeds from its specific class interests in improving economic relations, there are, nevertheless, common requirements which can be more effectively satisfied by developing mutual economic ties. The socialist countries try to make use of long-term economic ties to successfully meet the targets of their planned economies, to more effectively exploit their various natural resources, to most fully satisfy their populations' needs and to further develop socialist integration.[8]

Soviet economic modernisers have also argued for greater decentralisation within the foreign trade system and for more flexibility in the state monopoly of foreign trade, to facilitate contacts between Western firms and Soviet foreign trade enterprises. A 1978 Council of Ministers' decree went some way toward encouraging greater decentralisation in foreign trade but, like most Soviet economic reforms, this one did not alter the fundamentally centralised nature of the foreign trade bureaucracy.[9]

Although we have increasing evidence of Soviet debates about economic relations with the West, there is a major methodological problem in discussing Soviet economic strategy toward Western Europe. The Soviets in fact publish more economic data on foreign trade than they do on many other areas of their economy, but it is insufficient for determining key questions such as how important the contribution of West European technology and other imports are for the Soviet economy. It is thus impossible to give definitive answers about the economic impact on the USSR of commercial ties with Europe, and one can only speculate on these basic problems. The first question is how important foreign trade in general is for the Soviet economy, and here Western scholars are divided in their interpretations of Soviet data. A recent study by the US Department of Commerce, for instance, which evaluates Soviet trade dependence in terms of domestic ruble prices, concludes that foreign trade plays a much more important role in the Soviet economy than has hitherto been recognised. In 1980, according to this report, foreign imports represented 20 per cent of Soviet net material product (GNP minus services and depreciation).[10] Another study disputes these findings. Using world market prices which, it says, are more appropriate than ruble prices, it claims that imports represent only 4.1 per cent of Soviet GNP.[11] These latest debates echo long-standing Western discussions over the importance of foreign trade for the Soviet economy, debates that are often highly charged politically.

Perhaps a more significant question relates to the importance of Western technology for the Soviet economy and for Soviet economic growth. Foreign trade represents about 5 per cent of Soviet GNP, and direct imports from the West about 1.6 per cent.[12] However, both Soviet and Western statistics indicate that Western technology and machinery are disproportionately important for certain sectors of the Soviet economy, particularly the capital goods sector.[13] Some authors have argued that practically every single military innovation in the USSR since 1917 has been possible only because of Western technology.[14] Others dispute this view, claiming that, while technology imports are significant for certain industrial sectors, they are not the key to Soviet modernisation.[15] Nevertheless, it is indisputable that West European technology and product imports have had a significant effect on Soviet economic development. However, there is increasing evidence that technology imports may have a net resource-demanding effect on the Soviet economy, even though they may release some domestic resources for military use. Technology transfer consumes domestic resources in the process of adapting Western machinery to Soviet conditions. It is quite difficult for the Soviet economic system to absorb and diffuse technology that originates in another country. For instance, the Soviet-produced Fiat, (Zhiguli) required modification of 65 per cent of its parts in order to perform adequately under Soviet conditions.[16] In the absence of Soviet data on these problems one must assume that, whilst West European technology has undoubtedly fostered Soviet economic development, its importation has also created problems for the Soviet economic system.

Soviet Economic Goals Toward Western Europe Since 1970

IMPORTS

The primary Soviet economic interest in Western Europe over the past decade has been on the import side. The USSR has sought to import technology – that is, product and know-how – which it does not possess or cannot manufacture in the quantity and quality required. Initially, the USSR attempted to buy as much as it could from the United States, because it regarded the USA as the most desirable trade partner, for both economic and political reasons. The Kremlin has always hankered after the prestige and legitimisation that a significant US–Soviet trade relationship might bring.[17] Soviet hopes were disappointed when the US Congress in 1974 tied the passage of the US–Soviet trade bill to the Jackson-Vanik and Stevenson amendments. These linked the granting of most-favoured nation status to Soviet concessions on emigration and also set a limit of $300 million on Export-Import Bank credits to the USSR. The USSR cancelled this trade bill in 1975 and thereafter it turned increasingly to Western Europe for technology imports. In 1981 Western Europe accounted for 80 per cent of the USSR's trade with the industrialised West.

The Ninth, Tenth and Eleventh Five-Year Plans stressed technology and machinery imports. According to Soviet statistics, imports from the industrialised capitalist countries were 2.5 billion rubles in 1970, and rose to 15.7 billion in 1980 and 18.1 billion in 1981.[18] Some of the most visible trade deals with Western Europe have been the Fiat plant in Togliattigrad, various petrochemical projects, the Kursk/Oskol steel plant and, of course, the gas pipeline deals discussed below. Clearly, the Soviet strategy of selectively importing Western technology for certain sectors has brought results. However, technology imports have been falling in real terms since 1978. Machinery imports from the West were $5 billion in 1975, $5.7 billion in 1978, $5.2 billion in 1979, and $4.6 in 1981 (measured in 1975 prices.[19] The USSR still imports much more machinery from Eastern than from Western Europe.

Despite the success of the Soviet strategy of technology imports, therefore, the USSR has realised that there are constraints on its ability to achieve its economic objectives *vis-à-vis* the West. When the Soviets write about this, they cite CoCom as one of the barriers to increased economic relations with Western Europe. For instance, discussing the American pipeline sanctions, a Soviet commentator referred to CoCom 'blacklists' and reminded West Europeans that it was not in their interest to 'imitate the American cowboy policy'.[20] In reality, however, it is doubtful that CoCom has significantly affected the USSR's ability to import non-military Western technology. The Soviet Union prefers to purchase standard equipment rather than state-of-the-art technology, because the latter is often too sophisticated to be comfortably integrated into the Soviet system. Moreover, there is increasing evidence that the Soviets are able to obtain illegally what they cannot import officially.[21]

A far more serious constraint on Soviet machinery imports is the lack of hard currency, which means that it is becoming increasingly difficult for the USSR to finance its imports from Western Europe. In the substantial growth of Soviet trade with Western Europe since 1970, Soviet imports from the West increased more rapidly than did exports to the West. Apart from 1974, when the large increase in oil prices enabled the Soviet Union to expand its hard currency earnings, the USSR has had chronic balance-of-payments deficits in its trade with the West. In 1980, net Soviet debt was $10 billion, and its hard currency debt service ratio (the ratio of interest and principal repayments in relation to hard currency earnings) was less than 10 per cent.[22] Thereafter the Soviets began to cut back in imports, but in 1981 these efforts came undone because of the necessity of importing large amounts of grain. In addition, hard currency reserves were strained because the USSR had to give Poland a substantial amount of hard currency aid, at the same time as world market prices for oil were falling. Net debt in 1981 was $12.5 billion.[23] The USSR is still considered to be a good credit risk, as opposed to many other CMEA nations, but there is some evidence that the Soviets themselves are wary of incurring too great a debt and are conscious of the constraints that this places on their ability to pursue their economic objectives toward Western Europe. Moreover, the Soviet balance-of-payments situation is likely to deteriorate in the 1980s because of the Polish crisis, rising imports of grain, and falling oil earnings.

Although the major Soviet interest in Western Europe involves the import of technology, grain and foodstuff imports have become increasingly important for the USSR in the last few years. In 1981, food and food-related imports consumed 45 per cent of Soviet hard currency earnings and formed 28 per cent of total imports from the developed West. Soviet imports of grain and other food from the West reached a record level of $13.7 billion, of which $7.6 billion were imports of grain flour. The West accounted for 65 per cent of total Soviet grain imports.[24] Western Europe has become an increasingly important supplier of grain to the USSR since the USA imposed a grain embargo and even after it was lifted. In the fiscal year 1980–1 (July–June), the EEC exported 1.5 million metric tons to the USSR, in 1981–2 2.4 million, and it is anticipated that the 1982–3 figure will exceed 5 million tons.

EXPORTS

Traditionally, the USSR's comparative advantage has been in the production of fuels (oil and gas), minerals, metals and other resources, and the Soviet Union has exported these to Western Europe primarily to pay for its imports of machinery. Since 1970, oil has become the Soviet Union's major hard currency earner, providing 55 per cent of total Soviet hard currency earnings in 1981, while energy exports altogether accounted for 78 per cent of hard currency earnings.[25] The Soviet Union has been the world's leading oil producer since 1974 and the second largest exporter, after Saudi Arabia, since 1980. Natural gas has since 1980 become a major hard currency earner, and will eventually constitute the greatest single source of hard currency from Western Europe. The OPEC oil embargo greatly helped the USSR to achieve its economic objectives in West Europe after 1973. First, oil prices rose, and the Soviet Union was able to increase its hard currency earnings without having to export greater quantities of oil. Secondly, the European experience with the embargo made Western Europe wary of continued dependence on Arab oil, and eager to diversify sources of energy. The USSR appeared to be an attractive partner for the realisation of these goals.

Although energy will continue to be the most important Soviet export item to Western Europe for the rest of the decade, there are various constraints that may affect the USSR's ability to keep up the volume of exports. The first of these is the uncertain energy situation within the Soviet Union. There has been much discussion in the West about whether the USSR will face a major energy crisis by the end of the decade, or whether it will be able to utilise its resources well enough to avoid it. The US Central Intelligence Agency in 1977 predicted that the USSR would become a net importer of oil by 1985.[26] The CIA subsequently revised its estimates and recognised that owing to increased investment allocations in West Siberia, Soviet oil production would decline by 17 per cent by 1985, instead of the 40 per cent figure predicted in 1977. The US Defense Intelligence Agency has consistently disagreed with the CIA, and claims that 'continuation of the USSR as a net oil exporter for the foreseeable future is anticipated'.[27] Most European estimates – for instance, that by the British Economist Intelligence Unit – are also optimistic about Soviet oil production in the 1980s.[28]

Although Western estimates of Soviet oil reserves and production capabilities differ, there is widespread agreement that natural gas holds the key to the Soviet energy future. The Soviet Union has the world's largest natural reserves, over 45 per cent of total proven gas reserves in the world. Soviet natural gas production is projected to rise at an annual rate of 7–9 per cent in the 1980s, and export growth will reach more than 15 per cent annually.[29] As long as the USSR can develop its natural gas fields quickly, gas will replace oil as the principal Soviet energy export to Western Europe, and eventually the USSR will play a more important role in world trade in natural gas than it ever did in petroleum. The Soviets' ability to produce enough natural gas will, however, depend on continued imports of West European energy equipment.

Another major constraint on Soviet energy exports to Western Europe is the USSR's need to supply Eastern Europe with much of its energy needs. Energy exports are one of the areas where there is a direct conflict between Soviet goals toward Western and Eastern Europe. Not only does the USSR export approximately 1.7 million barrels of oil a day and 33 billion cubic meters of gas a year to Eastern Europe, but the East Europeans pay below world market prices for energy, mainly in soft currency. Thus, the USSR forfeits potential hard currency earnings by supplying Eastern Europe with much of its energy. The Soviet Union has in recent years cut back on deliveries to its CMEA partners and has raised the prices they pay for oil and gas, although these remain below world levels.[30] The CIA has estimated that the USSR could earn as much as an extra $1 billion annually if it were to export to Western Europe the 10 per cent of oil deliveries that it cut to Eastern Europe in 1981.[31] However, some of this oil has been used domestically. The USSR now requires payment in hard currency from some CMEA countries for up to 10 per cent of their oil purchases, and is encouraging CMEA to purchase oil from OPEC nations in barter deals. The USSR faces conflicting economic and political pressures. If it were to maximise its economic options, it would export all its energy to Western instead of Eastern Europe. However, it needs to maintain these energy exports to Eastern Europe for political reasons.

Another factor that may adversely affect the USSR's ability to pursue its economic *Westpolitik* is the fluctuation in world oil prices. Like other monocultural economies, the Soviet Union is vulnerable to falling world commodity prices, and Soviet hard currency earnings are affected by these unpredictable trends. Moreover, the USSR does not have the capacity to compensate for falling earnings by significantly increasing quantities of exports, because it faces declining oil production.

The USSR has attempted to alleviate its financial problems

partially through the exports of gold. These sales reached substantial levels in the first half of the 1970s, around $1 billion per year, but falling gold prices after 1976 and reduced gold stocks in the USSR made this a less promising prospect. In 1981, Soviet gold sales were valued at $2.75 billion and still represent one major means of alleviating payment difficulties. Ten per cent of Soviet foreign exchange earnings come from gold, and the USSR is vulnerable to fluctuations in world market prices.

There is one major area where the USSR has not achieved its economic objectives toward Western Europe in the past decade, and that is in the export of machinery. The Soviet Union has consistently sought to relieve the problems of being primarily a raw materials exporter, and has tried to sell machinery to the West, partly because equipment is not subject to the same price fluctuations as are raw materials. However, so far, Western Europe has been reluctant to purchase Soviet finished goods because of their inferior quality, although some Soviet industrial licences have been sold.

It is customary for Soviet writers to reiterate that Western Europe has not explored the full dimensions of East–West trade because it does not import enough Soviet machinery. Often European Community 'discriminatory' measures are blamed.[32] However, a careful perusal of Soviet literature and of speeches at the 25th and 26th Party Congresses reveals that many Soviet officials are aware of the quality control problems. A major article in the early 1970s by a Deputy Minister of Foreign Trade emphasised, for instance, that if the Soviet Union were ever to participate fully in the international market it must produce machinery and other finished goods that were truly competitive for export.[33] It is unlikely, barring major economic reform in the USSR, that the Soviet Union will be able to alter the essentially complementary structure of its economic relations with Western Europe by the end of the decade, and this will mean that Moscow's major exports will remain raw materials.

In view of the payments constraints outlined above, the most popular form of economic co-operation with Western Europe from the Soviet perspective is the compensation deal. Compensation deals usually involve the export of West European equipment to the USSR, paid for by Soviet exports of products produced by the Western machinery. An example of this arrangement is the Kursk/Oskol steel complex, where the Germans and other European sub-contractors are constructing a steel mill utilising German technology for reduction of ore pellets which will be used to manufacture steel. The Soviets will pay for part of this factory by exporting iron ore pellets to the Germans. There are many similar Soviet–West European projects, but they are restricted by the European concern that such arrangements have only limited scope and are not conducive to dynamic economic relations.

The most promising area for Soviet economic relations with Western Europe in the 1980s will continue to be the energy field, where a series of barter deals will ensure continued hard currency for the USSR. Gas-for-pipe projects are essentially triangular compensation agreements, in which the three participants on both sides are equipment exporters and importers, gas exporters and importers, and the banks. The Europeans have been importing Soviet gas since the early 1970s, but it is the Urengoi export pipeline, scheduled to be completed by 1985, that has caused so much controversy within the Atlantic alliance. The Soviet Union is to construct six natural gas pipelines during the Eleventh Five-Year Plan (1980–5), one of which will be the export pipeline to Western Europe. The pipeline will increase Soviet hard currency earnings by an estimated $8 billion per annum, although a sizeable proportion of these earnings will replace income currently derived from oil. It is indisputable that these extra earnings will ease trade-offs between guns and butter for the Kremlin. This pipeline, which will supply 40–60 billion cubic meters of gas per year (depending on whether one

216

or two strands are constructed) to ten European nations, will be the key to Soviet economic *Westpolitik* in the late 1980s.[34]

Although the USSR possesses vast natural gas reserves, its ability to produce and export natural gas is inhibited by a lack of infrastructure, particularly the shortage of pipeline capacity to transport the gas from Siberia to the Western part of the USSR and to all of Europe. It is in this context that Western Europe plays a crucial role, because the Soviet Union needs West European standard equipment – particularly pipe and compressors – in order to fulfil its goal of increasing gas production by 40–50 per cent in its current Five-Year Plan. Indeed, it is using West European equipment for all six pipelines. Moreover, if the USSR wants even to maintain its oil production, it will have to make substantial Western purchases of exploration equipment, submersible pumps, gas lift equipment and offshore technology. The Soviets, in response to the American pipeline sanctions, spent much time and energy insisting that they themselves could produce the equipment for the gas pipelines.[35] As a result of the sanctions, they do indeed appear to have assigned military priority to the development of their own compressor stations and other equipment. They have also charged some other CMEA members, particularly the German Democratic Republic, with producing compressor technology. But despite Soviet assertions about their ability to complete the pipeline if necessary without Western equipment, it is undeniable that the production of their natural gas resources would be substantially delayed were Western Europe not to participate in the pipeline.

The USSR has considerable economic interests in increasing its energy trade with Western Europe. Its gas exports bring it valuable hard currency earnings – $3 billion in 1980 – which it will need even more by the end of the 1980s. Western equipment imports are indispensable if it is to produce its natural gas. Economic factors would, therefore, indicate a growing Soviet interest in increased energy trade with Western Europe, all other things being equal. This should be borne in mind for the subsequent discussion of Soviet political objectives in the pipeline deal.

Apart from energy, there are few promising areas for Soviet–West European economic relations in the 1980s. Future possible energy contracts could involve coal liquefaction plants, nuclear power stations or more gas pipelines. However, unless the CMEA nations can substantially alleviate their hard currency problems, the prospects for Soviet–West European economic relations are not bright. In addition to the socialist countries' economic difficulties, of course, the economic crisis in the capitalist world has also had a dampening effect on East–West economic relations. High Western interest rates and growing inflation have made trade with Western Europe more costly for the Soviets.

Economic relations with Western Europe have undoubtedly brought the USSR substantial economic benefits since 1970, particularly in the energy sector and in certain technological fields. However, they have done little to alleviate the basic structural problems of the Soviet economy. They may have prevented the Soviet growth rate from further declining, but they clearly cannot solve the problems of what remains essentially a modified Stalinist economic system. Both Western opponents of East–West trade and, one suspects, some overly optimistic members of the Soviet economic elite, may have exaggerated the potential impact of trade with Western Europe on the Soviet economy. Economic *Westpolitik* has not proved to be a panacea for Soviet economic ills.

The Politics of Soviet Economic Relations with Western Europe

SOVIET POLITICAL GOALS

It is impossible to decouple Soviet economic and political objectives when discussing Moscow's economic strategy toward

Western Europe. The Soviets themselves have emphasised this theme since the Bolshevik revolution. They have consistently claimed that economic and political relations interact dialectically, and reinforce peaceful ties between nations of different social systems. As a recent article put it, 'There is considerable evidence that in Western Europe, including the EEC countries, people are aware of the importance of trade and economic relations as a factor of stability and more lasting peace on the continent'.[36] Indeed, many Soviet writings imply that the USSR is not only interested in trade with Western Europe for mutually beneficial détente purposes, but is altruistically assisting Western Europe in dealing with its difficult economic problems. Regardless of whether the Soviet leaders believe that trade promotes peace, it is indisputable that the political and economic aspects of Soviet strategy toward Western Europe are closely interconnected.

The USSR essentially pursues four sets of political objectives in its economic relations with Western Europe. Moscow has discovered that it can enjoy significant economic benefits from these relations and at the same time reap considerable political gains. The main political objective is to strengthen continued West European interest in détente, and, if possible, to induce an even more accommodating West European policy toward the USSR. By creating a substantial West European interest in long-term economic relations, and fostering economic interest groups that lobby for East–West trade in these societies, Moscow has calculated that it can maintain or even increase its influence in Western Europe.

Opponents of East–West trade in the West have suggested a closely related second goal. Some have argued that a major long-term goal of Soviet economic policy toward Western Europe is to create significant economic dependencies, particularly in the energy field, which will eventually render Western Europe susceptible to Soviet political pressure or even blackmail. While this argument supposes a degree of long-term bureaucratic co-ordination and planning that may well be unlikely in the Soviet system, it is not inconceivable that some elements of the leadership have considered this as a possible strategy.

A third Soviet goal, about which there is more agreement in the West, is the desire to separate Western Europe from the United States and thereby weaken the Western alliance. It is a core Soviet political objective in Western Europe, but has significant economic dimensions. This may not have been an original objective of Soviet economic *Westpolitik*, because in the early 1970s the USSR hoped to intensify its economic relations with both Western Europe and the USA and this was arguably more important than profiting from transatlantic quarrels over Washington's more restricted East–West trade policy. However, after the Carter Administration took office, transatlantic disputes over trade with the USSR greatly increased, and under the Reagan Administration have arguably been one of the major sources of alliance tension, influencing non-economic areas as well.

A final and related, although less important, set of goals has been to encourage differences between individual European nations, prevent the emergence of a united European Community policy on East–West trade, and play one country off against the other, thereby maximising the USSR's bargaining leverage.

These Soviet policies add up to one major objective, which is as valid for economic as for political goals: the desire to divide and influence, if not conquer, Western Europe.[37]

WESTERN EUROPE'S INTEREST IN ECONOMIC RELATIONS
WITH THE USSR

In order to evaluate the extent to which the USSR has fulfilled its political objectives in pursuing economic ties with Western Europe, it is instructive to examine briefly the West European stake in economic relations with the USSR. The Europeans are as interested in pursuing these ties as is the Soviet Union. The first, and probably the most important, reason for West European interest in economic relations with the USSR is on the export side. All EEC members are trade-dependent, with foreign trade contributing as much as 30 per cent of GNP for some nations. Most countries consider that export-led employment has been a major foundation of post-war economic and political stability. Facing the highest post-war unemployment rates, all European countries are acutely aware of the need to maintain or increase exports and thereby guarantee employment. They also have effective business and trade union groups that lobby for this. In addition, Europe's steel industry confronts major problems, not the least of which are with the United States. The USSR is an attractive export market for European steel producers because of its need for West European goods. In order to facilitate these exports, most EEC members grant subsidised credits.

The second source of West European interest in trade with the USSR is on the import side. Most EEC members are deficient in indigenous energy sources, and one of their primary national security goals is the diversification of imported energy sources and the securing of new suppliers. This is, of course, less important for the UK or the Netherlands, but it is very significant for the Federal Republic of Germany, France and Italy. Since these three countries will remain overwhelmingly dependent on imported hydrocarbons for the foreseeable future they are particularly concerned to secure new sources, and the USSR appears to be an especially promising supplier of natural gas, both because it has the resources, and because it is eager to sell them for hard currency.

The third source of West European interest in trade with the USSR is political, but the Federal Republic is in a unique category here. Most European nations, particularly the British and French, have always been sceptical about the political benefits that can be gained through commercial ties with the Soviets. They have always tried to separate their political and economic relations with the USSR. The governments of both

Prime Minister Thatcher and President Mitterrand have adopted a more critical stance toward the USSR than those of their predecessors, but both Britain and France have pursued economic ties since the invasion of Afghanistan for largely economic reasons. The Italians have also tried to decouple politics and trade.

The Federal Republic, however, has always recognised that its economic relations with the USSR are politicised. A divided country, seeking to improve ties with the GDR and to strengthen links with West Berlin, West Germany is inevitably more dependent on the Soviet Union than are any of its other EEC partners. The USSR has more to give – and to take away – from West Germany than any other West European nation. Former Chancellor Schmidt recognised this when he said, in response to questions about the Soviet invasion of Afghanistan, 'Our economic relations with the Soviet Union have been built up through many years of co-operation, and primarily for political reasons'.[38] The CDU–CSU generally shares this view, and FDP Foreign Minister Genscher has also stated that trade can act as a political incentive to the Soviet Union.[39] German politicians believe that economic relations can act as an incentive to maintain the Soviet interest in European détente. The FRG is also the USSR's most important capitalist trading partner (see Tables 7.1–7.4) and trade with the Soviet Union employs about 100,000 people. West Germany is the key country for Soviet economic strategy in Western Europe.

There is, therefore, an asymmetry between Soviet and West European objectives in pursuing bilateral trade. Both the USSR and Western Europe have significant economic reasons for trading with each other. The USSR, however, expects to gain politically from this trade, whereas most EEC members, with the exception of the FRG, do not. A closed society with a vast military arsenal, the Soviet Union is in a relatively more advantageous position in terms of achieving its political objectives, since it is dealing with smaller democratic nations who are militarily inferior to it and are competing for the

Table 7.1 Soviet Trade With Selected West European Countries 1970–81 (in million rubles and percentage of total Soviet trade)

	1970	1971	1972	1973	1974	1975	1976	1977	1978	1979	1980	1981
Belgium	149.0	157.7	174.5	354.3	603.4	529.8	541.3	572.5	660.8	818.7	1,225.3	1,196.4
	0.7	0.7	0.7	1.1	1.5	1.0	1.0	0.9	0.9	1.0	1.3	1.1
United Kingdom	641.4	606.8	557.8	715.2	889.8	959.3	1,232.8	1,332.3	1,525.6	1,903.8	1,811.8	1,503.6
	2.9	2.6	2.1	2.3	2.2	1.9	2.2	2.1	2.1	2.4	1.9	1.4
Italy	471.8	494.6	463.5	613.6	1,136.8	1,426.8	1,778.5	1,880.8	1,970.8	2,155.1	3,034.3	3,486.0
	2.1	2.1	1.8	2.0	2.9	2.8	3.1	3.0	2.8	2.7	3.2	3.2
Netherlands	222.9	224.1	222.3	356.3	570.7	451.0	541.7	565.0	461.8	1,145.7	1,387.5	1,477.5
	1.0	0.9	0.9	1.1	1.4	0.9	1.0	0.9	0.7	1.4	1.5	1.4
Federal Republic of Germany	544.0	666.6	827.3	1,210.2	2,208.7	2,777.3	3,008.8	2,967.3	3,304.2	4,246.6	5,780.0	6,009.3
	2.5	2.8	3.2	3.9	5.6	5.5	5.3	4.7	4.7	5.3	6.1	5.5
France	412.8	476.2	544.3	721.6	941.0	1,296.5	1,697.0	1,723.9	1,814.0	2,623.5	3,752.7	4,189.4
	1.9	2.0	2.1	2.3	2.4	2.6	3.0	2.7	2.6	3.3	4.0	3.8

Source: Vneshniaia Torgovlia SSSR (Moscow: Izdatel'stvo Mezhdunarodnye Otnosheniia) for the years 1970, 1972, 1974, 1976, 1978, 1980, 1982.

Table 7.2   *West German Exports to the USSR by Category of Goods, 1981* [1]

Goods or categories of goods	Exports	Change[2]	Composition of exports	Export weights[3]
	DM million		*per cent*	
Exports, total	7,622	−321	100	1.9
of which:[4]				
Food	945	+263	12.4	4.1
Raw materials	45	−7	0.6	0.6
Semi-manufactures	234	−60	3.1	0.7
Finished manufactures	6,366	−530	83.5	1.9
of which:				
Primary products	2,340	−272	30.7	3.4
Finished products	4,026	−258	52.8	1.5
Selected sub-categories[5]				
Meat and meat products	158	+46	2.1	5.6
Cereal products	179	+22	2.4	31.2
Sugar	276	+78	3.6	17.7
Chemical primary products	1,015	+308	13.3	3.2
Hardware	1,757	−442	23.1	6.6
Steel tubes	296	−66	3.9	7.5
Machinery	2,142	−158	28.1	3.1
of which:				
Machine tools, rolling mills	700	−131	9.2	7.7
Electrical engineering products	370	−90	4.9	1.0
Motor vehicles	133	−7	1.7	0.2
Chemical finished products	281	+10	3.7	4.0

Notes: [1] Provisional figures. [2] Change on previous year. [3] Share in respective total West German exports. [4] Excluding returns and replacements. [5] The categories of goods cover 87 per cent of total exports.

Source: Federal Statistical Office, Wiesbaden, *Foreign Trade*, Technical Series 7, Sets 1 and 3.

limited economic possibilities presented by the Soviet market.

A Balance Sheet of Soviet Political Gains

Despite the Soviet invasion of Afghanistan, the imposition of martial law in Poland and the Soviet conventional and nuclear military build-up in Europe, West Europeans believe that détente has brought concrete results and that it is worth con-

Table 7.3 *West German Imports from the USSR by Category of Goods, 1981* [1]

Goods or categories of goods	Exports	Change [2]	Composition of exports	Export weights [3]
	DM million		per cent	
Imports, total	9,223	+1,706	100	2.5
of which: [4]				
Food	78	+1	0.8	0.2
Raw materials	938	−740	10.2	1.5
Semi-manufactures	7,368	+2,402	79.7	11.1
Finished manufactures	769	+99	8.3	0.4
of which:				
Primary products	647	+150	7.0	1.7
Finished products	122	−51	1.3	0.1
Selected sub-categories [5]				
Crude oil	581	−765	6.3	1.2
Wood for construction, timber and sawn wood	202	−27	2.2	10.6
Fuels, lubricants, natural gas	6,076	+2,217	65.9	17.2
Tar and tar distillation products	378	+76	4.1	18.6
Gold for commercial use	311	+152	3.4	14.9
Chemical primary products	446	+147	4.8	2.6

Notes: [1] Provisional figures. [2] Change on previous year. [3] Share in respective total West German imports. [4] Excluding returns and replacements. [5] The categories of goods cover 87 per cent of total imports.

Source: Federal Statistical Office, Wiesbaden, *Foreign Trade*, Technical Series 7, Sets 1 and 3.

tinuing. The Europeans had limited, regional expectations of détente, and the Soviet Union has largely abided by its original commitments to them. Western Europe, unlike the United States, never expected that détente would constrain Soviet activities in the Third World, and thus there has been less disappointment in Europe about Soviet foreign policy in the 1970s. The USSR has consciously lived up to its side of the European détente bargain in order to retain European interest in co-operative relations. Of course, one must distinguish the Federal Republic from other EEC nations. Whereas the British and French have become critical of the USSR and more sceptical about the value of détente, the Germans stress that it has worked, because the situation in West Berlin and contacts

Table 7.4   *Franco–Soviet Trade, 1979–81 (in millions of francs)*

Exports	1979	1980	1981	Per cent total	80/81 change
Food and agriculture	933	2,643	3,414	34.0	+29
Energy	16	67	90	0.8	+34
Minerals	2	3	5		+66
Metals	2,567	3,089	2,685	26.7	−13
Chemicals	651	1,017	1,032	10.3	−1.4
Industrial goods and equipment	3,708	2,736	1,825	18.2	−33
Household	28	11	10		−9
Private vehicles	20	17	10		−41
Spare parts, other	72	123	84	0.8	−32
Consumer	503	712	880	8.7	+23
Total	8,501	10,418	10,037	100	−3.6
Imports					
Food and agriculture	676	760	1,033	5.6	+36
Energy	4,662	11,510	15,243	82.8	+32.4
Minerals	50	80	63	0.3	−21
Metals	1,502	1,723	1,009	5.4	−41
Chemicals	204	324	405	2.2	+25
Industrial goods and equipment	98	95	85	0.5	−11.7
Household	7	4	15		+275
Private vehicles	163	130	197	1.0	+51.5
Spare parts, other	8	11	13		+18
Consumer	358	415	340	1.8	−18
Miscellaneous	12	13	3		−76
Total	7,741	15,067	18,406	100	+22

Source: US Embassy, Paris, based on French Customs data.

between the two Germanies have greatly improved. All parts of the mainstream German political spectrum are convinced that the USSR has fulfilled its promises to bring more stability and predictability to Europe.

Most European nations, and especially the FRG, acknowledge that the promise of closer economic ties has been one element in the continued Soviet interest in détente. The USSR itself has stressed this point. According to Foreign Trade Minister Patolichev, 'Apart from the advantages of international division of labor, business co-operation between the USSR and West European countries tends to create an atmosphere of mutual confidence, thus consolidating and strengthening peaceful interstate relations'.[40] The Soviets also stress that the Final Act of the Conference on Security and Co-operation in Europe institutionalises the linkage between the economic and political aspects of détente. West Europeans have tried to utilise this linkage in their dealings with the Soviet Union at the various CSCE follow-up conferences, because they realise that Soviet implementation of 'Baskets' I and III is partly dependent on West European willingness to proceed with basket two.

There is little evidence, however, that the second Soviet objective – that of creating economic dependencies that might render Western Europe susceptible to Soviet political pressure – has been achieved. Whereas the USSR has used oil supplies as a form of political pressure in its relations with Eastern Europe, China, Israel, and Finland, there is no evidence to date that it has ever attempted to influence Western Europe through the direct use of the gas lever. There were some reports to this effect after President Carter announced the imposition of sanctions on the USSR in reaction to the invasion of Afghanistan. Soviet Deputy Minister of Foreign Trade, Yuri Krasnov, apparently warned the Germans at the Hanover Fair that, if they complied with US sanctions, the USSR 'could turn off the natural gas tap' in an extreme case.[41] Most Europeans, however, claim that shortfalls of Soviet natural gas in the past few winters have been due to climatic, not political, exigencies. Moreover, Europeans are systematically examining alternatives to Soviet energy supplies and developing safety nets to make themselves more immune to potential Soviet pressure.[42] As Soviet–West European energy interdependence increases, the potential for Soviet leverage will grow. However, assuming that the Europeans are aware of this and make alternative arrangements for a potential loss of Soviet gas, it will be difficult for the USSR to gain significant political leverage from its raw materials exports to Western Europe. Moreover, if the USSR were to cut back gas supplies for political purposes, it would forfeit hard currency earnings.

In terms of separating Western Europe from the United States and weakening the Western alliance, the USSR must have considerable cause for satisfaction in the past few years. The alliance disarray over economic relations with the USSR has, of course, been caused by changing American policy, as opposed to any concerted Soviet strategy. American and European policies were only in harmony in the first half of the 1970s. Europeans have always been wary of using economic sanctions as a means of dealing with the USSR. They are convinced that sanctions do not alter Soviet behaviour, and can even have a negative effect on future Soviet policy. More importantly, sanctions disrupt Western economies, make Western nations unreliable business partners and usually impose more economic costs on the West than on the Soviet Union. Twenty years ago, the Germans, unlike other European nations, complied with the US order to cancel retroactively shipments of large-diameter pipe to the USSR.[43] Today, the Germans are no longer willing to jeopardise their commercial relations with the Soviet Union by following an American embargo policy.

The heightened US–European conflict began after the invasion of Afghanistan, when the United States introduced a grain embargo and high technology sanctions. Although all EEC members complied with a tightening of COCOM policies toward the USSR, none of them were willing to cut back on their machinery exports to the Soviet Union and the French even took over some contracts that had originally been won by American corporations.[44] Beginning in 1980, the Europeans, with a far greater stake in East–West trade than the Americans, refused to follow US sanctions. The Soviet Union responded with outrage over US sanctions and reminded the West Europeans that America was acting to their political and economic detriment in attempting to restrict their trade with the USSR.[45]

The pipeline sanctions were, however, the most divisive for

Atlantic unity, and appear to have had little effect on the USSR. Some Western sceptics, indeed, argued that in imposing the sanctions, the United States had succeeded in disrupting Western harmony to an extent of which the Soviet Union could never have dreamed. Shortly after his election, President Ronald Reagan lifted the grain embargo, for largely domestic reasons, but tried to dissuade the Europeans from going ahead with the Urengoi pipeline. He used the imposition of martial law in Poland in December 1981 to embargo all American shipments for the pipeline; and in June 1982, following an unsuccessful attempt to gain allied unity on this issue at the Versailles Conference, he extended these sanctions extraterritorially, to affect European companies that were producing compressors under American licences. These sanctions were finally lifted in November 1982, after acrimonious intra-allied debates, and the Europeans agreed to study East–West trade issues as a *quid pro quo* for the USA lifting of sanctions. Not only did the sanctions cause disagreements between the allies over trade, but they inevitably spilled over into other issues, and appear to have reinforced European suspicions of all aspects of American policy toward the USSR, including the question of the stationing of intermediate-range missiles in Western Europe.

Although this is not the place to discuss in detail the US objections to the pipeline, suffice it to say that the Europeans rejected American arguments that increased dependence on Soviet gas would make them vulnerable to Soviet political pressure. More importantly, they disagreed with the American assertions that it was dangerous to construct the pipeline because this would increase Soviet hard currency earnings and thereby enable it to continue its unprecedented military build-up.[46] The Soviets engaged actively in this debate and provided the Europeans with a series of arguments against American claims. Soviet press and radio commentaries cited critical West European media extensively and praised those European firms that defied US sanctions. *Izvestiia*, reminding its readers of the severe economic crisis in Europe, claimed: 'The United States' selfish financial and economic policy and blatant diktat against its allies inflicts new hardships for West European workers'.[47]

The USSR need hardly have reminded the Europeans that the USA was pursuing a policy that was harmful to their interests, but it is indisputable that the Soviet Union benefited politically from the pipeline dispute, even if only in an indirect way. The sanctions did impose some economic costs on the USSR. Although the Soviet media were full of reports about how pipeline targets had been completed on time or even ahead of schedule,[48] there was undoubtedly some disruption to the project. However, on balance the political gains from the pipeline dispute outweigh the economic costs, partly because the sanctions controversy will have long-term reverberations within the alliance and possibly impede future US–European co-ordination on East–West economic issues.

One of the Reagan Administration's arguments in favour of the pipeline sanctions was that they finally persuaded the USA's allies that NATO must rethink its economic strategy toward the USSR. In return for lifting the sanctions, Washington apparently secured a European promise to re-evaluate East–West trade strategy. The four multilateral studies to be conducted in 1983 – on technology transfer, credits, energy alternatives and overall definitions of security – were designed to gain agreement to restrict credits and possibly prevent the construction of a second strand of the export pipeline. If these studies were indeed to affect West European policy, and if the alliance were to arrive at a new consensus about restricting trade with the USSR, then prospects for future Soviet economic strategy would not be bright. It is highly unlikely, however, barring a Soviet attack on Western Europe, that European Community members will significantly restrict their trade with the USSR in the 1980s, even if they further tighten the CoCom lists and reassess credit conditions. The gap between American and European positions on these issues is sufficiently wide to guarantee future Soviet success in benefiting from intra-allied disputes.

The USSR has succeeded to some degree in using economic

relations to create competition between European states and prevent any EEC unity on East–West trade policy. However, this is probably as much a product of the inability of the European Community to agree on such a strategy as of direct Soviet policies. Certainly, the Soviets were able, in the negotiations for the pipeline, to use their monopolist bargaining leverage and play off different companies and countries against each other. The USSR sent three separate negotiating teams – one from the gas industry, one from the bank, and one from the machinery-importing organisation – to each country. In the end, the Federal Republic did not receive as many orders as it had originally anticipated, because it was underbid by France and the UK.[49] The Soviets can profit from the competitive nature of capitalism in hard economic times.

The USSR has always criticised the EEC, has only recognised it *de facto*, and has sought to prevent the emergence of any unified Community policy toward the USSR.[50] The Soviets continually stress the contradictions both between the USA and the EEC, and between individual EEC members.[51] Many Soviet comments about the inability of the EEC to evolve a viable policy on a variety of issues are in fact quite perceptive.[52] Given the enormous difficulties that the EEC will face as the Community is enlarged in the 1980s, it is unlikely that the Soviet Union will have to fear the potential power of European integration.

Moreover, the Community so far has been unable to develop a unified East–West trade policy. Members have been forbidden, since 1974, from concluding bilateral trade agreements with the Soviet Union. However, they have circumvented this provision by signing scientific co-operation agreements. For instance, the 1978 Twenty-Five Year German–Soviet Treaty is a co-operation agreement, but it includes a variety of provisions for bilateral trade. The French signed a similar accord with the USSR in 1979. There was one exception to this, however, when the EEC imposed modest sanctions on the USSR after martial law was declared in Poland. However, these sanctions were largely symbolic, and did not affect any Soviet raw material exports to Europe.

Given their attitude toward the EEC, the Soviets have always been ambivalent about the desired outcome of the EEC–CMEA negotiations which have been carried on in a desultory fashion since 1975. The Eastern European members of CMEA would like the EEC and CMEA to sign a treaty, because it might give them more room for manoeuvre. The traditional Soviet approach is to stress the USSR's interest in such a treaty and blame the EEC for the delay.[53] The conclusion of an EEC–CMEA treaty is apparently not of great economic or political concern to the Kremlin at the present time.

The USSR has undoubtedly made political gains from the economic strategy; has it incurred any political losses? One major Soviet objective has been to avoid being the object of Western linkage strategies. Although the USSR itself has no qualms about linking economic and political relations with any nation over which it has preponderant power, it has done all it could to avoid making political concessions in return for trade benefits. The Kremlin has largely succeeded in this goal, although there are some areas where it has been willing to make compromises in return for trade. It has allowed a few hundred thousand Soviet Jews and ethnic Germans to emigrate from the USSR in return for promises of Western trade or financial benefits or, in the American case, in the anticipation that this might mollify the US Congress. However, in recent years the numbers for both Soviet Jewish and ethnic German emigrants have significantly fallen. Given the contrast between the state of Soviet–American and Soviet–German relations, this suggests domestic reasons for this change. Similarly, the Soviet Union has included West Berlin in its trade agreements with the FRG, which involved a compromise with the traditional Soviet insistence that West Berlin is not a part of the FRG.[54]

Other than these concessions, however, the USSR has not been willing to compromise on any major political goal in return for trade. It has also tried to ensure that greater trade with

Western Europe does not lead to any undesirable multiplication of contacts between Western businessmen and Soviet citizens which might infect Soviet people with dangerous capitalist bacilli. So far, it has contained the potential disruptions to Soviet society created by increased East–West commerce.

Soviet Economic Strategy in the 1980s

The future of Soviet economic strategy toward Western Europe will depend on political and economic developments within the USSR and within Western Europe in the next decade. Continuity in all of these areas appears likely, but it is important to examine the possibilities for change.

The Andropov era has begun with a stress on continuity with the goals of the Brezhnev era, but with a more assertive and coherent policy toward Western Europe. Andropov has given no indication so far that the USSR might move toward a more isolationist, neo-Stalinist stance. It is likely, therefore, that the Soviet Union will continue to pursue a policy of economic interdependence with Western Europe, given its goal of maintaining good relations with Western Europe and promoting US–European dissension. The Soviet Union will not, however, in the near term significantly increase its economic intercourse with Europe for both political and economic reasons. The current generation of Soviet leaders is still part of the group that rose to power under Stalin and retains a healthy suspicion of excessive contacts with the West.[55] Perhaps the second phase of the Brezhnev succession, when the next generation comes into office at the end of the decade, will produce a more innovative outlook toward interdependence with the West.

Economic factors will also inhibit a qualitative change in the nature of economic relations with Western Europe. Although the Soviet economy is considered to be far more creditworthy that most East European economies, the Soviet debt may increase by 40 per cent in real terms between 1980 and 1985, and this will constrain Moscow's ability to finance more imports.[56] If the USSR is able to speed up the development of its natural gas resources and improve its oil production, then it might be able to finance more trade with Western Europe, but it is unliklely that it will be able to accomplish either of these goals before the end of the decade. If Eastern Europe were able to purchase large amounts of oil from the Middle East, then this would free some Soviet hydrocarbon resources for hard currency export. However, even these extra exports are unlikely to alter substantially Soviet trading policy. The income from the Urengoi pipeline will improve the Soviet hard currency situation, and, as long as Europe wants to sell its steel products to the USSR, the prospects for trade will continue much as they are in mid-1983. Economic constraints might, however, limit this trade. Unless the USSR is able to cut back on its grain imports it will spend large amounts of hard currency for agricultural purchases. In addition, the Soviet domestic economic outlook is not favourable, and growth rates are projected to decline during this decade.[57] The USSR's ability to increase its economic relations with Western Europe will, therefore, largely depend on whether Andropov is able to improve the performance of the Soviet economy, as he has promised to do.

Western Europe's continued interest in economic relations with the USSR will partly depend on its political will to maintain co-operative ties with the East. Most European governments, whether conservative or socialist, appear to believe that a minimum form of détente is worth pursuing, and they are likely to resist American attempts to abandon this policy. Thus, a new cold war is not a Western European option. It is conceivable that, if public opinion in Europe succeeds in preventing the stationing of the INF missiles and there is no Soviet–American arms control agreement, then US–European relations could significantly worsen and the Soviets might be able to increase their influence in Western Europe. However, past evidence suggests that US–European problems do not necessarily translate directly into Soviet gains. The most likely political scenario is for a continuation of European interest in economic relations with the USSR as part of a policy of reduced détente expectations.

Economic problems in Western Europe may, however, act as a constraint on expanding trade with the Soviet Union. Certain European banks are already over-exposed in Poland, and are wary of making further loans to some CMEA nations. Even though the USSR is considered a better credit risk, there will be a general reluctance in Western Europe, in a time of recession, to make major new loans to the Soviet Union. Moreover, if the USA does succeed in securing an allied agreement on credits, even one that falls below American maximum goals, there is likely to be a general tightening in European credit policy toward the Soviet Union. It is also conceivable that a second strand of the pipeline may not be built, in which case the Europeans will have limited their dependence on Soviet gas. The most likely area for future European interest in economic relations with the USSR is in the manufactured goods export sector, particularly steel.

The outlook for the 1980s is, therefore, mixed, and depends as much on the fate of the international economic system as on the byzantine manoeuvres of Soviet domestic and foreign policy. So far, Soviet economic strategy toward Western Europe has brought considerable economic and political dividends, and has incurred few economic or political costs. As long as the Western alliance remains in disarray over East–West trade, the USSR will continue to reap these benefits. Its ability to profit from them will, however, be constrained by the rigidities of its own domestic economic system and by Western Europe's determination to resist Soviet encroachments on its independence and sovereignty.

Notes to Chapter 7

The author thanks Mark Kimbrell for his research assistance.

1   Western Europe, for the purpose of this chapter, is the European Community.
2   See Herbert S. Levine, 'Soviet Economic Development, Technological Transfer and Foreign Policy', in Seweryn Bialer (ed.), *The Domestic Context of Soviet Foreign Policy* (Boulder, Colorado: Westview Press, 1981).
3   See Gunnar Adler-Karlsson, *Western Economic Warfare, 1947–1967* (Stockholm: Almquist and Wiksell, 1968), p. 84; Marshall Shulman, *Stalin's Foreign Policy Reappraised* (Cambridge, Mass.: Harvard University Press, 1963), pp. 186–7.
4   Science and technology agreements were signed with France and Italy in 1966, the UK in 1968 and West Germany in 1973.
5   For a detailed discussion of the Kosygin reforms, see Gertrude Schroeder, 'Soviet economic reform at an impasse', *Problems of Communism*, vol. 20, no. 4 (1971), pp. 36–46.
6   See John P. Hardt and Kate S. Tomlinson, 'Soviet Economic Policies in Western Europe', paper presented at University of Washington, October 1982, pp. 6–12.
7   For a discussion of these views, see John Lenczowski, *Soviet Perceptions of U.S. Foreign Policy* (Ithaca: Cornell University Press, 1982), ch. 7.
8   *Western Europe Today: Economics, Politics, the Class Struggle, International Relations* (Moscow: Progress Publishers, 1980), pp. 390–1.
9   See Erik P. Hoffman and Robbin F. Laird, *The Politics of Economic Modernization in the Soviet Union* (Ithaca: Cornell University Press, 1982), ch. 9.
10 Vladimir Treml and Barry Kostinsky, *Domestic Value of Soviet Foreign Trade: Exports and Imports in the 1972 Input–Output Table* (Washington, DC: US Department of Commerce, October 1982).
11 Jan Vanous, 'Dependence of Soviet Economy on Foreign Trade', Wharton Econometric Forecasting Associates, Centrally Planned Economies, *Current Analysis*, 14 July 1982. A CIA report agreed with these findings. See *New York Times*, 9 January 1983.
12 Jan Vanous, 'Soviet Participation in Western Trade and its Impact on the Domestic Economy', statement prepared for the workshop on 'The Premises of East–West Commercial Relations' organised by the Congressional Research Service for the Senate Foreign Relations Committee, 14–15 December 1982, Washington, DC.
13 See Philip Hanson, *Trade and Technology in Soviet–Western Relations* (New York: Columbia University Press, 1981).
14 See, for instance, Anthony Sutton, *Western Technology and Soviet Economic Development* (3 Vols) (Stanford: Hoover Institution Press, 1973).
15 See Thane Gustafson, *Selling Them the Rope* (Santa Monica, Cal.: The RAND Corporation, 1981).
16 Hardt and Tomlinson, *Soviet Economic Policies*, pp. 13–16.
17 For an account of Soviet–American economic relations in the early 1970s, see Marshall I. Goldman, *Detente and Dollars: Doing Business with the Soviets* (New York: Basic Books, 1975).
18 *Ekonomicheskaia Gazeta*, no. 14, 1982.
19 Vanous, 'Soviet Participation', p. 6.
20 Radio Moscow in German to Germany, 12 October 1982, in FBIS, *Daily Report: Soviet Union*, vol. 3, no. 200, 15 October 1982.
21 The United States government, which has published numerous studies documenting illegal technology transfer, introduced 'Operation Exodus', which

involved a tightening of customs controls on all points of exit from the USA and in California's Silicon Valley, to stem these illegal transfers from the USA. However, the USA also claims that illegal transfers occur in Europe.

22 Robert Campbell, 'The Economy', paper written for the Georgetown University Center for Strategic and International Studies' Soviet Project, August 1982, p. 66. Poland's debt service ratio in the same year, by contrast, was 100 per cent.

23 Hardt and Tomlinson, *Soviet Economic Policies*, p. 18.

24 Vanous, 'Soviet Participation', p. 5.

25 Vanous, 'Soviet Participation', p. 2.

26 US Central Intelligence Agency, *Prospects for Soviet Oil Production*, ER 77–10270 (Washington, DC: April 1977).

27 Statement of Major General Richard X. Larkin and Edward M. Collins, Defense Intelligence Agency, before the Joint Economic Committee, Subcommittee on International Trade Finance and Security Economics, 'Allocation of Resources in the Soviet Union and China – 1981' (8 July 1981).

28 David Wilson, *Soviet Oil and Gas to 1990* (London: Economist Intelligence Unit, 1980).

29 Statement of Major Larkin, 'Allocation of Resources'.

30 See US Congress, Office of Technology Assessment, *Technology and Soviet Energy Availability* (Washington, DC: Government Printing Office, 1981), ch. 9.

31 Hardt and Tomlinson, *Soviet Economic Policies*, p. 24.

32 *Western Europe Today*, p. 392.

33 N. Smeliakov, 'Delovye Vstrechi', *Novyi Mir*, no. 12, 1973, pp. 203–39.

34 For a detailed discussion of the pipeline, see Angela E. Stent, *Soviet Energy and Western Europe*, The Washington Papers no. 90 (New York: Praeger, 1982).

35 *Pravda*, 25 August 1982.

36 V. Gorsky, 'European trade: progress and difficulties', *International Affairs* (Moscow), August 1981, p. 81.

37 See Angela Stent, 'Accommodation: the USSR and Western Europe', *The Washington Quarterly*, vol. 5, no. 4 (Autumn, 1982), pp. 93–105.

38 Statement by Chancellor Schmidt, 28 February 1980, quoted in 'Der Bundes-minister fuer Wirtschaft', *Der Deutsche Osthandel 1980* (Bonn, 1980) p. 62.

39 Hans Dietrich Genscher, 'Toward an overall Western strategy for peace, freedom and progress', *Foreign Affairs*, vol. 61, no. 1 (Autumn, 1982), p. 54.

40 N. S. Patolichev, 'The USSR – for equal and business cooperation', *Foreign Trade* (Moscow), July 1982, p. 4.

41 Reuters, *East–West Trade Newsletter*, nos 17 and 18 (April 1980).

42 See Stent, *Soviet Energy and Western Europe*, pp. 86–96.

43 For a complete description of the 1962–3 NATO pipe embargo and its con-sequences, see Angela Stent, *From Embargo to Ostpolitik: The Political Economy of West German–Soviet Relations 1955–1980* (New York: Cambridge University Press, 1981), ch. 5.

44 For instance, the French sold a computer to TASS for the 1980 Olympics which had originally been contracted by the US company Sperry-Univac. President Carter in 1978 denied Sperry-Univac a licence to show disapproval of the Soviet treatment of dissidents. The French also took over a contract to build a steel mill in Novolipetsk, after the USA forced Armco to cancel the deal following the in-vasion of Afghanistan.

45 See G. Stepanov, 'East–West business ties: a sphere of cooperation, not an instrument of blackmail', *International Affairs* (Moscow), December 1981, pp. 41–9.

237

46 For a full discussion of the American objectives, see Stent, *Soviet Energy and Western Europe*, pp. 78–86.

47 *Izvestiia*, 7 September 1982.

48 See, for instance, TASS International Service, 3 September 1982, which says of a new compressor factory in Leningrad, 'This is the Leningraders' response to the embargo imposed by the US administration on supplies of this equipment to the Soviet Union'.

49 *Financial Times*, 30 September 1981.

50 For more on this, see Ebehard Schulz, *Moskau und die Europaeische Intergration* (Munich: R. Oldenbourg Verlag, 1975).

51 N. Klimenko, 'Nekotorye Aspekty Vozdeistviia Kapitalisticheskoi Integratsii, na Obostrenie Protivorechii EES i SShA', *Ekonomika Sovetskoi Ukrainy*, January 1981, pp. 78–84; V. Baranovskii, 'EES: Realnosti "Politicheskogo Sotrudnichestva"', *Mirovaia Ekonomika i Mezhdunarodnye Otnosheniia*, pp. 96–105.

52 See, for instance, Yuri Shishkov, 'EEC in the eighties', *New Times*, no. 19, 1981, pp. 22–4.

53 See Alexei Chertanov, 'CMEA–EC relations: two approaches', *New Times*, no. 35, 1979, pp. 18–20.

54 See Stent, *From Embargo to Ostpolitik*, chs 4 and 8.

55 Seweryn Bialer, *Stalin's Successors: Leadership, Stability and Change in the Soviet Union* (New York: Cambridge University Press, 1980), Pt 11.

56 Daniel Bond, 'CMEA Growth Projections for 1981–85 and the Implications of Restricted Western Credits', cited in Hardt and Tomlinson, *Soviet Economic Policies*, p. 61.

57 Growth rates are projected to decline to about 2.5 per cent per annum in the late 1980s.

8

Arms Control Strategies

Jane Sharp

Soviet arms control diplomacy toward Western Europe appears to be guided by the same long-term objectives as Soviet defence policy, namely:

- to maintain Eastern Europe as an ideological and military buffer against both destabilising ideas and traditional enemies from the West;
- to limit the military potential and undermine the political cohesion of NATO in general, and to curb the Bundeswehr and weaken the Bonn–Washington axis in particular – not only to reduce the threat to the physical security of the Soviet homeland but to deny NATO the capability to interfere with Soviet control of Eastern Europe;
- to limit foreign and military bases around the Soviet perimeter, most especially American forward-based nuclear weapons in West Germany; and
- to gain recognition of the Soviet Union as a superpower co-equal with the United States and to demonstrate the positive trend in the 'correlation of forces' in favour of socialism.

Given the geography and historical experiences of Tsarist Russia and the Soviet Union, these are rational objectives. Charles III, Napoleon, Kaiser Wilhelm and Hitler all invaded

239

through the territory of the states which now comprise the northern tier of the East European buffer zone; despite the temporary alliance against Nazi Germany in the 1940s, the Western powers have generally been hostile to the Soviet Union and interfered in the Russian civil war in an effort to defeat the Bolsheviks; the suffering at German hands in two world wars inevitably bred a generation of Soviet leaders paranoid about a new German threat; and the ring of alliances formed around the Soviet Union in the late 1940s and 1950s reinforced traditional Russian fears of foreign encirclement.

This chapter will try to assess how the Soviet Union has pursued these security goals in Europe at four specific negotiating forums: the multilateral Conference for Security and Co-operation in Europe (CSCE), the inter-alliance negotiations on mutual and balanced force reductions (MBFR); and the bilateral talks on strategic arms limitation (SALT) and intermediate-range nuclear forces (INF).

The Conference on Security and Co-operation in Europe

The Conference on Security and Co-operation in Europe (CSCE) stemmed from a Soviet initiative designed to secure Western recognition of Soviet control over Eastern Europe by codifying the political and territorial changes effected during, and immediately following, the Second World War. A pan-European security conference was first proposed in 1954 by Molotov, revived in 1964 by the Polish Foreign Minister Adam Rapacki (whose government had good reason to seek the international recognition of its new borders), reiterated with increasing frequency at Warsaw Pact gatherings through the mid and late 1960s, and finally convened as the CSCE in Helsinki in 1972.[1]

Initially, Soviet objectives for such a conference appeared to be consolidation of their political hegemony over the East and confirmation of post-1945 borders; it was to be, in effect, the Second World War Peace Conference. Another declaratory objective through the mid-1960s was dissolution of the two military blocs to reduce American influence on the continent, and the establishment of a new pan-European security system. After the Czechoslovakian crisis of 1968 and the Sino–Soviet clashes on the Ussuri River in March 1969, the Soviets seemed more ready to embrace the military as well as the political status quo in Europe.

Before the CSCE was convened, most of what the Soviets had sought at the conference had already been achieved through the *Ostpolitik* of Chancellor Willy Brandt, the essential feature of which was acceptance of the political and territorial realities in Europe, however painful these were in terms of perpetuating the division of Germany. A series of mutually reinforcing concessions by West Germany on the one hand and East Germany, Poland, Czechoslovakia, and the Soviet Union on the other, made possible a set of treaties which resolved a number of formerly contentious issues. For the Federal Republic, it meant abandoning the insistence on progress toward German re-unification as a precondition for East–West détente, acceptance of the Oder–Neisse line which explicitly recognised the post-war transfer of territory from Germany to Poland, acknowledging the invalidity of the 1938 Munich Treaty, and embracing Willy Brandt's ingenious concept of two states within one nation which made possible the Basic Treaty accepting both halves of Germany. These concessions were balanced by a more secure Western position on Berlin in the Four Power Berlin Agreement, conclusion of the Final Protocol of which, in June 1972, was one of the preconditions for Western participation at CSCE; another being Eastern participation in the Vienna talks on mutual force reductions (MBFR).

Three 'baskets' of issues make up the (CSCE) agenda. Basket I deals with military security and Basket II with economic relations, both high priorities for the Soviet Union. In Basket III, however, the NATO and non-aligned states managed to insert fundamental issues of human rights, thereby providing an unusual opportunity to call Soviet and East European governments to account for their domestic practices in an international forum.[2] In addition, CSCE commissions and Helsinki watchdog committees were established in most of the thirty-five participating countries – including more than one of the Soviet republics – which were a source of considerable embarrassment to East bloc regimes, particularly in Czechoslovakia and the Soviet Union.[3] A communiqué issued in late 1976 by the Warsaw Pact Political Consultative Committee reflected concern that East–West détente and the CSCE process might be getting out of hand. It noted, *inter alia*, that:

- The 1975 Helsinki Accords had made a positive contribution to East–West détente in Europe, but the West was exploiting the human rights issue in Basket III at the expense of security and co-operation in Baskets I and II;
- East–West co-operation in humanitarian and cultural fields must not be confused with ideological capitulation by the socialist states to capitalist values;
- if the East is to fulfil its CSCE obligations to promote further East–West co-operation it must consolidate its unity both in foreign policy and ideological cooperation.[4]

Two new issues were raised at the Bucharest meeting for consideration at the CSCE review conference scheduled for November 1977 in Belgrade: that both NATO and the Warsaw Pact should pledge 'no first use' of nuclear weapons, and that neither alliance should expand its current membership. The first was a long-standing Soviet position, designed to undermine NATO's flexible response doctrine which relies on deterring the threat of a Soviet conventional attack by threatening a nuclear response. The timing coincided with an effort by the United States Defense Secretary Schlesinger to increase the credibility of extended deterrence over NATO by acquiring more accurate, 'cleaner' nuclear warheads capable of 'limited' nuclear strikes.[5] The stipulation that neither alliance should increase its membership was an obvious effort to prevent Spain from joining NATO and perhaps a veiled threat that the Soviets would then have the right or even the obligation to expand membership of the Warsaw Pact.

In the interval between the signing of the CSCE Final Act in Helsinki in July 1975 and the convening of the first review conference in Belgrade in November 1977, Helsinki 'watchdog' committees in Moscow, as well as in Armenia, Georgia, Lithuania and the Ukraine produced over 200 reports on Soviet compliance with the CSCE, including problems of emigration, conditions of political prisoners, and religious persecution. These reports were smuggled out to the West and beamed back to the Soviet Union by radio. Together with President Carter's human rights campaign, which began in early 1977, this activity soon became intolerable to the Soviet regime which began to clamp down on the monitoring committees. By early 1978 almost half the membership had either been deported or imprisoned, though trials of the more prominent activists like Orlov, Scharansky and Ginzburg were delayed until after the Belgrade conference.[6]

With respect to Basket I, security issues, all CSCE participants were deemed to have complied adequately with the modest confidence-building measures (CBMs) in the Helsinki Final Act; namely, to give twenty-one days' prior notice of military manoeuvres involving more than 25,000 men. Many CSCE participants would have liked the Belgrade conference to beef up these CBMs; though with different emphases. The Soviets wanted a separate conference to discuss pan-European security measures and urged a ban on large exercises to curb the NATO practice of large annual 'reforger' exercises involving American and West European forces each autumn; the Western states wanted requirements to notify smaller exercises, to provide fuller information, and to increase the number of observers; Romania wanted to deny manoeuvres close to the borders of another state, presumably in an attempt to curb the Soviet practice of harassing exercises, and ideally would like to see a ban on any increase in foreign-stationed troops to prevent any redeployment of Soviet troops from central Europe nearer to Romania – as a result of an MBFR agreement, for example. All these issues were debated at Belgrade but little was achieved except to publicise the poor Soviet record of compliance with human rights issues. While obviously embarrassing for the Soviets, this was not, however, wholly satisfactory to the West European, Canadian and non-aligned participants, who sometimes were hard put to hide their irritation with the Carter Administration's holier-than-thou attitude to human rights. Many felt that, while the Soviet record was indeed deplorable, the remedy lay in quiet diplomacy rather than public castigation. Chancellor Schmidt and Premier Trudeau of Canada, in particular, warned the United States in July 1977 that an over-zealous campaign on human rights threatened East–West détente.[7]

Between the Belgrade and Madrid review conferences, the impact of the CSCE on the Soviet bloc continued to be felt, most notably in Poland, where, for example, Gdansk shipyard workers seeking independent trade unions invoked the Helsinki Final Act as rationale for their demands. But if the CSCE seemed to foster more interest in free expression in the East, East–West relations were not noticeably enhanced. In May 1978, responding to steady improvements in Soviet forces, NATO countries agreed to increase defence budgets by 3 per cent annually and to establish a new long-term defence programme (LTDP), and in December 1979 to deploy new long-range American nuclear weapons in Western Europe which could hit targets on Soviet territory; after which Brezhnev withdrew an earlier offer to negotiate limits on medium-range missiles. Later the same month the Soviet Union invaded and occupied Afghanistan which in turn had a negative impact on both SALT and CSCE. President Carter withdrew the SALT II Treaty from consideration by the United States Senate, effectively suspending the ratification process indefinitely, while the Madrid CSCE review conference in September opened with a barrage of criticism of the Soviet Union both for its continued occupation of Afghanistan and increasingly harsh repression of CSCE monitoring groups.

A New European Disarmament Conference?

At the first United Nations Special Session on Disarmament in May 1978 French President Giscard D'Estaing proposed a new European Disarmament Conference (CDE), initially envisaged as quite separate from the CSCE process although the participants would be the same thirty-five countries. The emphasis was to be on a first stage agreement imposing mandatory, verifiable, and militarily significant confidence-building measures (CBMs), as distinct from the modest, voluntary CBMs of the 1975 Helsinki Final Act. This would be followed by a second stage agreement on reductions of conventional forces. In line with the long-standing French position that their own nuclear arsenals were non-negotiable, nuclear arms control was explicitly excluded from the CDE. Finally, and most importantly, the CDE aimed to curb the geographical advantages enjoyed by the Soviet Union at CSCE and MBFR by extending the European CBM zone to the Ural mountains.

Initially, both the Carter Administration and the West German government were lukewarm to the French initiative, believing such a conference might not only let the Soviets off the hook on the human rights issue, but could also undermine the MBFR negotiations. Eventually, after the French agreed to link their proposal more firmly to the continuing CSCE process, all the NATO and EEC countries endorsed the CDE.[8]

For precisely the reason that some Western governments were sceptical of a new pan-European arms control conference – insulation from the human rights issue – the Soviets thoroughly approved of the idea and had indeed suggested such a conference at Belgrade in October 1977.[9] Warsaw Pact foreign ministers meeting in Budapest in May 1979 reiterated the Soviet call for a separate Conference on Military Détente and Disarmament in Europe (CMDDE), a proposal which was further refined through 1979 and 1980 and formally presented by Poland to the Madrid CSCE review conference on 8 December 1980.

At this stage there were a number of differences between the Eastern CMDDE proposal and the French CDE. In terms of scope, the Warsaw Pact envisaged a conference devoted to military détente quite distinct from the economic and human relations encompassed by Baskets II and III at the CSCE. The confidence-building measures envisaged in the French proposal would be more militarily significant, more binding and more easily monitorable than those proposed by the East, and would apply to a greater geographical area. The CBMs proposed by the East would only apply to a narrow 250km strip inside the Soviet border, whereas the French proposal would include all the Soviet western military districts. As initially proposed in Bucharest in 1976, the Eastern proposal also included a treaty prohibiting the first use of nuclear or conventional weapons in Europe and another agreement prohibiting the expansion of either NATO or the Warsaw Pact.

In a number of articles and speeches through 1981 the Soviet position on the geographical zone for new European CBMs was modified, most notably by President Brezhnev in his address to the 26th CPSU in February and in his interview with *Der Spiegel* in November. In February he said that the Soviets could accept a European CBM zone stretched as far east as the Urals, but hinted that there would have to be a corresponding expansion of the Western zone, to include, for example, the reporting of naval and air force activities in the Atlantic and maybe even on the Eastern seaboard of North America. In Madrid in July Western delegates agreed to include those military activities in contiguous sea and air space which were integral to operations on the continent, but this did not appear to satisfy the Soviet CSCE delegates who suggested that the Western maritime zone should be as wide as the continental portion of the zone. But in Madrid in October, and in the *Der Spiegel* interview in November, the Soviets adopted a more modest position, suggesting that the CBM zone should include 'island territories adjacent to Europe, respective sea and ocean areas and the air space over them'.[10] This formulation would include islands like the Portuguese Azores which are to be used as fuelling stations for the operation of the new United States Rapid Deployment Force.

The bridging of differences on the geographical zone was complemented in February 1981 by the Reagan Administration's rationalisation of the French CDE proposal as a new surprise attack conference, and by a Yugoslav initiative in March which suggested that the new CBMs should be designated Confidence and Security-Building Measures (CSBMs) to emphasise the need for more substantial measures than the existing CSCE CBMs. By July, a substantial measure of consensus had been reached on the goals for a new CDE, and the non-aligned countries were drawing up a draft Final Document for the Madrid review of the CSCE.

The imposition of martial law in Poland in December 1981, however, put a damper on all CSCE activities as the Reagan Administration in particular, but the Western states in general, used the Madrid forum to castigate the Soviets for menacing military manoeuvres on the Polish border, and the Jaruselski regime for harassment and repression of Solidarity. Max Kampelman, the United States delegate, threatened to break off all CSCE business until martial law was lifted. Not all the West Europeans were equally enthusiastic about this course of action, the West Germans being the most reluctant, and through 1982 the United States stand was gradually softened, though even as late as October the Americans were threatening not to participate in the Madrid sessions scheduled for the following month.

During November, however, President Brezhnev died and

was replaced by Yuri Andropov, Lech Walesa was released from custody along with several hundred other Solidarity detainees, and the Polish government was promising to ease martial law. At least in its opening sessions the 1982–3 conference in Madrid proceeded in a businesslike manner markedly different from the confrontational atmosphere which characterised the 1981–2 forum. Whether Soviet tactics have changed with the new leadership, or whether a new pan-European conference will be any less of a human rights trial for the Kremlin, remains to be seen.

The Vienna Talks on Mutual (and Balanced) Force Reduction

The Vienna talks on M(B)FR stem from a NATO initiative launched in June 1968, but the antecedents can be traced to various disengagement proposals after the Second World War, when the crucial problem for both East and West was how to reabsorb Germany into the international system. In the early 1960s, when the demilitarisation and reunification of Germany were no longer at issue and after the Berlin and Cuban crises had subsided, Soviet leaders joined officials of the Kennedy and Johnson Administrations in a series of informal discussions about the feasibility of mutual troop withdrawals. Some reductions were effected during this period, though apparently only of the extra forces each had deployed to the two Germanies during the 1961 Berlin crisis.[11] After Khrushchev's fall from power and the onset of heavy American military involvement in Vietnam, these 'mutual example' talks were discontinued, in part because of Soviet sensitivity to Chinese criticism that the Kremlin was easing the withdrawal of American troops from central Europe to fight communists in Asia.[12]

The United States was not the only NATO ally with extra-European commitments in the mid-1960s. France, Belgium,

Portugal, Britain and the Netherlands were all tidying up remnants of Empire, and these extra-alliance activities, combined with a general easing of East–West tensions on the continent, led to a steady trickle of combat forces away from the central front. In all the NATO countries, but particularly in the United States, this process was encouraged by fiscal conservatives like Senator Mansfield who first proposed legislation for the return of foreign-based US troops in 1966. In 1967, after France had left NATO's integrated military command, and when even the West Germans were contemplating force reductions, West European leaders (most notably Denis Healey in Britain and Willy Brandt in West Germany), suggested a formal reduction agreement between NATO and the Warsaw Pact. Thus the invitation to the Soviet Union and the East European countries to negotiate a mutual and balanced reduction of forces, issued from the North Atlantic Council meeting in Rejkyavik in June 1968, was primarily a device to halt further unilateral withdrawals of NATO troops. It also served as a pragmatic counter-proposal to the repeated, but somewhat vague, Soviet proposals for a pan-European security conference.

The crisis in Czechoslovakia in the summer of 1968 delayed not only the Soviet response to the Reykjavik invitation, but also the beginning of the Soviet–American Strategic Arms Limitation Talks (SALT) which had been scheduled for August 1968, but did not get under way until November 1969. The first sign of Soviet interest in MBFR came at a meeting of Warsaw Pact foreign ministers in Budapest in June 1970. A second signal emerged at the CPSU conference in Moscow in March 1971, when President Brezhnev tied force reductions in Europe to the long-standing Soviet campaign to abolish foreign military bases. Six weeks later, speaking in Tbilisi on the 50th anniversary of the Georgian Republic, the Soviet leader called explicitly for negotiations on force reductions, chastising the NATO countries for their lack of resolve 'to taste proposals that interest you'.[13] Many political analysts suspect that Brezhnev's speech was timed to defuse the latest Mansfield amendment before the United States Senate, and thereby avoid any precipitate unilateral withdrawal of American troops from Europe.

This may seem paradoxical, since Soviet writings have often stressed the pernicious effects of the American military presence on the continent and especially of the threat represented by the Bonn–Washington axis. This was a dominant theme, for example, in the Soviet campaign for a pan-European security conference in the early 1960s. After the turbulence in Czechoslovakia in 1967 and 1968, however, the Soviets showed more interest in preserving the status quo in Europe than in ridding the continent of American troops. This Soviet interest was so obvious by the early 1970s that United States Senator Eugene McCarthy suggested in congressional hearings – one suspects only half in jest – that the Kremlin should be asked to bear half the cost of keeping the United States 7th Army in West Germany.[14]

Soviet Objectives at MBFR

Despite their declared interest in MBFR, the Soviets would not commit themselves to a firm date for negotiations until the Western powers had agreed to participate in a European security conference, and the West German government had recognised East Germany as an independent state and accepted the Oder–Neisse line as the post-war German–Polish border. Once the MBFR negotiations began in 1973, however, the Soviets embraced the initiative as their own, claiming that the Vienna talks stemmed from repeated Soviet proposals for force reductions since 1946.[15] Soviet tactics in Vienna suggest, however, that rather than seeking force reductions, the Kremlin sees MBFR as useful to maintain a *droit de regard* over NATO force planning, to prevent the emergence of a West European Defence Community led by a stronger, more independent West Germany, and to maintain the equilibrium of military force which has kept the peace in Europe since 1945.[16]

Pursuit of formal arms control agreements and the prospect of contractual limits on force levels tends to focus attention on the asymmetries between the force postures of potential adversaries. This encourages the matching of force beyond what otherwise might seem necessary for military purposes. Once engaged in MBFR, the Soviets probably saw at least four interlocking balances in need of maintenance. First, a rough parity between NATO and the Warsaw Pact, to deter NATO from attempting to interfere with any police action the Soviets might need to undertake in Eastern Europe. Secondly, to ensure that West Germany is not tempted to intervene in support of any future uprising in East Germany, the Soviets need some kind of balance between Soviet forces in East Germany and the Bundeswehr; thirdly, as Brezhnev's helping hand to the Nixon Administration in dealing with Senator Mansfield demonstrated, for the near future at least, the Soviets also want to retain American troops in Western Europe and a certain ratio of foreign forces to indigenous forces in West Germany, as a constraint on the Bundeswehr. Retaining American troops on the continent also helps of course to rationalise Soviet forces in Eastern Europe. This brings us to the fourth essential component of the balance, which is the equilibrium between stationed Soviet and indigenous East European forces, to prevent any individual East European country from acquiring the capability to resist the kind of Warsaw Pact military action which subdued Czechoslovakia in 1968.

MBFR offers the Soviets an opportunity to maintain all four components of the European balance at current, or even lower levels of force. Troop reductions might seem attractive in theory, especially since the Soviets face a serious downfall in the supply of draft age manpower in the 1980s.[17] In practice, however, the force requirements for controlling potential disruptions in Eastern Europe, especially after the upheavals in Poland through 1980 and 1981, suggest little hope for an MBFR agreement that goes much beyond codifying the status quo.

The Impact of MBFR on Perceptions of the NATO/Warsaw Pact Balance

Maintaining the status quo was also the original NATO objective for MBFR in 1967–8. At that time the US Central Intelligence Agency (CIA) estimated that NATO and Pact forces were approximately balanced in Central Europe, and the four guidelines for the negotiations issued in June 1968 suggested that the objective was to maintain the same balance at lower levels.[18] This perception of parity persisted despite the Pact invasion of Czechoslovakia because the five divisions of Soviet occupation troops – some 70,000 men – which remained there were offset in NATO by the steady build-up in the Bundeswehr through the late 1960s.

In late 1968 the CIA was estimating between a 10,000 and a 35,000 manpower advantage for the Pact,[19] but in late 1969 Helmut Schmidt, then Defence Minister of the Federal Republic, obviously felt this was close enough to parity. In a speech to the West European Union Assembly on 10 December 1969, outlining the principles to be observed at MBFR, Schmidt said:

> . . . force reductions on both sides of the iron curtain must be carried out along comparable lines; in other words, the ratio of relative force capabilities must not be changed.[20]

The Nixon Administration inherited the MBFR proposal when it took office in January 1969 and, though preoccupied with Vietnam, eventually undertook its own review of general purpose force needs in relation to MBFR.[21] In his February 1971 Foreign Policy Report to the Congress, the President still referred to NATO/Pact parity:

> The economic strength of the NATO nations, we found, makes us considerably stronger in military potential than the Warsaw Pact. We and our allies collectively enjoy a threefold

advantage in gross national product and a twofold advantage in population. The actual balance in conventional military forces in Europe is much closer, however. NATO's active forces in peacetime are rougly comparable to those of the Warsaw Pact.[22]

By the spring of 1972, however, with formal MBFR negotiations now definitely on the horizon, official Western estimates of Pact manpower shot upwards to declare a Pact advantage of more than 100,000 men. Sceptical legislators in the United States, who later found it hard to believe that the Warsaw Pact could have increased its forces so dramatically without anyone having noticed, were told by intelligence analysts that the new estimates did not necessarily reflect increased Pact strength but simply better CIA counting methods.[23] Whatever the rationale for the new estimates – the accumulation of useful political bargaining chips by NATO or more accurate intelligence gathering – the Soviets have consistently maintained that Pact manpower has not increased in the MBFR guidelines area since the late 1960s.[24]

Thus, when MBFR negotiations began in 1973, the Soviets asserted that the existing balance must be preserved, while NATO officials now spoke not of maintaining but of 'improving' the balance. When Ambassador Stanley Resor made his opening statement in Vienna, he said three kinds of imbalance were in need of correction: a Pact advantage in manpower, a Pact advantage in tanks and a geographical advantage in the sense that returning Soviet troops to the central front across land was a much simpler operation than the transatlantic crossing required for returning American forces.[25]

Soviet officials denied an overall Pact advantage in manpower though obviously did not dispute the preponderance of stationed Soviet troops in Eastern Europe over stationed American troops in Western Europe. For them the more critical balance, as already noted, was between stationed Soviet forces and the indigenous West German forces. The Soviets acknowledged a Pact advantage in tanks but rationalised this as part of the stable status quo and necessary for the defence of Eastern Europe. With respect to the geographical factor, the Soviets acknowledged the asymmetries between the two alliances but denied that this translated into a military advantage for the Pact, noting that many military bases in the United States were closer to Western Europe than many Soviet military districts were to Soviet garrisons in Eastern Europe.[26]

Converging Positions in Vienna

The proposals each side presented in Vienna reflected these fundamentally different views of the balance, with NATO arguing for asymmetrical reductions to achieve a more stable equilibrium and the Soviets insisting on equal percentage cuts to preserve the status quo. NATO's opening position called for a two-stage reduction to common manpower ceilings. In the first stage 68,000 Soviet troops would be withdrawn from Eastern Europe, 29,000 Americans from Western Europe. In the second stage all national forces would take cuts to reach common alliance ceilings of 700,000 ground forces and 900,000 ground and air forces combined. By contrast, the Pact called for equal percentage cuts in both alliances, setting national sub-ceilings on residual forces to prevent West German increases making up for possible shortfalls in other NATO national contributions.

The NATO proposal was augmented in December 1975 with the offer to withdraw fifty-four nuclear capable F-4 aircraft, thirty-six Pershing IA ballistic missiles, and 1,000 nuclear war-heads, and to place residual ceilings on remaining holdings of these weapons, in exchange for the withdrawal of a Soviet tank army of 68,000 men and 1,700 tanks and reductions of man-power to common ceilings. This proposal, often referred to as 'option III', was first discussed within NATO in early 1972 when the revised CIA estimates of Warsaw Pact forces suggested that the Soviets would have no incentive to reduce their perceived advantage in manpower and tanks unless NATO offered to reduce its own advantage in battlefield nuclear weapons.[27]

Consistent with their view of the balance the Soviets responded in February 1976 by calling for symmetrical reductions: fifty-four American F-4s to be offset by fifty-four Soviet SU-7 Fitter aircraft, thirty-six Pershing IAs to be offset by the same number of Soviet SCUD-B missiles, as well as equal numbers of nuclear warheads and air defence missiles.[28] At this stage the Soviets still did not accept common manpower ceilings and made no effort to offset their tank advantage, and NATO rejected the Soviet offer outright.

In June 1976 the Soviets produced their first numerical data for Warsaw Pact manpower: 805,000 for total Pact ground forces plus 182,000 airmen to make a combined manpower total of 987,300 in the MBFR guidelines area. Though it was something of a breakthrough for the Soviet Defence Ministry to release any data, these numbers resembled NATO estimates of Pact forces prior to the Spring of 1972, and were some 150,000 less, on ground forces alone, than NATO's current working estimates at MBFR. Thus in June 1978, when the Soviets offered another 'concession' by agreeing to NATO's common manpower ceiling for each alliance, Western delegates were not very favourably impressed because Soviet data suggested something so close to parity that the Warsaw Pact delegates could still insist on their earlier goal of equal percentage reductions to reach the common ceiling. More data on the East European and Soviet forces was released in 1978 and again in June 1980, when it became clear that NATO estimates for East German and Czechoslovak forces were close to those acknowledged by the Soviet Defence Ministry, and that the greatest discrepancy between Eastern and Western estimates was in Soviet and Polish forces. As of early 1983, however, the Soviets were unwilling to further disaggregate the data to allow Western analysts to pinpoint exactly how their counting methods differed, and which if any military units the Soviets were not counting. It was determined that Polish amphibious forces were counted by

NATO and discounted by the Pact, but this was not sufficient to account for the whole discrepancy.

In the late 1970s, with little movement toward resolution of the data problem, the emphasis in Vienna shifted from quantitative reductions and residual limitations to measures designed to give warning of sudden reinforcements and concentrations, the so-called 'associated measures' by which an MBFR agreement might be monitored and which would also serve to reduce the risk of surprise attack. In December 1979 NATO proposed a package of such measures in Vienna which included provisions for pre-notification of entry of large numbers of troops into the reduction area and of major 'out of garrison' activities; restriction of entry to and departure from the reduction area only through posts permanently manned by observers of the opposing alliance; periodic exchanges of force data; an annual quota of inspections by each alliance of the others' forces; and the establishment of a standing consultative commission to resolve any ambiguity about compliance with an MBFR agreement.[29]

Since this package was offered in Vienna only two days after the decision to modernise NATO's long-range theatre nuclear weapons was announced in Brussels, the response from the East was lukewarm at best, the more so since some of the systems being upgraded by the double-track decision in Brussels had been offered in the Option III proposal in Vienna some four years earlier. With the December 1979 TNF modernisation decision, NATO's Option III proposal was formally withdrawn, and since then NATO has been unwilling to consider any limits on armaments in MBFR.

Over the next two years, however, coincident with renewed pressure in the United States Congress to withdraw American troops from Europe, the Soviets adopted a more conciliatory attitude at MBFR, much as Senator Mansfield's efforts to effect unilateral withdrawals appear to have influenced Leonid Brezhnev in 1971. In February 1982 a new draft treaty was presented in Vienna which reversed several earlier Pact positions and came close to the NATO position on a number of issues: a common alliance ceiling for manpower; a consultative commission to monitor compliance; pre-notification of major military movements into the reduction area; and agreement not to redeploy forces withdrawn from the reduction zone near the borders of the northern and flank states of each alliance.[30]

Some troublesome differences remain. For example, the Soviets have agreed only to temporary manning of observation posts to oversee troop movements in and out of the reduction zone, and have not yet agreed on the quota of on-site inspections necessary for adequate monitoring of compliance with an MBFR agreement. While backing away from their earlier insistence on national sub-ceilings, the Soviets have not given up hope of setting some *de facto* limits on the size of the Bundeswehr, and have proposed the so-called 50 per cent solution.[31] This was first raised informally in the mid-1970s by British and American officials at MBFR, in an effort to resolve at one stroke both West European apprehension about Soviet tank armies and the Warsaw Pact's apprehension about the Bundeswehr. The proposed solution was that within a common alliance ceiling, no single state could provide more than 50 per cent of the manpower. This had the added advantage that it essentially codified the status quo since Soviet forces and the Bundeswehr make up 50 per cent of the manpower in their respective MBFR reduction zones. Even Chancellor Schmidt publicly endorsed the concept in the Bundestag in March 1979, but Foreign Minister Genscher apparently vetoed it and NATO has not formally approved the plan although it originated on the Western side.

Prospects for Resolving the Data Discrepancy

By late 1982, the Soviets and their allies had agreed to almost half the provisions which NATO would like to see in an MBFR agreement.[32] Why then should the Soviets be so reluctant to take the necessary steps to resolve the discrepancy over troop data? A number of explanations seem possible. First, as many Western analysts claim, the Soviets may be deliberately falsifying the numbers so as to maintain an existing superiority.[33] These assertions seem to be based on statements attributed to East European military spokesmen in the mid-1960s and early 1970s to the effect that Pact superiority over NATO was necessary to deter a NATO attack,[34] as well as to earlier Soviet statements in Vienna that reductions to common NATO and Pact manpower ceilings would diminish Soviet security, implying that existing security rested on Pact superiority. No one has yet produced an authoritative Soviet or Warsaw Pact statement, however, which explicitly admits that Pact forces are more than marginally superior numerically to NATO, either globally, in Europe generally, or in the smaller MBFR guidelines area. The Soviet line on the data discrepancy is that NATO is exaggerating Pact forces, but this does not explain why NATO can estimate some Pact forces quite accurately and be so off-base with others.

A more benign explanation of the data problem is that there may have been genuine miscalculations, after which no one in the Soviet leadership was prepared to cope with the loss of face involved in admitting previous errors. Some Western delegates have suggested that this could be resolved by a tacit 'steal away in the night' whereby surplus Soviet troops are quietly withdrawn, and NATO can then agree to the Soviet data, providing there is adequate monitoring. A third possibility is that the Soviet military may not want to further disaggregate their data because to do so would disclose weakness – undermanning of divisions, for example. In any event, helping Western analysts to refine their estimates goes against the long-standing Russian belief that details of the force posture represent highly sensitive military intelligence which should not be disclosed to an adversary. This attitude is reflected in an interview which Lt General Nikolai Chervov, the member of the Soviet General Staff in charge of arms control negotiations, gave to a Bulgarian newspaper:

. . . the request of the Western side for additional data on the Soviet ground forces is amazing. We have been submitting an increasing amount of data but no concrete results have come out of this. The question justifiably arises why the Western states are so stubbornly trying to obtain data on the organizational structure and number of detachments, and groups of units of the Soviet ground forces.[35]

A fourth explanation is that tension in Poland may have increased Soviet reluctance to provide more information, since the major discrepancies were in Soviet and Polish forces. Indeed, the fear of further unrest throughout Eastern Europe may have stiffened military resistance to the idea of any contractual limits on Soviet forces in the MBFR guidelines area.

Finally, and most plausibly, the Soviets may see further disclosures as bargaining chips to be cashed in stages in exchange for Western concessions. Delegates in Vienna report that the Soviets have complained that earlier disclosures (which though minimal by Western standards were dramatic for the Eastern bloc) did not generate any corresponding conciliatory gestures from NATO. The Soviets are still hoping the West will relax NATO requirements for verification, be willing to impose limits on arms and equipment as well as manpower, give some official recognition in NATO estimates of recent increases in US forces into the MBFR guidelines area as well as the unilateral withdrawal of 20,000 Soviet troops from East Germany in 1980, and agree to freeze indigenous forces when stationed forces are reduced to prevent the West Germans making up for US reductions.

Some Soviet representatives at MBFR have argued that previously agreed data on overall force levels is unnecessary as long as reductions come to an agreed ceiling which could be verified. The verification/disclosure trade-off implied in this position is an interesting possibility. Many Western defence experts have said that they are less troubled by possible East–West force imbalances – since it is common knowledge that

Soviet troops in Eastern Europe serve a major police function for which there is no analogy in Western Europe – than about restrictions on monitoring troop activity. From the perspective of Western security it can be argued that it would be more advantageous to accept Soviet data and insist on more rigorous verification provisions, than to relax the latter in exchange for more accurate troop numbers.

Persuading NATO to impose limits on arms and equipment as well as manpower in a first-stage agreement will be more difficult. Although nuclear-capable arms featured in the Option III proposal in December 1975, this was a one-time offer which has now been overtaken by the December 1979 double-track modernisation decision and formally removed from consideration in Vienna. There is little enthusiasm in the Reagan Administration for complicating the draft MBFR treaty NATO presented in early 1982. On the other hand, some former members of the United States MBFR delegation have argued publicly that MBFR is the appropriate forum in which to negotiate a follow-on agreement limiting battlefield nuclear weapons, i.e. those with ranges below 1,000 km which are beyond the scope of the INF talks in Geneva.[36]

While blocking NATO's plans to preposition equipment for six extra United States divisions in West Germany may be the underlying motive, the Soviet rationale for urging limits on arms and equipment at MBFR focuses on three other factors. First, that arms are destructive, and omitting them results in purely symbolic reductions which do not really address the NATO/Pact confrontation; secondly, that manpower-only agreements are inherently unfair, because NATO's advanced technological base allows it to extract more defence capability out of fewer men than does the Pact; and thirdly, that both sides agreed to include forces and their equipment in MBFR limits when the talks began in 1973, and NATO is now reneging on that earlier commitment by restricting the agreement to manpower only.

With respect to force adjustments in the guidelines area

parallel to the negotiations, it would be both instructive and constructive for both alliances to disclose how their force levels have fluctuated since 1973. Senator Stevens of Alaska has claimed that American forces in Western Europe have increased by more than 58,000 since 1975, but these have been partially offset by reductions in some West European forces.[37] In the Warsaw Pact, during 1980 20,000 Soviet troops and 1,000 tanks were withdrawn from East Germany and redeployed in the western military districts of the Soviet Union, a fact acknowledged by Western intelligence agencies but not recognised in NATO estimates of Pact forces at MBFR. There has been no adjustment, for example, in the number of Soviet troops that NATO would like to see withdrawn in the first stage of an agreement. NATO still proposes a 13,000-man reduction for the United States and 30,000 for the Soviet Union. The Soviets argue that would make a total reduction of 50,000 for them, and propose a compromise whereby they would reduce another 20,000 on top of the 20,000 already withdrawn.

In conclusion, difficulties remain in Vienna, but none of them seem insurmountable. The biggest problem to date has been lack of high-level political interest in either Washington or Moscow for an early agreement. Furthermore, many European participants view the MBFR process itself as useful both for confidence-building and intelligence-gathering and the need to conclude an agreement has not been paramount. Early 1983 brought new leadership in Moscow and an upheaval in the United States arms control bureaucracy which could change the pace in Vienna. Both Yuri Andropov and Ronald Reagan need an arms control success, and the replacement of political appointee Richard Staar by a respected professional, Morton I. Abramovitz, as the US Ambassador to MBFR, suggests more serious interest in an agreement in Washington. As in 1971, the pace may also be forced by the threat of unilateral American withdrawals rather than by any East–West dynamic.[38]

The Soviet Campaign Against NATO's Nuclear Weapons

Whether driven by an ideology which asserts the inevitable momentum in the correlation of forces in favour of socialism, or more pragmatic security considerations, the Soviet Union has consistently sought to counter each new nuclear development in NATO either through arms control diplomacy, or by matching nuclear capability in Western Europe with equivalent, if not necessarily symmetrical, Soviet capability in the East.

Until the Soviet Union began to catch up with the United States in nuclear capability, arms control was their best hope of reducing the American advantage. In the late 1950s and early 1960s the Soviets and their Warsaw Pact allies sought to hinder NATO nuclear force planning by proposing a number of regional nuclear free zones in Europe. These proposals were clearly designed to curb the number of American forward-based nuclear weapons which could reach targets in the Soviet Union and, in particular, to limit if not totally prevent Federal German access to nuclear weapons. Though the nuclear free zone concept made no headway towards formal adoption, and did not even generate serious negotiations, some of NATO's more provocative land-based missiles were replaced by Polaris sea-launched missiles based in the Mediterranean. This should, arguably, have been more reassuring to the Warsaw Pact in general and to the Soviet Union in particular, since submarine-based systems are less vulnerable and less provocative, being better suited to retaliatory than pre-emptive missions. Unfortunately, from the Soviet perspective, the switch in emphasis from a land to a sea-based deterrent was coupled with the Kennedy Administration's proposal for a NATO manned and owned sea-based multilateral nuclear force (the MLF). The French opposed the MLF idea and the British were lukewarm, but West German enthusiasm was profoundly disturbing to the Soviet Union. As the MLF came to look increasingly like a bilateral German–

American venture the Soviets grew correspondingly more energetic in pursuit of nuclear free zones to thwart it.[39]

In the event, neither the MLF nor any other nuclear sharing scheme ever came to fruition. West Germany's enthusiasm for the project was not only threatening to the Soviets but also a very divisive issue within NATO and President Johnson cancelled the project in late 1964. West German interest in the scheme lingered on through 1965, however, and the Soviet Union then sought to prevent future West German access to nuclear weapons by negotiating a Non Proliferation Treaty designed to preclude the kind of nuclear control sharing envisaged in the MLF.

The Soviet Campaign Against American Forward-Based Systems at SALT

After conclusion of the NPT in the late 1960s, the Soviet Union mounted a major effort in the bilateral Strategic Arms Limitation Talks (SALT) to limit American nuclear weapons based in Europe and elsewhere around the Soviet perimeter – the so-called forward based systems (FBS). There is considerable justification for claims that nuclear weapons based in Western Europe threaten Soviet security more than intercontinental range systems based in the United States, because they offer less warning time and may be more accurate. But focusing on FBS also serves useful political interests for Moscow.

With no analogous forward bases which threaten the United States, calls to close down nuclear bases can be made from morally superior ground in international forums and serve as useful diplomatic ploys. In addition, emphasising the FBS threat to Soviet territory, while discounting both the long-standing NATO threat to Eastern Europe and the Soviet missiles targeted on Western Europe, suggests that the security of Europe is less important than that of either superpower, thereby emphasising the dependency of the smaller NATO powers on, and undermining their confidence in, the United States as security guarantor.

Propaganda which focuses on nuclear weapons on German soil can always be counted upon to stir up both intra-NATO feeling and traditional European anxieties about Germany and specifically about German fingers on nuclear triggers. Finally, as long as the United States refused to negotiate limits on its FBS, the Soviets could justify not accepting limits on their own medium-range systems targeted on Western Europe.

At the first SALT negotiating session in Helsinki in November 1969, the chief Soviet delegate, Vladimir Semyenov, defined as offensive strategic systems any Soviet weapons which could strike the United States and any American weapons capable of striking the Soviet Union. This definition embraced not only bombers and missiles of intercontinental range based in the United States and at sea, but also American nuclear weapons based in Europe and the Far East within range of the Soviet Union. By 1969 the USA had withdrawn all its medium-range land-based missiles from the continent and American FBS remaining in Europe were almost exclusively nuclear-capable aircraft: F-111 bombers based in Britain, F-4s at USAF bases in West Germany, Spain, Greece and Turkey, and A-6s, A-7s and F-4s based on carriers in the Mediterranean, the North Atlantic and the Western Pacific. The American delegate, Gerard Smith, told Semyenov that the effort to limit American nuclear-capable aircraft based in Europe was doomed to fail because these systems were deployed to counter the SS-4 and SS-5 missiles targeted on Western Europe. Smith asserted that the NATO Allies would have to participate in any talks aimed at limiting FBS, a point worth remembering in 1983 in view of American reluctance to include British and French forces or participants in the Geneva INF talks.

Despite having argued in November 1969 that SALT should focus on centrally-based intercontinental-range strategic systems, in April 1970 in deference to the NATO Allies the United States did make a half-hearted effort to impose limits on

Soviet systems which threatened Western Europe, including not only medium-range SS-4 and SS-5 ballistic missiles, but also some of the Soviets' 1950s vintage tactical cruise missiles. By 1970, however, the United States had deactivated all its own land and sea-based cruise, retaining only the obsolescing air-launched Hound Dog missile. Imposing limits on either side's cruise was thus not taken very seriously at this stage of the negotiations.[40]

Consistent with their definition of strategic systems as being only those which can threaten the homeland of either super-power, the Soviets resisted American suggestions that their SS-4s and SS-5s should be limited in SALT. Indeed when the United States delegation pointed out that some Soviet medium-range missiles threatened Alaska, the systems in question – deployed on the Chukotsk peninsula – were dismantled.[41] The Soviets persisted, however, in their effort to limit American FBS, and at the second negotiating session called for the withdrawal of all American forward-based nuclear-capable aircraft and associated facilities, as well as the closing down of the submarine bases at Rota, Spain and Holy Loch, Scotland. Later, the Soviets offered the more modest proposal that ceilings for Soviet strategic force levels should include compensation for the extra threat posed by FBS, as well as British and French strategic arsenals. A variant of this formula was implied by the SALT I Interim Agreement on offensive systems which allowed the Soviet Union a greater number of missiles than the United States. The same principle was embodied in the Soviet proposals at the INF talks in Geneva in 1982.

West European satisfaction that no limits had been imposed on FBS in the SALT agreements signed in May 1972, was soon diluted during the ratification debate, as Nixon Administration spokesmen rationalised higher permitted levels of strategic launchers for the Soviet Union on the grounds that the United States enjoyed an advantage in FBS and long-range bombers.[42] Some European defence analysts were troubled by this trade-off, seeing it as an example of the American tendency to undercut European interests. Uwe Nerlich, for example, charged that Administration testimony at the SALT hearings would encourage the Soviet Union to jump back on the FBS issue early during SALT II. Others recommended negotiating FBS not at SALT but at MBFR where the Allies were expected to participate on an equal basis with the superpowers. Still others suggested that the best way of dealing with FBS and Soviet medium-range systems was to freeze both sides' forces, and it is worth recalling the IISS judgement of late 1973 that:

> In political and strategic terms, the most feasible arrangement on both sides is probably a freeze of existing systems. The United States could probably agree to a freeze on her current levels of FBS, and the Soviet Union apparently plans no increase in her MRBM and IRBM forces targetted on Western Europe, so that this would offer few difficulties for her.[43]

Alastair Buchan floated a more radical 'zero option' solution, namely, that the Soviets dismantle all their old SS-4 and SS-5 missiles without replacement, in exchange for the withdrawal of all American land-based nuclear-capable aircraft from the continent, though retaining carrier-based systems.[44]

SALT I made 1973 a critical juncture in Soviet missile modernisation, when an agreement or tacit understanding to freeze American FBS and Soviet medium-range missiles might well have found favour in the Kremlin. The fixed land-based SS-4 and SS-5 missiles had been growing progressively more obsolete as satellite reconnaissance improved American target acquisition capabilities, and the first attempts to replace these systems was development of the mobile land-based SS-14 and SS-15 missiles.[45] Technical problems prevented these systems from being deployed in any numbers, however, and the Soviets' next effort was to adapt the variable range SS-11 ICBM to a theatre mission. By 1970 some 120 SS-11s were deployed in the old SS-4 and SS-5 sites in the Western military districts. As

ICBMs, however, after the summer of 1972, these missiles were subject to SALT limits. The Soviets then faced the problem of finding new medium-range systems to replace the ageing SS-4s and SS-5s. Having to accept SALT limits on the SS-11 while failing to impose limits on American FBS no doubt encouraged the Soviets to convert their three-stage SS-16 intercontinental ballistic missile into the two-stage medium-range ballistic missile which became the SS-20. A freeze on both sides' medium-range forces in the early 1970s might have been a sufficiently attractive option for the Soviets to cancel the SS-20 project. The consensus in NATO, however, was that a FBS freeze would reduce flexibility and overly constrain the conventional missions of American dual capable aircraft based in Europe.

When SALT II negotiations began in earnest in March 1973 the Soviet delegation again rejected the American definition of 'central' strategic systems and, repeating their consistent position throughout SALT I, insisted that FBS be either withdrawn or included in the ceiling imposed on strategic systems. By the year's end SALT seemed at an impasse and through the first half of 1974 the Soviets were disinclined to conclude an agreement or even seriously negotiate while President Nixon was under threat of impeachment as a result of the Watergate burglary. Once President Ford was installed in late summer, things moved relatively quickly as the Soviets no doubt then saw advantages in concluding an agreement before the United States became embroiled in preliminaries to the 1976 elections.

In Moscow in October Kissinger and Brezhnev reached an understanding that SALT II would be based on equal aggregates of strategic delivery vehicles including heavy bombers. This understanding was further refined at the Ford–Brezhnev summit meeting in Vladivostock the following month and incorporated in an aide-memoire, the main points of which were:

• Both sides should be limited to 2,400 intercontinental-range

strategic delivery vehicles, of which 1,320 could be mirved;
- Air-launched missiles of ranges more than 600km on heavy bombers were to count in the 1,320 mirv limit;
- Heavy bombers were understood to include American B-52s and Soviet MY-4 Bison and TU-95 Bear bombers.
- the Soviet Union would drop its earlier insistence on FBS limits in exchange for the United States giving up its effort to impose a special sub-ceiling on Soviet heavy missiles.[46]

Though hailed initially as a major breakthrough in the negotiations, the Vladivostock understanding was to prove a bone of contention over the next several years, in particular the definitions of 'heavy bombers' and 'air-launched missiles', and the trade-off between concessions on American FBS and Soviet heavy missiles. These differences were eventually resolved to the satisfaction of each side's delegation, and a SALT II treaty was signed in June 1979. But the compromises involved generated so much dispute in Washington that, at the time of writing, the treaty remains unratified. Moreover in NATO, resentment that the treaty did nothing to limit the SS-20 missile or the Backfire bomber while imposing some, albeit temporary, limits on cruise missile technology, generated pressure to deploy new longer-range American missiles in Europe which could directly threaten Soviet targets.[47]

Soviet Motives at the INF Talks

Concurrent with the intra-NATO debate on nuclear force modernisation was a more muted debate in the Warsaw Pact on how to cope with the prospect of a new generation of forward-based American weapons and, presumably, on the merits of further SS-20 deployments. Reports from Eastern Europe hint at attempts in late 1976, by both the Romanian and the Hungarian governments, to dissuade the Soviets from deploying SS-20 missiles against West European targets, on the grounds that a

new generation of nuclear weapons in Europe would undermine the East–West détente just codified in the 1975 Helsinki
Final Act. The Soviet rationale for SS-20 missiles was as modern
replacements for, rather than additions to, the medium-range
SS-4 and SS-5 missiles first deployed in the 1960s to counter
American FBS. Since these FBS, as well as more recent British
and French strategic nuclear arsenals, are constantly being
improved and modernised, the Soviets argue that their own
analogous systems must also be upgraded to maintain the East–
West equilibrium.

These arguments are not completely devoid of merit, and the
extent to which the European-based nuclear threat to the Soviet
Union has increased since the early 1970s is often overlooked.
At the same time, various offers since late 1979 to freeze SS-20
deployments during negotiations, and even a willingness to
reduce the number targeted on Western Europe, suggest that a
redundancy of force was deployed for bargaining purposes,
even though in megatonnage the SS-20 force is less of a threat
than the old SS-4 and SS-5s. It was certainly clear during SALT
II that the Soviets intended to press for limits on American
forward-based systems at SALT III, and President Brezhnev
acknowledged the need to accept limits on Soviet medium-
range missiles on a visit to Bonn in May 1978. The Soviets may
not have anticipated at this stage, however, having to deal with a
new generation of American forward-based systems which
could reach Soviet targets, and through 1978 and 1979 mounted
an intensive campaign against NATO's proposed new longer-
range nuclear missiles. After the somewhat clumsy propaganda
barrage against the neutron bomb in 1977, the campaign against
the longer-range missiles was relatively sophisticated. Nevertheless, all the articles and speeches, the diplomatic missions to
Western European capitals, and the direct appeals to increasingly anti-nuclear publics only served to strengthen the
resolve of the NATO defence establishment.

It was not until 6 October 1979 that the Soviets came through
with a constructive offer to restrain SS-20 deployment and

negotiate limits on all medium-range systems in Europe. The offer was made conditional on cancellation of NATO's proposed modernisation decision, but by then the momentum in NATO for deploying the longer-range systems was unstoppable. Even those officials who had earlier been sceptical about the military rationale for the new missiles, now argued for deployment to preserve Alliance cohesion. The 'double decision' to both deploy and negotiate was formalised on 12 December 1979. One hundred and eight Pershing II extended range ballistic missiles would replace 108 Pershing IA missiles with US forces in West Germany, and 464 Tomahawk ground-launched cruise missiles under American control would be hosted by several NATO Allies and would replace an equal number of existing nuclear warheads based in Western Europe. In addition, the United States offered to withdraw 1,000 of the 7,000 land-based nuclear warheads on the continent, and to negotiate limits on medium-range nuclear systems in the framework of SALT III.[48]

Except for Mrs Thatcher's government in Britain, which argued that NATO's nuclear forces needed upgrading regardless of the SS-20, most other NATO governments would have preferred to avoid new nuclear deployments and assumed that as soon as the United States Senate had ratified SALT II, SALT III negotiations would proceed to deal with medium-range systems deployed in and targeted on Europe. In the event, the Soviets withdrew their offer to negotiate when NATO formalised its deployment decision on 12 December. Then, following the Soviet invasion of Afghanistan at the end of the month, President Carter withdrew the SALT II treaty from consideration by the United States Senate, thereby undermining the foundation – an ongoing SALT dialogue – on which the Allies had voted for the NATO 'double decision'.

The Soviet position softened through the spring of 1980. Initially the Soviets said they would negotiate only if the NATO modernisation decision was revoked, and that any agreement reached on limitation of medium-range missiles could only go into effect after ratification of SALT II. Eventually, after a visit to

Moscow by Chancellor Helmut Schmidt in early July, President Brezhnev agreed to negotiations without preconditions and talks began with the Carter Administration in Geneva in October, only to be suspended when President Carter was defeated in the November elections.

West European apprehension about the double-track decision increased through 1981 as the Reagan Administration conducted its own threat assessment and review of US theatre nuclear policy. Richard Perle, Assistant Secretary of Defense for International Security Affairs reported to NATO's Special Consultative Group in the spring of 1981 that the Administration considered 572 warheads a mere token response to recent Soviet force improvements, and tried to persuade the Allies to accept a larger number of Pershing missile reloads. The Allies, now hard-pressed by their anti-nuclear movements, refused to change the terms of the double decision and in turn pressed for early resumption of negotiations. Soviet–American INF talks reconvened in Geneva in November 1981.[49]

Meanwhile the Kremlin had stepped up its propaganda campaign against the new NATO missiles, raising five main arguments: the new missiles would undermine the SALT II treaty signed in June 1979; as qualitatively new systems, Tomahawk cruise missiles and Pershing II extended range ballistic missiles posed a new, more serious threat to the security of the Soviet homeland and upset Soviet–American strategic parity; the new systems suggested that the United States was preparing to engage in limited nuclear strikes and to confine future nuclear exchanges to the European continent; by assigning such a prominent role to West Germany as host nation for the new missiles NATO was undermining the gains of *Ostpolitik* and East–West détente in Europe; and, finally, the new missiles would undermine a long-standing nuclear equilibrium in Europe which would have to be re-established.[50] Since these arguments form the basis for the Soviet negotiating position at INF, it is worth addressing the implications of each in turn.

Defining the new NATO missiles as strategic is consistent with the Soviet position throughout SALT that any American system which can hit Soviet territory should be considered strategic no matter where it is based. In keeping with the criteria of equal security in all bilateral arms control arrangements, the Soviets argued that deployment of new American missiles would require additional medium-range Soviet missiles which could hit American targets; in Cuba, for example.[51] The qualitative new threat posed by the American systems rests in the accuracy of their guidance and the drastically reduced warning time, especially of a Pershing II attack on the Soviet Union as compared to an attack from centrally based American systems. The Soviets hinted that the appropriate response to counter this threat was to adopt a launch-on warning doctrine for their own missiles; an admittedly destabilising move but one for which, they argued, the onus would be on the United States.

The Soviet assertion that the United States's intention in deploying new missiles was to limit any future nuclear exchange to the European continent seemed designed to undermine NATO cohesion and play on traditional European fears about being drawn in to a nuclear conflict between the two superpowers. It no doubt also reflects genuine anxiety in the Kremlin that the United States might develop military capabilities which could deny the Soviets control over their East European buffer. Soviet spokesmen are quick to deny the feasibility of limiting a nuclear exchange by threatening a massive nuclear retaliatory strike in response to any initial strike on Soviet territory by American nuclear weapons no matter where they were originally based. Ironically, this parallels West European interests in maintaining the credibility of the American nuclear umbrella. For the Soviets, promising a strategic response to any nuclear strike is a useful deterrent since the perception that limited NATO nuclear strikes were possible, on rear echelons of Soviet troops, for example, could seriously undermine Soviet control over East European armies. It thus appears that both the Soviet Union and Western Europe are anxious to couple American forward-based systems as closely as possible to central strategic systems based in the continental United States.

Chancellor Schmidt anticipated that the Soviets would raise the spectre of German fingers on the nuclear button, and sought to pre-empt the ensuing political fall-out by laying down four conditions that must be met before the new missiles could be deployed. First, unlike the shorter-range missiles now deployed with the Bundeswehr which are under double-key (i.e. German and American) control, the new longer-range systems must be under single key (i.e. American only) control; secondly, other continental non-nuclear states in NATO must share the risks of deployment; thirdly, the deployment decision must be taken by NATO as a whole and not as a series of bilateral arrangements between the United States and individual European countries; and, finally, that the missiles would only be deployed if the negotiations failed.[52]

These conditions were by no means easy to meet. Though Italy was willing to accept cruise missiles, neither Belgium nor the Netherlands were enthusiastic and kept putting off the final decision into the early 1980s. Relations among the West European members of NATO were complicated by the separate carrot and stick dialogue on nuclear issues between the Soviets and the West Germans. The Russians alternatively offered conciliatory gestures of nuclear restraint and threatened dire countermeasures if new American missiles were deployed on German soil. On several occasions, for example, the Soviets chose state visits to Bonn, or when the German Chancellor was in Moscow, to announce a new Soviet arms control initiative. These 'peace offensives' have also proved irritating in trans-Atlantic relations and between the two main political parties in West Germany. The Americans resent efforts by West Germany to act as intermediary between the two superpowers, while CDU spokesmen accuse the SPD of undermining NATO's bargaining position. In April 1981, an editorial in the *Frankfurter Allgemeine Zeitung* claimed that the Soviet peace offensives were designed 'to play West Europe against the United

States and to let the Federal Republic become the rotten apple of the Western alliance'.[53]

The issue of balance in European military forces is particularly difficult to assess since NATO and Soviet forces are so asymmetrical as to make numerical comparisons almost meaningless. Nevertheless, balances must be contrived for arms control agreements, and in 1981 the Soviets asserted that NATO and the Soviet Union were balanced at approximately 1,000 systems each in nuclear delivery vehicles of between 1,000 and 3,000km range. Just as at MBFR the Soviets appear to divide the manpower balance into several components, so at the INF talks Soviet tactics suggest the need to balance European nuclear forces on three levels. At the first level, 300 modern Soviet systems – the SS-20 missiles and the Backfire bomber – are offset by 300 modern British and French systems. At the second level, approximately 700 older systems – SS-4 and SS-5 missiles, Badger and Blinder bombers – are balanced against some 700 United States forward-based aircraft (F-111s, F-4, and carrier-based A-6s and A-7s). The third Soviet balancing act, and the one the United States and most of her allies find the hardest to accept, is based on equilibrium at the other two levels such that any additional NATO missiles – specifically the proposed package of 572 Pershing II and Tomahawk ground-launched cruise missiles – will require new Soviet missiles to maintain European stability.[54]

As the INF talks opened in November 1981, Soviet and American versions of the balance and scope of the proposed limitation were far apart. In contrast to the Soviet view that systems in the range 1,000km to 3,000km were roughly balanced, the Reagan Administration discounted British and French systems and claimed that the Soviets enjoyed a 6:1 advantage over the United States in medium-range systems. This was computed by counting 560 forward-based nuclear capable aircraft against a package of 3,825 Soviet systems which included more than 2,000 short-range tactical aircraft.[55] It should be noted that this data discrepancy is of a different order from that at MBFR. At INF there is little dispute about what actually exists, only which of the systems are relevant, a particularly thorny question when dual-capable systems are involved.

With respect to the scope of the negotiations, the United States initially wanted to set global Soviet and American limits on a narrow category of forces – intermediate-range land-based ballistic missiles – while the Soviets wanted to limit a broad range of weapons, with freedom to mix between categories, in a narrowly defined geographical zone.

The opening American proposal, as announced by President Reagan on 18 November, was the so-called 'zero option' in which the United States would not deploy any of the proposed new long-range missiles in Western Europe, if the Soviets would dismantle all their SS-4s, SS-5s and SS-20s. The Soviets' opening proposal was for a two-stage agreement: by 1985 both the Soviet Union and NATO would reduce by approximately one third the 1,000 systems outlined in the Soviet view of the balance, with each side having freedom to choose which systems to dismantle. The Soviets insisted that both British and French forces count in the NATO forces, but emphasised that NATO could decide which systems (American, British or French) would be reduced. By 1990, another third of the systems would be withdrawn, preferably dismantled, leaving a minimum force on each side of 300 systems.[56]

The Soviet proposal floated informally in Geneva in November 1982, confirmed in a major speech by Yuri Andropov in Moscow on 21 December, and endorsed by the Warsaw Pact Political Consultative Committee in January 1983, was a variation on this theme. The chief innovation was a concession toward the American position of a first-stage agreement limiting missiles only; setting aside yet again the vexed question of forward-based American nuclear-capable aircraft. Specifically, the Soviets offered to reduce the number of SS-20 missiles targeted on Western Europe to the number of British and French medium-range missiles.[57] This proposal also seemed to

275

embrace an informal American proposal which sought to match the restraint expected of the two superpowers.[58] The Soviet Union would withdraw 580 warheads (assuming they pulled back 100 SS-20s with 300 warheads, and dismantled 280 SS-4s and SS-5s) if the United States would not deploy the 572 new warheads proposed in the double decision. It was not clear in January 1983 exactly how the Soviets would modify their proposal to account for the proposed mirving of British and French strategic systems, but they did pick up the Western proposal to count warheads, not missiles.[59]

The immediate reaction from the United States, Britain and France was to reject the Soviet proposal out-of-hand by insisting on a Soviet–American rather than a Soviet–NATO balance; but many West European leaders found considerable logic in the Soviet position and began to call for more flexibility from the United States at the Geneva talks; certainly to move away from the Reagan Administration zero option proposal.[60] The argument that the Soviets were justified in offsetting European-owned nuclear forces seemed irrefutable not only to the anti-nuclear movement but to a growing number of defence analysts and political leaders. In Britain, opposition leaders Jim Callaghan and David Owen called for British and French participation at the Geneva talks, a call echoed in the United States by Ambassador Jonathan Dean, former head of the US delegation MBFR, who proposed that not only the European nuclear weapons powers but all the NATO Allies scheduled to host the new American missiles should sit in on the INF negotiations.[61]

Conclusion

In conclusion, a balance sheet on the contribution of Soviet arms control diplomacy to Soviet security during the Brezhnev era presents a mixed picture. There has been more success in maintaining Eastern Europe as a military buffer than in securing the bloc from destabilising political and economic influences from the West; more success in straining the Bonn–Washington axis than in undermining NATO as a whole; and more success in encouraging Western opposition to destabilising new nuclear weapons than in securing recognition either of a positive trend in the correlation of forces in favour of world socialism, or of the Soviet Union as a superpower co-equal with the United States.

The Soviets sought to stabilise their East European buffer zone by seeking broader acceptance of the post-1945 political and territorial status quo in Europe through the CSCE, an initiative in which the NATO countries agreed to participate with reluctance in the early 1970s. Yet it is the Eastern bloc which has been most on the defensive at CSCE, as the Western and non-aligned states used this forum to call the Soviet Union and Eastern Europe to account for their repressive domestic practices. Results have been better for the Soviets in Basket II where they sought greater access to Western technological benefits, but even here there have been problems due to over-reliance of Eastern Europe on Western credits. Most CSCE participants have been satisfied with the military confidence-building measures incorporated in the 1975 Helsinki Final Act, but the Soviets have not yet succeeded in using CBMs to limit the size of NATO's large annual autumn reforger exercises, an objective they will no doubt continue to pursue if and when a new pan-European Disarmament Conference ever gets under way.

At MBFR, which was a NATO initiative, the Soviets have negotiated seriously and fared relatively well. There has been a convergence of NATO and Pact positions on a number of important issues and, while serious differences still remain, the Vienna talks have proved a useful framework for détente and East–West confidence-building. There have been fewer opportunities to probe intra-NATO differences than the Soviets might have wished, but they continue to seek separate limits on the Bundeswehr through the 50 per cent solution and they may yet be able to secure reciprocal NATO reductions for withdrawals the Soviet military seems to be planning in any event.[62]

The most persistent Soviet arms control effort since the late 1950s has been to limit American nuclear weapons in Western Europe and to limit West German access to nuclear control-sharing. This began with attempts to establish regional nuclear-free zones, continued with the NPT, and was maintained as an integral part of Soviet policy at SALT I and SALT II, and most recently at the INF talks in Geneva. Here again the picture is mixed. Having missed the window of opportunity to freeze both American FBS and Soviet medium-range missiles in the early 1970s, the Soviets decided to replace the obsolescing SS-4 and SS-5 missiles with the mobile Mirved SS-20. This in turn encouraged some NATO leaders – those anxious about the impact of strategic parity on the American nuclear guarantee – to seek a renewed American security commitment to Europe in the form of new missiles which could reach targets in the Soviet Union. The Soviet effort to halt this development with an arms control initiative was both too little and too late, and the increasingly sophisticated public campaign waged against the new NATO missiles through the early 1980s was not particularly cost-effective. While the Soviets probably saw some political dividends in the West European anti-nuclear movement, it was by no means clear that the loss of Chancellor Schmidt as Chancellor of West Germany was in the Soviet interest; a loss which could probably have been averted had the Soviets been more restrained in their SS-20 deployments and more imaginative in their arms control diplomacy in the late 1970s. Furthermore, the anti-nuclear mood spilled over into both East Germany and the Soviet Union generating some awkward backlash among the military establishments there.[63]

One of the major obstacles to negotiated arms control has been the closed nature of Soviet society and the traditional Russian and Soviet reluctance to accept any form of on-site inspection or disclose military data. SALT I was negotiated purely on the strength of data supplied by the United States, and even then it was reported that military members of the Soviet delegation did not want their civilian colleagues exposed to information about Soviet strategic forces.

Since then, however, there has been an encouraging trend toward more openness and the Soviets have been more forthcoming both in disclosing military data in arms control negotiations and to the wider public. The SALT II treaty signed in June 1979, for example, provides for maintenance of an agreed data base which, as one Soviet delegate quipped, 'reversed 400 years of Russian history'. More recently, data on Soviet and East European combat manpower was disclosed at MBFR, and on intermediate nuclear forces at the INF talks in Geneva; at the CSCE, the Soviets offered to open up the western military districts to a new CBM regime; at the second United Nations Special Session on Disarmament in June 1982, Foreign Minister Gromyko proposed on-site inspections in connection with a proposed ban on chemical weapons, and offered to open up civilian nuclear power plants to IAEA inspections; and the Political Declaration issued by the Warsaw Pact summit meeting in Prague in January 1983 endorsed the concept of 'international procedures' to verify arms control agreements.

Furthermore, information on the East–West military balance has been made available to publics in East and West in a remarkable series of pamphlets issued simultaneously in Russian and English. While much of this newly published material is Western data re-issued with a Soviet seal of approval, the fact that it is being disclosed and distributed suggests more serious Soviet interest in arms control agreements as distinct from arms control posturing.

Agreements to limit forces in Europe can only succeed, however, to the extent that Soviet and West European security interests overlap. This chapter suggests that Soviet security goals are not necessarily antipathetic to the security needs of Western Europe, and that at least two aspects of the military status quo seem to be in the common interest and worth preserving in the near term: the maintenance of American

279

troops in Europe and the tight coupling of American security guarantees to centrally-based American nuclear systems. Under these conditions the Soviets can be reasonably confident that West Germany will not be tempted to take independent military action in Eastern Europe, that the United States will not be tempted to launch limited nuclear strikes, and that the European members of NATO will not be tempted to acquire an independent West European nuclear force.

On the other hand, Soviet domination of Eastern Europe, suppression of human rights throughout the bloc, and efforts to demonstrate a correlation of forces in favour of socialism are all aspects of Soviet behaviour which, while not directly threatening to Western Europe, do not sit well with NATO governments. Western efforts to gradually ease economic and political conditions in the East will thus doubtless continue, just as surely as NATO will refrain from any attempt to liberate Eastern Europe by military means.

The task for NATO in the 1980s and beyond is to engage the Soviets in a constructive dialogue on European security; to search for areas of common interest on which lasting and equitable agreements can be built; and to make umambiguously clear to the new leadership in Moscow which Soviet goals are considered provocative and threatening to long-term stability in Europe.

Notes to Chapter 8

1 Stephen J. Flanagan, 'The CSCE and the Development of Detente' in D. Leebaert (ed.), *European Security: Prospects For The 1980s* (Lexington, Mass.: D. C. Heath, 1979), pp. 189–233.
2 Basket I – Questions Relating to Security in Europe – has two parts. The first part comprises ten principles guiding relations between states. The second relates to specifically military security issues. Principle no. 7 of the ten guiding principles calls on participating states to respect human rights and fundamental freedoms, including the freedom of thought, religion or belief. Human rights are therefore very much a part of Basket I as well as Basket III.
3 For accounts of the persecution of the Helsinki monitoring committees in the Soviet Union and Eastern Europe, see the semi-annual reports on *Implementation of the Helsinki Final Act* issued by the United States Department of State.

4 *Declaration of Warsaw Treaty Members Countries* issued by the Warsaw Pact Political Consultative Committee meeting in Bucharest, 24–6 November 1976; cited by Robert R. King and James F. Brown (eds), *Eastern Europe's Uncertain Future* (New York: Praeger, 1977), pp. 15–17.

5 Defense Secretary Schlesinger's policy on limited nuclear options is discussed in Robert Art and Simon Lunn, *NATO in the age of Strategic Parity* (Washington, DC: The Brookings Institution, forthcoming).

6 Flanagan, 'The CSCE', p. 223.

7 International Institute for Strategic Studies, *Strategic Survey 1977* (London: IISS, 1978), p. 126.

8 The EEC endorsed the CDE on 1 November 1979 and NATO ministers in June 1980.

9 IISS, *Strategic Survey 1977*, p. 140.

10 *L. I. Brezhnev's Interview with Der Spiegel Magazine, November 1981* (Moscow: Novosti Press Agency, 1981); see esp. pp. 27–8.

11 These 'mutual example' discussions were re-examined by the United States Arms Control and Disarmament Agency in the late 1960s in preparation for MBFR. See the memorandum by J. E. Mayer, *Soviet–American bilateral talks on Mutual Example Force Reductions in Europe 1963–1964* (Washington, DC: USA ACDA, 8 December 1969).

12 'Overstretching the Americans', New China News Agency, 16 January 1966, reprinted in *Survival*, vol. VIII, no. 3 (March 1966), pp. 92–4.

13 'Address by CPSU General Secretary Brezhnev at Tbilisi (Extract)', 14 May 1971, *Documents on Disarmament 1971* (Washington, DC: USA ACDA, 1972), p. 293.

14 United States Congress, Senate Foreign Relations Committee, Hearings on *Detente 74*, Eugene McCarthy testimony at p. 144.

15 John G. Keliher, *The Negotiations on Mutual and Balanced Force Reductions: The Search for Arms Control in Central Europe* (New York: Pergamon Press, n.d.).

16 Coit D. Blacker, 'The Soviet Perception of European Security' in Leebaert (ed.), *European Security*, p. 142.

17 Ellen Jones, 'Manning the Soviet military', *International Security*, vol 7, no. 1 (Summer 1982), pp. 105–31.

18 'Mutual and Balanced Force Reductions: Declaration Adopted by Foreign Ministers and Representatives of Countries Participating in the NATO Defense Programme', Annex to the NATO Communiqué of 25 June 1968, *Documents on Disarmament 1968* (Washington, DC: USA ACDA, 1969), pp. 449–50.

19 Interviews with NATO delegates to the MBFR negotiations, conducted in London, Vienna, Washington DC and The Hague, September and October 1982.

20 Helmut Schmidt's speech to the West European Union Assembly, reproduced in *Survival*, vol. 12., no. 1 (January–February 1970), p. 44.

21 United States National Security Council, National Security Study Memoranda (NSSMs), nos 84 and 92.

22 Richard M. Nixon, *U.S. Foreign Policy for the 1970s: Building for Peace*, A Report to the Congress, 25 February 1971 (Washington, DC: US GPO, 1971), pp 34–5.

23 United States Congress, Senate Armed Services Committee, *Hearings on FY 1976 Military Appropriations*, March 1975, pp. 2241–2.

24 See, for example, President Brezhnev's remarks at a press conference at Bonn in May 1978, reported in the *Financial Times*, 3 May 1978; and statements in *Disarmament: Soviet Initiatives in Disarmament* (Moscow: Novosti, 1977), p. 24.

25 US Arms Control and Disarmament Agency, 'Statement by the United States Representative (Resor) on the Negotiations on Mutual Reduction of Forces and Armaments in Central Europe, October 31, 1973', *Documents on Disarmament 1973* (Washington, DC: US GPO, 1974) p. 721.

26 Yu Kostko, 'Mutual force reductions in Europe', reprinted in *Survival*, vol. XIV, no. 6 (September–October 1972), pp. 236–8.

27 Lothar Ruehl, 'MBFR: Lessons and Problems', *Adelphi Paper no. 176* (Summer 1982), pp. 3, 9, 14–17.

28 The Warsaw Pact proposals of February 1976 are discussed in detail in Keliher, *The Negotiations on MBFR*, pp. 67–73.

29 Discussions of the Associated Measures proposed by NATO at MBFR can be found in Jonathan Dean, 'MBFR: from apathy to accord', *International Security*, vol. 7, no. 4 (forthcoming); and Ken Scott, 'MBFR: Western initiatives seek to end deadlock', *NATO Review*, vol. 30, no. 4 (1982), pp. 14–19.

30 Stanley Sloan, *Policy Alert: Warsaw Pact Proposes New Draft Treaty in Vienna Force Reduction Talks* (Washington, DC: Congressional Research Service, 25 February 1982).

31 Chalmers Hardenburgh, *The Arms Control Reporter* (Brookline, Institute for Defense and Disarmament, 1982), p. 401-c-1.

32 Dean, 'MBFR'.

33 Ruehl, 'MBFR'.

34 A. Ross Johnson, Robert W. Dean and Alexander Alexiev, *East European Military Establishments; The Warsaw Pact Northern Tier* (Santa Monica, Calif.: The RAND Corporation, R-2417/1-AF/FF, December 1980).

35 Lt General Nikolai Chervov, interviewed in *Narodra*, 21 November 1980, p. 3, reprinted in FBIS/USSR, 26 November 1980, pp. AA4–AA6.

36 Jonathan Dean, 'Time for a revamped arms reduction push', *The Boston Globe*, 5 December 1982; John G. Keliher, 'Ground Force Nuclear Weapons and Arms Control', *European Nuclear Forces and Arms Control Prospects For the 1980s* (Center for Science and International Affairs, Harvard University, forthcoming).

37 The Department of Defense claims the correct figure for increased US forces in Europe since 1975 is 48,000; see Hardenburgh, *The Arms Control Reporter*, pp. B10–12.

38 Richard Halloran, 'Study calls on U.S. to bring ground troops home', *New York Times*, 11 July 1982; Reuters, 'Panel votes to thin out G.I. ranks in Europe', *New York Times*, 5 September 1982; Michael Getler, 'Frustration building up in Congress over NATO defense costs', *Manchester Guardian Weekly*, 2 May 1982; Bernard Gwertzman, 'Some Congressmen suggest bringing the boys back home', *New York Times*, 14 March 1982.

39 'Soviet Note to the United States on Proposed Multilateral Nuclear Force, April 8, 1963', *Documents on Disarmament 1963*, pp. 161–170; 'Soviet Note to the United States on Nuclear Free Zone in the Mediterranean; May 20, 1963', *ibid.*, pp. 187–193. For an account of proposals for Nordic Nuclear Free Zones see Kekkonen and Khrushchev proposals made in 1963 and 1964, *SIPRI Year Book 1969–1970* (Stockholm International Peace Research Institute, 1970), pp. 412–14.

40 Gerard Smith, 'The Negotiations Begin' ch. 3 of *Doubletalk: The Story of SALT I* (New York: Doubleday, 1980).

41 *ibid.*, p. 129.

42 'Remarks by Presidential Assistant Kissinger at Congressional Briefing on the Strategic Arms Limitation Treaty, June 15, 1972', *Documents on Disarmament 1972* (Washington, DC: US GPO, 1973), pp. 295–309, at p. 302.

43 IISS, *Strategic Survey 1973*.

44 Alastair Buchan, *The End of the Postwar Era* (London: Dutton, 1974), p. 309.

45 Robert C. Berman and John C. Baker, *Soviet Strategic Forces: Requirements and Responses* (Washington, DC: The Brookings Institution, 1982), pp. 171, see pp. 59–61; 90–3.

46 For details of the Vladivostock understanding see Thomas W. Wolfe, *The SALT Experience* (Cambridge, Mass.: Ballinger, 1979), pp. 95–6.

47 United States Congress, House Committee on Foreign Affairs, *The Modernization of NATO's Long Range Theater Nuclear Forces*, Committee Print prepared by Simon Lunn (Washington, DC: US GPO, 31 December 1981); Senate Committee on Foreign Relations, Subcommittee on European Affairs, *SALT and the NATO Allies*, A Staff Report (Washington, DC: US GPO, October 1979).

48 The 12 December NATO communiqué is reprinted as Appendix 4 of the House Committee Print, *The Modernization of NATO's LRTNF*.

49 Simon Lunn, 'Long range theater nuclear force negotiations in Geneva: problems and prospects', *Pugwash Newsletter*, vol. 19, no. 3 (January, 1982), pp. 102–12.

50 See, for example: the summary of 1979 statements from the Soviet press in Appendix 2 of *The Modernization of NATO's LRTNF*; Dimitry Ustinov, 'Against the arms race and the threat of war' *Pravda*, 25 July 1981, reprinted in Foreign Broadcast Information Service (FBIS), 27 July 1981, pp. AA1–AA10; Soviet Committee for European Security and Cooperation and Scientific Research Council on Peace and Disarmament, *The Threat to Europe* (Moscow: Progress Publishers, 1981); V. Boikov and L. Mlechin (eds), 'The arms race: the dangers, the burden, and the alternative', a special supplement to *New Times*, Moscow 1982.

51 Ian Mather, 'Press fights for arms talks clues', *The Observer*, 16 December 1981.

52 Catherine M. Kelleher, 'The present as prologue: Europe and theater nuclear modernization', *International Security*, vol. 5, no. 4 (Spring, 1981), pp. 150–69 at p. 154.

53 See also: Ernst-Otto Maetzke, 'Manuilski's belated triumph', *Frankfurter Allgemeine Zeitung*, 27 April 1981; FBIS/FRG, 29 April 1981, pp. J7–J8; James M. Markham, 'Bonn opposition tries arms talks ploy', *New York Times*, 16 December 1982; and 'Gromyko warns Germans of risk if new missiles are deployed', *New York Times*, 18 January 1983; Ye Greigoriev, 'Opportunity for FRG to play active role in detente', *Pravda*, 11 April 1980; Anthony Barbieri, Jr, 'NATO strain may be Soviet goal', *Baltimore Sun*, 19 March 1982.

54 Christopher D. Jones, 'Equality and equal security in Europe', *Orbis* (Fall, 1982).

55 For alternative perspectives on the European nuclear balance, see Jane M. O. Sharp, 'Prospects for Limiting Nuclear Forces in Europe' in M. Olive and J. Porro (eds), *Nuclear Weapons in Europe: Modernization and Limitation* (Lexington, Mass.: Lexington Books, 1983), pp. 65–79.

56 United States Congress, House Committee on Appropriations, Hearings, *Department of Defense Appropriations For 1983* (Washington, DC: NSGPO, 1982); the statement of Ambassador Paul H. Nitze, pp. 812–21 outlines the negotiations through 16 March 1982.

57 *New York Times*, 22 December 1982.

58 David Linebaugh, 'An arms reduction plan worth talking about', *Christian Science Monitor*, 14 January 1983.

59 John Burns, 'Soviet move on missiles', *New York Times*, 15 January 1983.

60 R. W. Apple, Jr, 'The "Zero Option": Margaret Thatcher softens her support', *New York Times*, 20 January 1983; Patrick Keatley and Alex Brummer, 'Britain cautiously welcomes Soviet offer', *Manchester Guardian Weekly*, 19 December 1982, p. 5; John Vinocur, 'Mitterand now favors a missile compromise', *New York Times*, 12 December 1982.

61 Jim Callaghan, *Manchester Guardian Weekly*, 28 November 1982, p. 4; Jonathan Dean, *Boston Globe*, 5 December 1982; David Owen, 'Negotiate and Survive', Chapter 11, *Facing the Future* (New York: Praeger, 1981), pp. 221–45.

62 See the passage on the MBFR negotiations in the Political Declaration issued by the

Warsaw Pact summit meeting in Prague, 5 January 1983, *Political Declaration of the States Parties to the Warsaw Treaty Prague, 5 January 1983* (Berlin DDR: Panorama, 1983) at p. 13.

63   Serge Schemann, 'Top Soviet soldier urges readiness', *New York Times*, 11 March 1982, which describes a new pamphlet entitled *Always Ready To Defend the Fatherland* by Marshall Nikolai V. Ogarkov, Soviet Chief of Staff, in which 'complacency and elements of pacifism among Soviet youth' are decried; also John Burns, '11 Russians Open Anti-Nuclear Drive', *New York Times*, 5 June 1982.

Index

DATE DUE